Differentiated Staffing -

The Key to
Effective School Organization

Differentiated Staffing-
The Key to
Effective School Organization

Bruce G. Caldwell

The Center for Applied Research in Education, Inc.

521 Fifth Avenue

New York, N.Y. 10017

Printed in the United States of America
C-1482-3

To my family for their support and understanding
and particularly to Sue,
the most important person in my life.

About The Author

Bruce G. Caldwell, Ed.D., assisted in the development of the nation's first comprehensive program of differentiated staffing in the schools of Temple City, California. In 1967, he was appointed principal of the demonstration school in Temple City and subsequently served as the city's director of secondary education, director of instruction, and assistant superintendent. During his five years with Temple City, Dr. Caldwell was retained as a consultant on differentiated staffing by school systems in 12 states and delivered many keynote addresses to professional conferences across the country. He also authored a series of articles on differentiated staffing in *Educational Technology*.

Dr. Caldwell's experience in education also includes ten years of teaching in California schools and a year as Coordinator of the Elementary and Secondary Education Act, Title I, for Los Angeles County. Upon beginning his work at Temple City in 1967, he was appointed to the U.S.O.E.'s advisory panel for More Effective School Personnel Utilization and served on this committee for three years.

Awarded his doctorate by the University of Massachusetts in 1972, after a year as Fellow in Residence at the Center for Leadership and Administration, Dr. Caldwell is presently superintendent of the Westfield, Massachusetts, Public Schools.

About This Book

This book will be useful to all persons connected with education who are interested in the reorganization of schools. It should be particularly useful to those who are currently in or moving toward leadership roles since it presents a broad range of rationale and support for the reorganization of schools and the role of leaders in the change process.

The term "differentiated staffing" adequately describes the major process this book suggests as a means of reaching toward the larger and more meaningful goal of organizational health. Undoubtedly other process terms could and have been used with equal fervor; but they, too, are less important than the goal of organizational health in schools.

Many models of differentiated staffing are now in operation throughout the United States. I have chosen to restrict most of my analysis to a hierarchical model which is vertical in nature. This was done for two reasons. First, I was personally involved in the development and implementation of such a model while a principal, project director, and assistant superintendent in Temple City, California; and second, Temple City committed itself to an extremely comprehensive model which had many unique and complementary facets. I will state now and reiterate several times within this book that Temple City provides the reader with a good point of reference relative to examples, job descriptions, procedures, and so on, but that Temple City is a small system in a white middle-class suburb of Los Angeles which has successfully implemented a project only after many years of intensive endeavor. No other system should consider Temple City as any more than "a" model of differentiated staffing. There are other models which have received less publicity but which may be as effective or better. Having said this, however, I feel the Temple City model is an outstanding one to study because it was planned so carefully, has received a great many commendations, and continues to prosper after six years of involvement.

This book emphasizes the rationale and justification for differentiated staffing as a process. A wide variety of resource people and documents are offered as supportive evidence. In addition, many practical suggestions and examples are provided. However, I have carefully avoided the development of a "cookbook approach" to differentiated staffing and continue to feel that local variables should be strongly considered in the development of any differentiated staffing model. It was my intention to interrelate theory and practice, assuming that either by itself is insufficient.

This book presents strong arguments regarding the need for reorganizing our schools. It also presents a structure for reorganization which emphasizes participative management within a goal-directed system.

Bruce G. Caldwell

Acknowledgements

This book could not have been written had it not been for the encouragement of many friends and associates.

Dr. M. John Rand, former superintendent of the Temple City Schools, was instrumental in providing me with the opportunity to lead and offering me his personal support.

The staff and students of Oak Avenue Intermediate School deserve much of the credit for implementing with skill and enthusiasm a comprehensive program which would have overwhelmed a less committed and competent group of individuals.

Wes Bosson, a long-time personal friend and professional colleague, encouraged me greatly and offered many excellent suggestions. I deeply appreciate his support and assistance.

Members of the Center for Leadership at the University of Massachusetts and particularly Professors Richard Clark, Kenneth Blanchard, Phil DeTurk and Bob Miltz were of great assistance. I thank them for their very helpful comments and their excellent advice.

I also thank Dean Dwight W. Allen for his support and personal aid in gaining me the time to do the research for this book.

Finally, I am grateful that a sincere but departed friend, Tony Melton, allowed me his counsel and advice. His influence lingers yet.

Contents

4. The Role of the Master Teacher (*Continued*)

5. Differentiated Staffing: What Is in It for Students?   98

6. Differentiated Staffing and the Process of Change   120

8. Problems with Differentiated Staffing (*Continued*)

9.   Financial Implications of Differentiated Staffing 187

10.   In-Service Education 204

In-Service Education *(Continued)*

APPENDICES

ONE

An Introduction
to Differentiated Staffing

Differentiated Staffing: A Means to Organizational Health

⌈Differentiated staffing is a *means* or a *process* by which schools may attempt to practice healthier management principles. It is an organizational plan—a strategy for change along predetermined lines—consistent with the best available current thinking about healthy organizations. It is a system which enables schools to function democratically and one which sees freedom and power as interdependent concepts. Differentiated staffing has a great deal to do with the issues of human dignity, trust, leadership and followership, autonomy, creativity, and accountability. Differentiated staffing is a plan which utilizes a comprehensive, interrelated set of delivery systems. It should not be an isolated thrust or innovation independent of the rest of the school system. It affects all of the participants in the educational enterprise.⌋

Some indication of the thesis behind differentiated staffing is found in this quotation from Abraham Maslow:

> To make growth and self-actualization possible, it is necessary to understand that capacities, organs and organ systems press to function and express themselves and to be used and exercised, and that such use is satisfying and disuse irritating. The muscular person likes to use his muscles, indeed *has* to use them in order to "feel good" and to achieve the subjective feeling of harmonious, successful, uninhibited functioning (spontaneity) which is so important an aspect of good growth and psychological health. So also for intelligence, for the uterus, the eyes, the capacity to love.

Capacities clamor to be used, and cease their clamor only when they *are* well used. That is, capacities are also needs. Not only is it fun to use our capacities, but it is also necessary. The unused capacity or organ can become a disease center or else atrophy, thus diminishing the person.[1]

Most schools in the United States, given their present hierarchical organizational relationships, are inhibiting the development of the potential of nearly all of the participants. There is abundant evidence that our present policies are largely ineffective. The schools of our nation are being attacked from without and from within by conservatives and liberals, students and taxpayers. The derogatory phrases one hears have become hackneyed expressions. "The schools are irrelevant," "Teachers are lazy," "The kids are undisciplined," "The administration is weak," "There is a crisis in our classrooms," and "There is no accountability in education." It is the position of this author that much of what is wrong in schools can be traced to the organizational relationships which exist within them.

The investigation of organizational relationships has been a subject of concern for many years. Most notably one hears of the "efficiency era," an era marked by time and motion studies and scientific management[2] and the "human relations era" introduced in part by Elton Mayo as he analyzed the Hawthorne Studies[3] and discovered the effects of personal attention and meaningful involvement on the behavior of the study's participants. More recently the focus of behavioral scientists has turned to the study of *theory* in regard to human relations. The present era is marked by studies related to system theory, leadership theory, and motivational theory. It was launched by Douglas McGregor and his now classical contribution known as Theory X or Theory Y.[4]

---

[1] Abraham Maslow, "Some Basic Propositions of a Growth and Self-Actualization Psychology," *ASCD Yearbook* (Washington, D.C.: The National Education Association, 1962), p. 40.

[2] Frederick W. Taylor, *The Principles of Scientific Management* (New York: Harper and Row, 1911).

[3] Elton Mayo, *The Social Problems of an Industrial Civilization* (Cambridge, Mass.: Harvard University Press,1945).

[4] Douglas McGregor, *The Human Side of Enterprise* (New York: McGraw-Hill, 1960).

McGregor's postulation is that the potential of men is viewed by organizations as either basically unambitious, needing direction and therefore needing "managing" (theory X), or as ambitious, creative, and capable of self-regulation (theory Y).

The United States Seems Ready for More Humane Schools

It would be an oversimplification to suggest that schools, being so "theory X" oriented, must hasten to become organized in ways more consonant with a "theory Y" philosophy. Many schools are formally and informally seeking to become more humane places; however, lingering images, traditions, and expectancies continue to inhibit the transitions for which some are hoping.

The problems which remain and which are viewed as significant by this author are basically organizational in nature. The *will* to solve them seems to exist. No longer are educators and the public in general viewing education in our country as indoctrination achieved through manipulation and regimentation. Most boards of education, school committees, educators, and legislators are supporting goals for the schools such as "maximum individual growth for each individual learner."[5]

The breach is substantially one of poor exemplary practices, not one of intent or attitude. The poor practices are perpetuated by organizational rigidities through "policies" that inhibit the institutionalization of desired new practices and result in the continuing gap between theory and practice.

An important advantage present today is that educators do not have to contend with the situation on the grounds of a progressive-traditional issue, a condition which greatly inhibited the growth of similar movements in the past four decades. This advantage seems to be owing to several factors including:

- Great financial investments by state and federal agencies as well as private foundations to stimulate change in education.
- The equalizing of educational opportunities, apparently on the basis that every individual has dignity and worth and should be given an equal chance to develop his skills and talents.
- Large numbers of influential leaders who endorse "promoting the growth of the individual" as a major role for schools.

---

[5]From a pamphlet, "Relevant Changes and Educational Direction," Temple City Unified School District, 1968.

- The efforts of behavioral scientists who continue to add credence to the importance of organizational relationships as a key to the accomplishment of corporate and individual goals.
- The rising militancy and strength among teachers who are demanding a greater voice in the establishment of educational policies, many of which deal with the right of the individual.

The Background for Differentiated Staffing

The impetus of differentiated staffing can be traced to a number of sources. The following is a partial list of what might be regarded as causative factors as viewed by various participants in the educational process.

The nonprofessional view of teaching

1. Teachers are labeled, paid, and considered as equal, interchangeable parts. Outstanding teachers are not adequately rewarded. Incompetent and inadequate teachers are automatically moved along toward the top of salary schedules which honor time and credit and pay no attention to performance.
2. The schools are not arranged in a manner which permits teachers to accept different levels of responsibilities.
3. Many administrators realize that they, as single leaders, are not able to effect in a meaningful way what goes on in classrooms. They recognize that they are generalists and lack the background to aid in the development of skills, methods, and curriculum in every field.
4. The situation as it normally exists permits apathetic teachers to be rewarded in the same manner as energetic ones.
5. Collegial relationships between teachers and administrators are difficult to maintain in today's struggle for policy-making power.
6. Principals are viewed as management and teachers as labor.
7. Principals have power, yet they know change must come in cooperation with the teaching staff, not in competition with it.
8. Principals are in the position of "headmaster" in a school setting which calls for a new distribution of power and leadership.
9. Students are affected by facts such as "65 percent of their teachers are getting Master's degrees in administration"[6] while they remain teachers of academic subject matter. The students' teachers are preparing for their professional future, not the present.

---

[6] Arthur D. Little, Inc., "Teacher Supply and Demand in California," 1965-76, a report to the California State Board of Education, 1967.

10. First-year teachers are generally isolated (some would say insulated) from their teaching colleagues and are forced to re-invent curriculum, methods, materials, and ideas as though they were the first to ever teach.

Artificial constraints and "sacred cows"

1. School schedules are a matter of administrative convenience and tradition. Most classes are 50 minutes in length, 30 students in each class, classes last for nine months and classrooms are 900 square feet in size.
2. Principals are "accountable" and therefore they must evaluate personnel and programs which exceed their knowledge base and which obviously are under the true direction of the teaching staff.
3. Students do not often progress at their own rates, participate in multiple-size learning groups, or have small group inquiry-oriented lessons. They are taught in standard-sized groups, not as individuals.
4. Students are asked to make relatively few decisions as they move through the daily structured program. Not until most students arrive at college or accept employment do they sense the degree of personal responsibility and accountability that life holds for them.
5. Even in a large school, with a staff of 50 to 75 teachers, students will have meaningful access to only one teacher in the case of a self-contained elementary school or perhaps six teachers in a secondary school.

The concentration of power and stifling of creativity

1. Teachers are selected and evaluated by generalist adminstrators. They labor in an environment loaded with hierarchical power, one which sees policies made at the top.
2. Creativity is neither encouraged nor rewarded unless the local principal is tolerant of it and the major criterion for measuring one's effectiveness is "a well-ordered classroom, not given to the need for administrative assistance."
3. Decision-making is centralized and generally in the hands of those the greatest distance from the students.
4. Students are clamoring to be heard and want to be included in decision-making.
5. Inventive teachers often draw back from new practices when it is anticipated the results may be non-normative.
6. Teachers are often viewed as passive, motivated only by rewards and penalties and needing to be controlled and manipulated for their own good.

Economic difficulties

1. Students see many of their favorite teachers leave the classroom to go to counseling and administration and higher salaries.
2. The education community often sees poor teachers obtain rewards with across-the-board raises and sees teachers who deviate from time-honored norms face penalties for "experimenting."
3. There is no longer a shortage of teachers, yet the law of supply and demand has no effect as annual salaries continue to increase.
4. There is a disproportionate annual increase in the cost of education due to the lack of turnover in schools and the subsequent increase of higher-paid, veteran teachers.

It is recognized that much of the rationale for the development of differentiated staffing is itself "normative." It has not and in some instances cannot undergo extensive tests for validation. Whether it is "right" that people should be treated as individuals with inherent rights and intrinsic values and that they "feel better when they play a major role in shaping their own futures" depends upon one's system of values. The author and many of his colleagues in Temple City do "value" the rationale for differentiated staffing as it will be presented here. This is another way of saying it is difficult to be completely objective about something to which one is personally committed.

Many years will have to pass before enough data exists to justify differentiated staffing. However, the author believes that the contributions of behavioral scientists such as Maslow and Carl Rogers, as well as the parallel testing of their postulations by organizational theorists such as Rensis Likert and Frederick Herzberg, are sufficient cause for the schools to immediately initiate changes consistent with their findings and/or conclusions.

Following a brief summary of the development and characteristics of the Temple City model, the remainder of this book is devoted to (a) describing the new roles and relationships which emerged in Temple City and (b) establishing a broad base of rationale for the Temple City model. In addition, the author will support most of the rationale with personal recommendations and comments which have been gained as an implementor, not a theorist.

It will be stated again at this point and reiterated many times that differentiated staffing is a method. It is not a goal. Goals are more important than methods. No attempt will be made to declare Temple City's method as more or less advantageous than other models of differentiated staffing. The author would argue here and expand on the statement later, that much of what is done under the banner of differentiated staffing fails to be goal oriented. In these cases, "methods" have replaced "goals" and, consequently, some individuals are excited about the wrong development.

The Birth of Differentiated Staffing in Temple City

The initial development of differentiated staffing in Temple City was not based on a comprehensive needs assessment which revealed all of the difficulties listed previously. To identify the specific incident in Temple City which launched the study and implementation of differentiated staffing, one would have to look back to a day in 1965 at a meeting between Dr. Jack Rand, Superintendent of the Temple City Unified School District and Dr. Dwight W. Allen, Dean of the School of Education at the University of Massachusetts. They were discussing the ills of a single salary schedule which honored time and credit and paid no attention to performance.

Both educators were also concerned about the lack of autonomy and the stifling of creativity among teachers. They discussed several options to what exists. The alternative that finally evolved on a napkin in a restaurant that day in Temple City has become known as *Differentiated Staffing*.

The rough model they developed was a hierarchical model which involved changing the single category of "teacher" under traditional systems to a classification system delineating four levels of teachers. These four levels began with a neophyte or beginner level and progressed upward to the level of skilled curriculum specialist. Each level had different responsibilities attached to it, and differing level of compensation. The system thus eliminated the notion of a single salary schedule.

Forming a Steering Committee

Dr. Rand took the basic idea to the leadership people in Temple City for a first hearing. They liked the concept and agreed it should be further studied. Dr. Rand suggested that a district-wide steering committee be formed which would consider the desirability and practicality of developing a program of differentiated staffing for Temple City. The steering committee's charge was to determine whether the idea should be pursued and in what manner. The principals of each school informed their staffs of the project and asked them to elect representatives to the district-wide steering committee. In addition to the teachers and administrators, the board of education and the two professional teachers' associations were asked to send representatives to the first meeting of the steering committee.

At the first meeting teachers tested their prerogatives by asking that the number of administrators on the steering committee be reduced. That was accomplished, as administrators elected their own representatives, and teachers now numerically dominated the steering committee. Study sessions then took place.

The work of the steering committee was greatly facilitated by a grant from the Charles F. Kettering Foundation. The total financial contribution of the Kettering Foundation was $56,840, sufficient funding to employ many staff members on a summer research and writing project as well as to sustain the administrative and support functions of the project.

As a result, the task forces which the steering committee had formed to consider issues such as salary schedules, job descriptions, evaluation procedures, school scheduling options, inter-task force linkage and policy development, each submitted position papers. Chairmen of task forces then met with the project coordinator and developed a "Proposal for a Differentiated Teaching Staff." This proposal was duplicated and distributed to every staff and board member by the opening of school, 1967. During preschool orientation, task force representatives met with small groups of teachers to solicit feedback on the proposal.

The steering committee found the teaching staff had mixed emotions about the proposal. Feedback ranged from "right on" to apathy. Some felt it was a great idea on paper but the potential for implementation was slim. No individuals or groups openly opposed differentiated staffing.

The introduction to the steering committee's proposal was a lengthy statement of purpose and rationale. A few paragraphs from it will give the reader some indication of its general contents.

When a school district sets in motion a complex study intended to bring about change, it is inevitable that there will be reaction to this change. This is perfectly reasonable. No staff should be expected to accept change to criticize, to participate in decisions, to demand justification for change without question. The Differentiated Staffing Project implies change: on this there can be little doubt or equivocation. If fully implemented, it will alter substantially all traditional school organization, methods of instruction, and the role of the majority of staff members. . . .

Of . . . importance in the considerations of many who leave the classroom, is the conviction that as teachers they are impotent to bring about any basic change or reform in education. Teachers are charged with the responsibility for classroom instruction but are almost never given any real authority to alter its nature based on their own convictions. They serve on innumerable committees and councils for this ostensible purpose only to discover with endless certainty that the ultimate decisions will be handed down from above. The sense of futility which this produces causes many who are genuinely concerned to seek positions where they will have a chance to put their convictions into practice; they become administrators or quasi-administrators. . .

This study is quite literally the first to propose a basic break in the accepted pattern of school organization, in which generalist administrators make all basic policy, and specialist teachers dance to the tune they play; rather like the tail wagging the dog. There are those who disagree with the philosophy implied here; they distrust the competence of teachers to make decisions of school-wide importance. Chief among these doubters are the majority of administrators themselves, whose attitudes on this matter are of questionable objectivity. . . [7]

It can be readily seen that administrators in particular might react defensively to the rationale for the proposed new organization. That reaction did occur in Temple City. Among those somewhat reeled back by its force and innuendo was this writer who at the time was a newly appointed principal at the Oak

---

[7]From a Temple City Unified School District publication, "Temple City Differentiated Staffing Project," 1967, pp. 1-4.

Avenue Intermediate School. After a short time and much debate, some consensus among the participants was achieved and the "general idea of differentiated staffing" was supported.

Funding the Temple City Model

On the basis of initial reactions, the proposal was reworked slightly and submitted to the U.S. Office of Education under the new Education Professions Development Act. That legislation had a particular subsection (Part D) which funded differentiated staffing proposals. The funding allotted to differentiated staffing was slight during 1967-68. Of the 270 proposals received during that funding period U.S.O.E. was able to fund only about ten which dealt specifically with differentiated staffing. Temple City was successful in receiving U.S.O.E. financial support.

It is important to note that U.S.O.E. funds under Part D of the Education Professions Development Act are for the training of teachers. Temple City's major task then was to prepare teachers to perform new differentiated roles. Of course, inherent within the total process was the development of new patterns of staffing schools.

A Training Program for New Roles

The steering committee's task forces identified some of the new roles which differentiated staffing would require. EPDA funds were used to offer various kinds of training programs relative to the new differentiated roles. The steering committee established the content of the programs and a procedure for recruiting/screening paraprofessionals, teachers, and administrators who wished to participate in the training. A partial list of the training programs offered include:

- Scholar/Teacher study with activities such as research methodology, procedures and instruments, curriculum theory, and development.
- Instructional management which covered such skills as writing behavioral objectives, system analysis, gaming and simulations, inquiry training, and behavior modification.
- Organizational analysis which focused on diagnosing organizational problems, understanding and using conflict, problem-solving, and decision-making.

- Model-building/Survey of innovations which involved training in race relations, micro-counseling, and alternate uses of time, space and staff.
- Group dynamics which dealt with conflict resolution, team building, and collaboration.
- Community career ladder which offered training in the skills of a paraprofessional, technology of the classroom, and the use of the library and media in the modern school.

Characteristics of the Temple City Model

Many schools around the country which have initiated some form of differentiated staffing possess various unique program characteristics. In some cases, these characteristics cut across many program lines and envelop the entire system. In others, less system-wide impact has occurred.

The Temple City Unified School District approached the problem of change in a comprehensive manner rather than supporting isolated, independent thrusts.

It will be helpful for the reader to view the following summary of Temple City's unique characteristics as an index of terms and definitions which will be referred to many times in the following chapters. In addition, these program characteristics are in part a substantive reply to the previous list of reasons for the emergence of differentiated staffing. These program characteristics are a direct result of the recommendations of the steering committee and its various task forces.

Multiple Salary Schedule

Salary schedules based upon differing levels of responsibility were established. The four basic categories of credentialed teachers are:

1. *Associate Teacher*—This is a person who is typically nontenured and possesses little if any experience. He teaches 100 percent of the time. He has a regular credential and earning power equal to an average teacher in any typical system during his first five years of employment. He must qualify for an advancement to the next level of teacher, and will have to compete with others who are of associate teacher status. It is possible that he may remain at his fifth-year earning level temporarily or indefinitely, depending on his desire or

ability to compete for a higher level. Openings at higher levels must exist in order for the associate teacher to advance. At this time, Temple City has set the number of associate teachers at 40 percent of the total teaching staff. All teaching levels maintain constant mathematical ratios to each other. It is anticipated that the associate teacher level will include some persons who are satisfied to retain that status since it entails fewer professional responsibilities and requires less effort and involvement than do higher levels.

2. *Staff Teacher*— This person is usually tenured, experienced, and totally involved. He teaches 100 percent of the time. His earning power is equal to that of any experienced teacher within the profession. Many people in this category are considered career teachers and may retire having never gone beyond the staff teacher status. This category also constitutes approximately 40 percent of the credentialed teaching staff.

3. *Senior Teacher*—A senior teacher is a person who is experienced and is generally considered to be the finest teacher in his area in the school. He is respected by teachers, students, and parents. He probably holds a master's degree and is considered an expert in a particular curriculum area. His position exists to provide services to the staff and associate-level personnel in his area and he assumes a major responsibility for the total direction of the school by being a member of the school academic senate. His monthly earning power is equal to that of a principal. He retains no tenure rights except at the staff level. He is selected by his peers and is evaluated by them. The senior teacher teaches formally approximately 60 percent of a staff teacher's load. He may be employed beyond the normal teacher work year. This category constitutes about 17 percent of the total teaching staff.

4. *Master Teacher*—A master teacher is a person who has experience at various levels which must include teaching and may include teacher training. He probably has a doctorate, due to the level of skills required; however, a doctorate is not a necessity. His primary function is to serve the needs of the senior teachers in his curriculum area, which means he would be a specialist as opposed to a generalist. His services revolve around a central theme referred to as the self-renewal function. He is a retrieval expert. His knowledge and professional affiliations are broad. He must be familiar with national projects and research. Since he serves senior teachers, grades K-12 in a particular discipline, his efforts are intended to be catalytic in nature, thus the ongoing input or self-renewal. His monthly earning power is equal to that of an Assistant Superintendent. He has no

tenure at the master teacher level. He too is selected by his peers and evaluated by those he serves. He teaches (as does everyone in the system, including administrators) about 20 percent of a staff teacher load. He is a member of the Instructional Council which is composed of all master teachers and the superintendent, and heads up his team of senior teachers when they meet as a vertical curriculum committee, grades K-12. About 3 percent of the total staff are master teachers.

Professional Self-Regulation

The steering committee carefully built in a number of specific controls intended to ensure professional self-regulation. These include:

1. Teachers who are to receive services from a member of the teaching hierarchy specify what personal training and service needs exist.
2. Recipients of services play the major role in the selection of service agents.
3. Those being serviced (for instance, associate teachers and staff teachers being served by a senior teacher) evaluate those who serve them.
4. Members of the teaching hierarchy evaluate those they serve. Senior teachers, not principals, evaluate staff and associate teachers.
5. Decision-making at the school and district level is no longer controlled by an administrator. Senior teachers and principals work as colleagues in a decision-making body called the academic senate.
6. No one has tenure above the staff teacher level except as a staff teacher. If people do not meet the needs of those they serve, they return to the level of staff teacher.

Diffused Power

The model developed in Temple City significantly diffused power which previously and traditionally had been concentrated in the hands of administrators. The model enables senior teachers to function within their curricular area as principals formerly did within the school. Senior teachers in collaboration with their team make all decisions regarding the deployment of human resources, the use of budget, the allocation of space, generation of student schedules, and so forth. Collaboration and cooperation is assured by the fact that the team they serve evaluates their services and leadership. Senior teachers have considerable power but they are accountable for the results of their efforts.

The senior teachers of each school meet with their principal to formulate school policy in a body called the academic senate. The principal serves as their executive secretary much as the superintendent serves as the executive secretary of the Board of Education; that is, the principal is the executor or administrator of senate policy. An in-depth look at the principal's role is presented in Chapter 2.

The schools in the district send their principal and two elected senior teachers to the "district senate" to meet with the superintendent in the same manner. Neither the principal nor the superintendent have veto power. Final decisions remain the prerogative of the Board of Education although they usually accept the recommendation of the superintendent who is chairman of the district senate.

Program Comprehensiveness

Change in Temple City was a comprehensive endeavor. The planners intended to effect many areas of the educational program. For reasons to be discussed in detail later, they felt a wide range of changes would gain more effective results than isolated thrusts. The changes could be categorized as follows:

The Use of Time and Space. "Flexibility" was the overriding concern. Specific changes included (1) variable course structures, (2) flexible uses of the school day and year, (3) flexible options for the use of physical facilities, and (4) converting regular classroom or blocks of them into resource centers, labs and media centers.

The Role of the Learner. Temple City wanted to emphasize the "active and collegial" role of the student in the learning process and to recognize them as "individuals" by providing (1) self-directed learning opportunities for students, (2) clearly defined and measurable baseline skills for all learners, (3) curriculum vitalization with a focus on concepts, not content, (4) access to trained paraprofessionals as well as teaching resources from the community, (5) alternative forms of reporting student progress, (6) credentialed persons to function as personal advisors and to supplement counseling services. (7) opportunities for students to function as teaching resources, and (8) educational experiences outside the walls of the school.

The Nature of Organizational Relationships. The key to meaningful relationships in the opinion of those in Temple City was the establishment of democratic, nonauthoritarian interaction. Methods employed included (1) providing school units, teachers and students with power over resources, thus increasing their autonomy, (2) involving professional associations in the development and implementation of all plans, (3) involving citizens, students, and teachers in the formal decision-making process, and (4) denying persons in administrative positions "veto power."

The Preparation of Teachers. Temple City felt that the training and retraining of teachers and administrators had to be an integral part of any change strategy. Changes included (1) the development of a year-long "school-site" teacher training program, (2) provision for the systematic in-service education of all credentialed persons, and (3) the establishment of a clinical, school-site role for professors of education.

In-Service Training

Traditional models offer little in the way of ongoing, updated training for teachers and require virtually no return from them in the way of instructional skills which are measurable. Temple City's model assumes that training and evaluation are perpetual; everyone serves students, from the superintendent down to the custodian, and must, in performance terms, have a job description that defines minimum skills and results. If improvement is needed, a service is rendered. Since improvement is forever needed by all, then so are training and services. All of the members of the Temple City hierarchy must serve others or cease to have a reason for existing as a leader. Thus a central premise of the differentiated staffing concept is that improved instruction will result in improved learning.

Key Factors of Differentiation

Figure 1-1 summarizes the key factors of differentiation among the four teaching levels. To emphasize a point, it is important to note that degrees are not a requirement to ascend. Curricular responsibilities and instructional skills as listed represent "minimal expectations." An associate teacher, for instance, may be performing far beyond the expectations for his role, as may a staff teacher. Advancements to higher ranks are determined by a teacher's colleagues for the most part; thus performance promotions which are not based upon time served or credits earned are in order.

Promotions are based on openings. Ratios within categories are constant; thus if one is to have 17 percent of the total staff at the rank of senior teacher, promotional opportunities occur when some of the 17 percent leave or are themselves promoted.

FACTORS OF DIFFERENTIATION

	MASTER	SENIOR	STAFF	ASSOCIATE
SALARY RANGE	18,000-22,000	14,500-17,500	9,500-13,000	7,000-9,500
WORK YEAR	12 months	11 months	10 months	10 months
%AGE OF TIME IN CLASSROOM	20%	60%	100%	100%
"TYPICAL" DEGREE HELD	Doctorate	M.Ed.	B.A. plus	B.A.
CURRICULAR RESPONSIBILITIES	Conceptualizer	Designer	Tester and refiner	Implementor
INSTRUCTIONAL SKILLS	Learning theorist	Expert in multiple modes	Capable in multiple modes	Capable in two modes

Figure 1-1

SUMMARY

Differentiated staffing is inextricably related to management principles and to concepts of organizational theory. Its proponents therefore are involved in the development of an organizational schema based upon the recent findings and postulations of many behavioral scientists. The direction being suggested advocates shared power, concern for the higher needs of men such as recognition, responsibility and autonomy, full-flow communication, tolerance for expressions of individuality, and responsible leadership characterized by a high concern for people with a minimum degree of authoritarian behavior. Quite obviously many schools today would not generally be considered "healthy" by those criteria.

A greater degree of readiness and receptivity to change exists now than in past decades. Enticements, if not demands, for change are in abundance.

Differentiated staffing is a means, an organizational method, of implementing a more individualized, humane, responsive environment for all of the people affiliated with schools.

Differentiated staffing evolved as an answer to pressing problems in education related to such issues as: (a) a career in the classroom, (b) shared power, (c) differing levels of responsibility, accountability, and remuneration among teachers, (d) promotions based on performance, not time and credits, (e) enforced normative behavior, (f) self-regulation among teachers, (g) better programs for students from more creative teachers with more accountability, (h) more flexible uses of time and space, and (i) better-trained teachers.

Differentiated staffing started in Temple City as a "rough idea" and has grown to a comprehensive model through teacher involvement and leadership.

The characteristics considered of key importance in the Temple City model are multiple salary schedules with differing levels of teaching and leadership responsibility, professional self-regulation through specialist-to-specialist evaluations, diffused power, program comprehensiveness, and perpetual in-service training.

It is the author's opinion that the problems Temple City has encountered are not atypical and that even though Temple City is the basic referent, readers will have little difficulty linking the situation to their own schools.

TWO

New Roles for Principals

A Structure for Leadership Behavior

The school principal has often been referred to as the middleman or the educational leader. Sometimes he has been called obsolescent. You, as reader, can think back over all of those you have known who occupied the role of principal and add many additional descriptive terms. The point is that roles for principals in the past have been as diverse as the numbers who have occupied that position. Undoubtedly, there have been autocrats, disciplinarians, martinets, despots, dictators, humanitarians, altruists, pragmatists, liberals, conservatives, and combinations of many of these.

Differentiated staffing attempts to give a principal an organizational structure to work within which constrains him from behaving in undesirable ways and facilitates his behavior along desirable lines. The question arises: what is desirable and what is undesirable?

Indices of Desirable Principal Behaviors

Maslow presents what seem to be some excellent indicators of desirable managerial behaviors. He lists 36 assumptions which underlie healthy management principles which must exist as preconditions of a healthy organization. Some key points in his list are:

1. "Assume everyone is to be trusted."
2. "Assume everyone is to be informed as completely as possible of as

many facts and truths as possible, i.e., everything relevant to the situation."

3. "Assume in all your people the impulse to achieve. . . "

4. "Assume that there is no dominance-subordination hierarchy in the jungle sense or authoritarian sense. . . . It follows that this is another principle of selection of personnel for the eupsychian organization. Authoritarians must be excluded or they must be converted."

5. "Assume that everyone will have the same ultimate managerial objectives and will identify with them no matter where they are in the organization or in the hierarchy."

6. "Assume the ability to admire . . ."

7. "Eupsychian management assumes that people are improvable. (This does not mean that they are perfectable.). . . ."

8. "Assume that everyone prefers to feel important, needed, useful, successful, proud, respected, rather than unimportant, interchangeable, anonymous, wasted, unused, expendable, disrespected."

9. "Eupsychian management assumes everyone prefers to be a prime mover rather than a passive helper. . . ."

10. "Assume a tendency to improve things, to straighten the crooked picture on the wall, to clean up the dirty mess, to put things right, make things better, to do things better."

11. "Assume the preference for working rather than being idle."

12. "All human beings, not only eupsychian ones, prefer meaningful work to meaningless work. . . ."[1]

Other behavioral scientists reinforce Maslow's thoughts concerning healthy management principles. For example, Saul Gellerman, in *Motivation and Productivity,* comments about the Pittsburgh Studies conducted by Frederick Herzberg and his colleagues at the Psychological Service at Pittsburgh. In these studies the researchers interviewed 200 engineers and accountants and asked them to recall specific incidents in their recent experience which made them feel particularly good or particularly bad about their jobs. Gellerman states:

> In effect, the Pittsburgh group found that both the traditional bread and butter motivators and the more sophisticated "human relations" motivators didn't motivate. With this group at least, these factors had become the minimum tolerable conditions for a job. To lift them above humdrum, satisfied but unexcited level of

---

[1] Abraham H. Maslow, *Eupsychian Management* (Homewood, Ill.: Irwin-Dorsey, 1965), pp. 24-26.

motivation required something else: the freedom to exercise
initiative and ingenuity, to experiment and to handle the problems of their jobs in their own way. Control of their own work
rather than the tangible rewards of their work, was the motivator.[2]

On the basis of these findings it is possible to conclude that
an authoritarian, power-oriented, patriarchal-type principal is unable to be a desirable leader.

Rensis Likert has undertaken to establish a data base to test
behavioral theories such as those of Maslow and Herzberg. Likert
and his colleagues at the Institute for Social Research at the
University of Michigan developed an instrument which enables
members to rate their organization's management system. This
instrument has been administered to hundreds of managers. Figure
2-1 is an example of three items from Likert's instrument which
consists of 22 items.

As Figure 2-1 indicates, a system 1 organization displays theory
X characteristics with low levels of self-actualization potential. On
the other end of the continuum is system 4 which is theory Y
oriented and offers great potential for self-actualization. A system
1 management philosophy views employees as immature and
motivated by extrinsic rewards. System 4 views them as mature
and concerned with intrinsic rewards as described by Herzberg.

Likert asked each group of managers who completed the
instrument to indicate next to each item where they thought the
most productive departments, divisions, or organizations fell on a
continuum which began with system 1 on the left and moved to
system 4 on the right. They then were asked to indicate for each
item where they felt the *least* productive departments, divisions,
or organizations fell. Each respondent was asked to mark *h* under
each organizational variable which was most productive and *1*
under each organizational variable which was least productive.

Likert summarized the results of his research by saying that
respondents:

> . . . varied in their descriptions of the most productive depart-
> ment; some are quite far to the right, the *h*'s being largely under
> System 4. For others, the most productive unit was largely under

---

[2]Saul W. Gellerman, *Motivation and Productivity* (New York: American Management
Association, Inc., 1963), p. 50.

System 3. The striking fact, however, is that irrespective of where the *h*'s describing the high-producing unit fall in the table, the *l*'s for the low-producing department fall to the left. Quite consistently, the high-producing department is seen as toward the right end of the table.[3]

These findings confirmed the hypothesis of behavioral scientists who felt that self-actualization, theory Y, and motivational factors should be considered most conducive from the point of view of leaders themselves to the increased productivity of individuals in an organization. The interesting question he raises is "What keeps them (managers) from using the management system which they recognize yields the highest productivity, lowest costs, and best performance?"[4] This same question can be asked of the public schools.

Schools, as most bureaucratic hierarchies, are usually system 1 oriented. If questioned about the desirability of moving toward system 4 management styles, most people, like the managers Likert studied, would agree that would be a more desirable and productive situation.

Differentiated staffing is an organizational plan which structures leadership personnel into a system 4 operational mode. There are those leaders who will have difficulty making the transition; however, the expectation and performance controls of differentiated staffing support them and in several instances (selection, evaluation, decision-making, budget controls, etc.) require them to utilize a system 4 style.

Schools: Theory "X" or Theory "Y" Orientation

Formalization of good leadership practices is a key component of differentiated staffing. Differentiated staffing represents an effort to institutionalize healthy management principles. It is an attempt to develop a system which, regardless of the inclinations of the leaders, is responsive to the higher level needs of individuals. McGregor has described a managerial philosophy capable of allowing participants, and particularly subordinates, to achieve

---

[3]Rensis Likert, *The Human Organization* (New York: McGraw-Hill, Inc., 1967), pp. 4-7.

[4]*Ibid.*, pp. 3, 11.

Organizational variable	System 1	System 2	System 3	System 4
Leadership process used				
Extent to which immediate superior in solving job problems generally tries to get subordinates' ideas and opinions and make constructive use of them	Seldom gets ideas and opinions of subordinates in solving job problems	Sometimes gets ideas and opinions of subordinates in solving job problems	Usually gets ideas and opinions and usually tries to make constructive use of them	Always gets ideas and opinions and always tries to make constructive use of them
Character of communication process				
Direction of information flow	Downward	Mostly downward	Down and up	Down, up and with peers
Character of decision-making process				
At what level in organization are decisions formally made?	Bulk of decisions at top of organization	Policy at top, many decisions within prescribed framework made at lower levels	Broad policy and general decisions at top, more specific decisions at lower levels	Decision-making widely done throughout organization, although well integrated through linking process provided by overlapping groups

Figure 2-1

these higher-level needs. As mentioned in Chapter 1, he calls this idea "Theory Y." Its points are:

1. Management is responsible for organizing the elements of productive enterprise—money, materials, equipment, people—in the interest of economic ends.
2. People are not by nature passive or resistant to organizational needs.

They have become so as a result of experience in organizations.

3. The motivation, the potential for development, the capacity for assuming responsibility, the readiness to direct behavior toward organizational goals are all present in people. Management to make it possible for people to recognize and develop these human characteristics for themselves.

4. The essential task of management is to arrange organizational conditions and methods of operation so that people can achieve their own goals best by directing their own efforts toward organizational objectives.[5]

To place Theory Y in perspective, one must examine what McGregor calls Theory X. It is his premise, and he is joined by virtually all behavioral scientists who have been active in the last decade of research, that most organizations practice Theory X principles, whether by design or default. Traditional management practices of the past 60 years have greatly influenced prevailing practices. Most of what exists was inherited from what is known as the "Taylorism era," fraught with time and motion studies and other factors of accountability.

Raymond Callahan, in *Education and the Cult of Efficiency,* cites the writings of Frederick Taylor, who authored *The Principles of Scientific Management,* published in 1911. Taylor lists four basic principles of scientific management. His first three emphasize the careful analysis of a task, training for efficiency, and a spirit of cooperation. His fourth principle is more indicative of his whole approach: "There is an almost equal division of the work and the responsibility between the management and the workmen. The management takes over all work for which they are better fitted than the workmen, while in the past, almost all of the work and the greater part of the responsibility were thrown upon the men." [6]

Callahan offers this analysis of Taylor's fourth point.

> When Taylor said that there was an almost equal division of the work and responsibility, he was probably literally correct, but the statement was misleading. . . . The worker's equal division of work was to do what he was told to do by management and his

[5] Douglas McGregor, *Leadership and Motivation* (Boston: M.I.T. Press, 1966), p. 15.

[6] Raymond E. Callahan, *Education and the Cult of Efficiency* (Chicago: University of Chicago Press, 1962), p. 27.

share of the responsibility was that responsibility to do what he was told. . . . Taylor justified this on the ground that "one type of man is needed to plan ahead and an entirely different type to execute the work." The whole attitude of Taylor in this respect was described by a mechanic who worked under him. In the discussion of the problems that come up in the shop, Taylor would tell him that he was "not supposed to think, there are other people paid for thinking around here." Apparently this mechanic was a rugged individualist, because he added, "I would never admit to Mr. Taylor that I was not allowed to think."[7]

Schools, following the lead of scientific management, did as the church and military had previously done and arranged themselves in a typical bureaucratic hierarchy. This hierarchy reinforces the management as thinker and worker as implementor point of view, and perpetuates an environment which demeans the value of most of the members of the organization by denying them access to power and self-reliance.

The mind-set necessary to manage a bureaucratic hierarchy of this type is characterized by McGregor as a Theory X view of man. The basic points of McGregor's Theory X are:

1. Management is responsible for organizing the elements of productivity enterprise—money, materials, equipment, people—in the interest of economic ends.
2. With respect to people, this is a process of directing their efforts, motivating them, controlling their actions, modifying their behavior to fit the needs of the organization.
3. Without this active intervention by management, people would be passive—even resistant—to organizational needs. They must therefore be persuaded, rewarded, punished, controlled—their activities must be directed. This is management's task—in managing subordinate managers or workers. We often sum it up by saying that management consists of getting things done through other people. Behind this conventional theory there are several additional beliefs—less explicit, but widespread.
4. The average man is by nature indolent—he works as little as possible.
5. He lacks ambition, dislikes responsibility, prefers to be led.
6. He is inherently self-centered, indifferent to organizational needs.
7. He is by nature resistant to change.
8. He is gullible, not very bright, the ready dupe of the charlatan and the demagogue.[8]

---

[7]*Ibid.*, pp. 27-28.

[8]Douglas McGregor, *Leadership and Motivation*, p. 5-6.

The Co-optation of Change Agents

School administrators, when given an opportunity to discuss Theory X (System 1), will almost universally agree that many of the characteristics of a Theory X philosophy are antiquated and inappropriate to deal with the sophisticated teaching staffs employed today. Some would question whether a Theory X management philosophy even exists in our modern world, which is another way of saying school administrators claim to be Theory Y people. They do not like to be characterized as bourgeois leaders, manipulating proletariat followers. That is why, as stated earlier, they seem to informally pursue Theory Y organizational structures such as advisory committees, executive committees, etc. It has been the author's experience when discussing differentiated staffing with most administrators that they seem to always get around to the conclusion, "Why that is what I have been practicing for years. I just never called it differentiated staffing." Thus by claiming to be proponents of change themselves, many such administrators (perpetuators of status quo) are co-opting the change agent. They, in effect, allow him to join *them.*

Libel by Label

One of the best replies to that situation is offered by Neil Postman and Charles Weingartner in their book, *Teaching as a Subversive Activity.* They quote Marshal McLuhan:

> McLuhan refers constantly to the human tendency to dismiss an idea by the expedience of naming it. You libel by label (here, MeLuhan connects again with Dewey, for no one stressed more than Dewey, the emptiness of "verbal knowledge"). Find the right label for some process and you know about it. If you know about it, you needn't think of it any further. "What is its name?" becomes a substitute for "How does it work?"[9]

Differentiated staffing, as well as many other innovations, suffers from the bandwagon phenomenon. As soon as it appears that an innovation is in vogue, no upstanding administrator is willing to run the risk of not being innovative. You will hear administrators say "Team teaching! Oh sure, we have been doing that for years," or "Individualized instruction? Why, that has

[9]Neil Postman and Charles Weingartner, *Teaching as a Subversive Activity* (New York: Delacorte Press, 1969), p. 6.

always been our primary concern." (At this point one often overhears those same people say, "Why aren't the desks all in straight rows?" or, "We try to stick to the state-adopted textbooks.") A frequent result of this phenomenon is that what started as a well-defined, thorough concept is eventually so prostituted that the originators shudder. Many worthwhile ideas become so copied by so many that, as in the case of an oft-told story, the original version is no longer discernible.

It would make the author grateful if no one could call what they are doing "differentiated staffing" unless they met 90 percent of some professionally agreed-upon basic criteria. It is likely that advocates of flexible scheduling, open schools, and Montessori schools would all appreciate protection of that kind. That is not a practical hope, but it does point out a frustration faced by people who are change oriented. A great many fabrications exist which are not a credit to the original concept. As they grow in number and diminish in potency, the result is obvious. People say, "Differentiated staffing, flexible scheduling, and so on—we tried those ideas. It was okay but not too different from what we have always done!"

As a case in point, the author was asked to evaluate a project proposal called "Differentiated Staffing." The plan is essentially the addition of paraprofessionals to the staff. Other plans operating under the differentiated staffing banner include some isolated portions of the overall concept, such as hiring some teachers to work an additional month, appointing department heads, creating school academic senates, or renaming coordinators and calling them master teachers. One plan limits itself to the utilization of credential candidates in an intern teaching role. Another was clearly an effort to reduce the salaries of most of the teachers.

All of this is to emphasize the point McLuhan made, "We libel by label." Principals have a responsibility to look past the name of something and to discover how it works.

Some principals, seeking to minimize the problems of offering leadership to specialists, long ago created alternatives which include ideas such as:

- Appointing an executive committee comprised of representatives from each department to accept some of the principal's responsibilities.
- Appointing department heads and giving them greater responsibilities.

- Appointing an advisory board to sit with the principal in decision-making.
- Delegating the curricular or instructional leadership to the vice-principal(s).
- Developing a no-evaluation policy, or retaining an evaluation policy but not practicing it.

These kinds of band-aid treatments carry with them some unfortunate liabilities. A few include:

1. Most appointments to a substitute leadership role are a form of reward for those who gain them and a form of penalty for those who do not. The side effect is a reinforcement of the undesirable, benevolent dictator role.
2. Executive committees, department heads, and advisory boards usually function as decision-makers except when they come to a point of disagreement with the principal. At that juncture, they become strictly advisory, which is, in reality, what they always were.
3. Substitute leaders seldom receive the remuneration or status of a principal. They accept greater responsibilities, such as program administration, interpersonal conflicts, and departmental accountability, but only in the hope they will ultimately be rewarded, or at least not to fall into disfavor with the principal and thus face penalties.
4. The effectiveness of the appointed leaders is reduced by the fact the principal determines whether they are doing a good or poor job of leading. Consequently, the people they serve may be justifiably dissatisfied with the substitute leader and further alienated by his retention.
5. Teachers are not evaluated. Wider gaps in communication between administration and teachers are created. Some woefully inadequate teachers gain tenure and students ultimately absorb the loss.

As mentioned previously, most principals are a combination of many characteristics, but even those who seem to possess an innate goodness are unable to formalize effective management practices to the degree that they become institutionalized. When the effective leader leaves, the risk of his replacement being an ineffective leader and getting away with it is imminent.

To Sustain or Propel

The educational lore says "A principal has a substantial impact on his staff." However, a study conducted by Harman Ziegler reported in his book, *The Political World of the High School Teacher,* finds otherwise. One part of Ziegler's study conducted in Oregon during 1965, involving 803 teachers, consisted of deter‑ mining how teachers felt about sanctioning agents. Included in the list of sanctioning agents were such categories as local cranks, P.T.A., school board, superintendent, other teachers, newspaper, principal, and so on. In determing severity of sanctions, Ziegler found:

> The superintendent and school board are believed to be capable of exerting extreme pressure. . . . The principal, in con‑ trast, is perceived to be a relatively mild sanctioner. In fact, the principal's sanctions are believed to be less severe than those of the other teachers. . . . and is comparable to the scores of stu‑ dents and business groups. Both students and business groups are perceived to sanction on fewer issues but far more intensely on each of these issues. Thus, the principal, although he is the most immediate and tangible symbol of authority for the teachers, is less frightening than other high-ranking sanctioning agents.
>
> . . . The perception of the principal which emerges seems to be one of benevolent authority. The principal would undertake punitive action in the same fashion that a father would discipline a mischievous child. Even students, while concerned with fewer issues, are perceived as being rougher than the principal.[10]

Ziegler's findings may lead to a number of alternative con‑ clusions; however, it seems that one could conclude that he has found the principal to be a less influential member of the power structure than he is traditionally considered to be. It is not necessarily the author's position that this is an "inherent" charac‑ teristic of the job, but that circumstances in the past 15 or so years have encouraged the principal to behave less dogmatically and powerfully.

Teacher militancy is on the rise. Principals are aware, more than ever before, that they cannot portray the role of a despot and remain secure in their job. It must be remembered that there was a time, and there are a few places still, when a principal could openly be dictatorial. Such problems as dismissing an ineffective new teacher or subduing the spirit of a wide-eyed liberal were easily disposed of by a strong principal. No longer is the path of "tough-minded leadership" an easy alternative.

---

[10]Harman Ziegler, *The Political World of the High School Teacher* (Eugene, Ore.: University of Oregon, 1965), p. 34.

Principals are retiring from overt leadership, according to statements offered by Keith Goldhammer and his associates in their 1967 study of *Issues and Problems in Contemporary Educational Administration.* They surveyed and interviewed 47 superintendents in 22 states and found that the superintendents:

> ...claim there are too many incompetent administrators operating schools and holding membership in administrators' associations. This lack of competence has been evidenced by: (1) not taking a stand on issues, (2) low esprit de corps within school and community, (3) inadequate educational leadership in the community, (4) little courage and vision, and (5) poor organization on the job with many functioning by the "seat of their pants."[11]

There are teachers saying the principal is about as influential as students and business groups and superintendents saying principals lack vision and courage. Both are acknowledging the role as lacking in leadership effectiveness. Yet there remains an air of expectancy for the principal to "lead."

A Viable Leadership Role for Principals

A new role capable of enabling the principal to lead and yet not dictate is called for. Differentiated staffing provides such an enabling environment. The principal shares his power with a group of teacher leaders who emerge from the ranks, are selected by their peers and whose roles are defined by their peers. The evaluation of these teacher leaders is done by their peers on the basis of the job description they have collectively developed. This new group of leaders then become colleagues with the principal (equal in power, status, income, and accountability). It has been the author's experience that these new teacher leaders turn out to be the most outstanding teachers in the school and usually the same people he would have hand-picked if he were looking for strong, independent people. The principal is augmented, challenged, and supported by the presence of such a group. A question as to his role emerges. Does he acquiesce to the urgings of individuals or factions within the group? Does he attempt to dominate them?

---

[11]Keith Goldhammer *et al., Issues and Problems in Contemporary Educational Administration* (Eugene, Ore.: Univ. of Oregon, 1967), p. 35.

It is proposed here that it is the principal's responsibility to continue to lead and coordinate the efforts of the group, but not to dominate it. He should not, as mentioned earlier, be in a position to veto the will of the group, but should be expected to give them *authentic* input on all issues. He must take a stand, lead when the situation calls for it (and that is when his expertise on the topic at hand is needed), and follow when he obviously is not the expert.

Differentiated staffing does not reduce the role of principal to that of a maintenance man. Healthy schools scarcely need a highly paid automaton responding to the commands of others or a chameleon-like leader who possesses no true color of his own. Principals are expected to exercise leadership, albeit in a collegial and cooperative manner. Ineffective leadership is exemplified by a statement the author once overheard a principal make to a group of parents, "If you want us to line your kids up and march them around the building, that is what we will do. We are here to serve the community and to be responsive to your request." The principal's intent was probably to win friends and influence people or to gain security in his job; however, principals do not exist for those reasons. They have a responsibility to assist in the design and implementation of an educational program for students and are supposedly expert (as compared to lay citizens) in doing so. Those who forfeit the responsibility to lead actually negate their training and preparation, declaring their input to be of no more value than that of the man on the street. Differentiated staffing does not place a principal in the position of abdicating his role as leader but it does provide a group of selected teacher specialists with whom to share leadership and responsibility.

It should be clearly understood that if the principal was not a good leader before differentiated staffing, the presence of differentiated staffing will not solve his problems, although it may make being a teacher more tolerable. Differentiated staffing creates few difficulties for effective leaders and creates havoc for ineffective leaders. Ineffective leaders would be characterized by behaviors such as being autocratic, fearful of change, possessive of power, unwilling to follow, or uninformed professionally.

The responsibilities of an effective leader include being well read professionally, aware of the latest research, ready to be open to new ideas and prepared to take a stand on an issue based upon his best thinking up to that time. He should have a clear understanding of group process, learning theories, motivational theories, and other ideas related to human interaction. He must be a good listener and be willing to follow others.

A principal does not exist to sustain or maintain a school. If he were to do that, it would imply rather boldly that the school system has arrived. It has become perfect and the task is to perpetuate what exists. No one believes that, yet actions speak louder than words, and there is a great deal of "maintaining" going on in schools. Rather, the task of the principal is to assist the school system as it propels itself forward, meeting new challenges and seeking better solutions.

The Growing Edge of a Principal

Vantage points never tend to quite allow one to see far enough ahead to anticipate emerging situations. The more one progresses, the broader becomes the field of options. Young teachers tend to become impatient with their older colleagues who fail to see the "simple, expedient solutions to problems" yet they too soon realize that knowledge coupled with experience increases the range of possible satisfactory solutions to a problem. The principal must communicate the idea to his colleagues that the whole human enterprise is constantly in a state of becoming, forever seeking to improve, realizing that as it reaches one goal, a higher goal comes into view.

A principal must have strong convictions about what he believes "now" and yet equally strong convictions that his beliefs are malleable and not set in concrete concerning "tomorrow." The author would not want to leave this thought without saying he personally holds absolute truths philosophically about the origin and destiny of man (Anno Domini) but finds no difficulty in taking an existential point of view of education and society.

Man, and systems that serve him such as education, should continually seek to create better services to meet emerging needs. Principals, by accepting the position, have agreed to join with those who are seeking better answers to what will always be tougher educational questions.

Leading requires risk taking in the sense that when you say, "I believe this is what we ought to do," you have, like the clay pigeon, stood still for a moment at least and thus become a fixed target for those who make it their business to challenge the ideas of others. There seems to be a hierarchy of roles in life which results in some thinking of better solutions, some implementing them with gusto, some not caring one way or another, and finally the group who can be counted on to cavil at the best ideas of the thinkers. One should not conclude that the last group is entirely negative or of no value to the others. They, in fact, do crush many ideas that need crushing and cause other ideas to go through the crucible of refinement. Thinkers need to recognize and accept the hierarchy and not to overreact. Dissenters play a useful role and are going to exist whether one likes it or not. Thinkers need to learn to adjust to discordance and to recognize its place in the system.

Functional Conflict

Differentiated staffing causes the number of opportunities for interaction on issues of importance among participants (principals, teacher leaders, teachers, clerks, students) to escalate drastically compared to the degree of such interaction in a traditional school. Top-to-bottom communication in a classical hierarchy generally reduces interaction and curtails the frequency and intensity of confrontation. Full-flow communication assumes by its presence that ideas and direction setting can emanate from any level of the organization.

Differentiated staffing is a full-flow communication model, thus increasing interaction considerably. Academic senates, team meetings, curriculum committees, peer-led in-service education, and teacher-student advisory groups all are vehicles which intensify communication in differentiated staffing.

If one accepts Homans' theory, described in his book *The Human Group,*[12] then there is agreement that increased interaction will lead to increased liking. However, one may feel that Homans overlooked the possibility that increased interaction may just as well bring about increased hostility, especially when the system is not prepared to accept divergent views.

---

[12]George C. Homans, *The Human Group* (New York: Harcourt, Brace & Co., 1950).

Conflict is naturally one byproduct of a system which provides channels for disagreement. It is essential that a school system considering differentiated staffing understands that interaction within groups escalates far beyond previous levels. Such escalation will intensify relationships. Whether these increased relationships are functional or dysfunctional depends in large part on the ability of the system to be receptive to dissent. Ill feelings, when suppressed either by overt actions of power figures or by implied coercion, tend not to disappear but to become magnified.

Therefore, the skillful principal will have to not only tolerate dissent, but develop an atmosphere of respect and admiration for minority points of view.

Lewis Coser addresses himself to those who feel conflict is always at the expense of harmony when he states:

> . . . no group can be entirely harmonious, for it would then be devoid of process and structure. Groups require disharmony as well as harmony, disassociation as well as association; and conflicts within them are by no means altogether disruptive factors. Group formation is the result of both types of processes. The belief that one process tears down what the other builds up, so that what finally remains is the result of subtracting the one from the other, is based on a misconception.[13]

It seems organizations such as schools, which provide few channels for dissent without unreasonable risk (sanctions, penalties, withdrawal of support and/or friendship) are moving towards a crisis of their own making.

One last comment about conflict. Groups which have grown to a close working relationship and who hold common goals, such as academic senates and teaching teams in a differentiated staffing school, need to be able to allow dissent to occur in an acceptable and constructive manner. Since hard-core dissent or harsh rejections tend to divide groups that have worked together in a fruitful relationship, an alternative and kinder means of disagreement is often sought. The display of a keen sense of humor seems to fill that need. A point can be made humorously and in an unobtrusive manner. A ready wit and the ability to jest allows the ambivalent (a desire to love but a need to hate or disagree) nature of a close relationship to be expressed.

---

[13]Lewis A. Coser, *The Functions of Social Conflict* (New York: The Free Press, 1956), p. 31.

People working closely together are going to disagree. If they do not disagree, it isn't because of homogeneity of thought. It is more likely to be due to the fact that the organization cannot tolerate dissent. Healthy groups often utilize a friendly repartee to make a strong point. Perceptive principals ought to learn to read between the lines of a poignant rebut sandwiched between smiles.

Good Leaders Do Not Always "Lead"

Principals who fear that their pet philosophy or hard-earned conclusions may suffer alteration are not good candidates for a differentiated situation. The very essence of differentiated staffing is wrapped up in the idea of collegial relationships, recognizing that one's colleagues cannot be rendered impotent and at the same time still remain colleagues. For those inclined to employ the Christian ethic in making decisions, note what Paul wrote to the Romans in the New Testament: "Let us have a real warm affection for one another as between brothers, and a willingness to let the other man have the credit." Or notice the physician, Luke's, statement, "The highest among you must bear himself like the youngest, the chief of you like a servant."[14] Platitudes? Yes, but essentially the basis of a healthy relationship among members of a group.

Differentiated staffing will probably be attempted by many who fail to accept the basic premises upon which the theory is built. The key assumption is, in the author's opinion, that people are inherently good and have considerable potential. Conversely, they are not inherently evil, lazy and indolent, and in need of protection from themselves by the enlightened few. It is not differentiated staffing that will fail, but its adherents who mean well and who capitulate to practices of the old regime when the pressure is on.

Maslow established the following points in formulating his theory known as *The Third Force in Psychology*,[15] which is summarized in a pamphlet entitled *Breakthrough in Psychology*, by Frank Goble and Peggy Granger.

---

[14]*The New Testament in Four Versions* (New York: The Iverson-Ford Associates, 1963), p. 487.

[15]Frank Goble, *The Third Force in Psychology* (New York: Grossman Publishers, 1970).

The recognition that the average individual is only using a tiny portion of his potential, including his potential to be creative, realistic, mature and responsible.

The conviction that man's needs are not merely physiological but include psychological needs for self-respect, respect and approval from others, freedom, justice, order, growth and achievement.[16]

Traditional organizational systems heavily laden with staff and line relationships and relying on authority instead of knowledge as a basis for decision-making, flatly deny there is any value in employing Third Force principles. They are often, by default, declaring their co-workers to be incapable of higher-order contributions. Likewise, the uninformed may tend to classify all conflict as harmful and dysfunctional rather than analyze its origins and provide for its insertion in normal group processes.

One point of view held by many advocates of differentiated staffing offers some hope for the principal who fears he is forfeiting his hard-earned right to lead. That point of view is that principals should behave persuasively and with conviction. They need not apologize for holding deep convictions about educational philosophy. Differentiated staffing advocates would want them to state their ideas as engagingly and strongly as possible. But that sort of behavior is what most people would like to see as typical for all members of the group.

The Integration of Personal and Organizational Goals

Any principal who truly feels coercion is a viable means of accomplishing organizational tasks simply does not understand the nature of fully functioning adults. Healthy organizations recognize the mutual interdependence of the goals of the organization and the goals (needs) of the individual. The probability of accomplishing goals is heightened as individuals within the organization function better. In other words, the growth of an organization is correlated (over long periods of time) with the growth of the individuals that comprise the organization.

---

[16]Frank Goble and Peggy Granger, *Breakthrough in Psychology* (Pasedena, Cal.: Thomas Jefferson Research Center, 1969), p.16.

Chris Argyris refers to organizations which behave in this manner as "organic organizations" which are characterized by:

> (1) decision-making widely done throughout the organization, (2) an emphasis on mutual dependence and cooperation based on trust, confidence, and high technical or professional competence, (3) a constant pressure to enlarge tasks and interrelate them so that the concern for the whole is emphasized, (4) the decentralization of responsibility for and the use of information, rewards and penalties, membership, (5) participants at all levels being responsible for developing and maintaining loyalty and committment at as high a level as possible, and (6) an emphasis on status through contribution to the whole and inter-group and interindividual cooperation.[17]

As one attempts to see the role of the individual in the Organic Organization, it is useful to consider the notion of *synergy* (also called synergism). This term is defined as "The action of two or more substances, organs or organisms to achieve an effect of which each is individually incapable,"[18] Ruth Benedict (1887-1948) uses the term when she refers to a condition "Where people cooperated together for mutual advantage, not necessarily because they were unselfish, but because the customs of society made cooperation worthwhile."[19] Maslow commented, "The society with high synergy is one in which virtue pays."[20]

It becomes the task of the principal to permit teachers and students to participate in an environment where it is possible that their contributions can be self-satisfying as well as beneficial to the goals of the school. When that happens it is likely people will enjoy their work and give themselves fully to it, or in Benedict's terms, achieve high synergy. Conversely, the lack of congruence between the goals of the individual and the goals of the school results in low or nonexistent synergy.

Paul Hersey and Ken Blanchard chart the corresponding relationship of the goals of management and the goals of subordinates indicating that the actual level of attainment depends

---

[17]Chris Argyris, *Integrating the Individual and the Organization* (New York: John Wiley and Sons, Inc., 1964), p. 185.

[18]*The American Heritage Dictionary* (New York: Dell Publishing Co., 1970).

[19]Frank Goble, *The Third Force in Psychology*, p. 108.

[20]*Ibid.*, p. 108.

upon the compatibility of the goals of the two groups. They summarily state, ". . . . the closer we can get the individual's goals and objectives to the organization's goals, the greater will be the organizational performance. . . ."[21]

In terms of a solution to the problem of independent and yet interdependent goals, Hersey and Blanchard suggest that one consider an approach referred to by many organizations as "Management by Objectives."[22] In essence, Management by Objectives (MBO) is a change strategy whereby participants in the organization come to agreement on the issue of goals and *jointly* establish means to accomplish the goals, specifying such processes as the dimensions of tasks, role of personnel, amount of dollar resources, time involved, and quality control. The key to MBO strategy is the mutual agreement on goals.

So whether one speaks of (a) an organization where one works for us rather than them, (b) an organic organization, (c) a condition of high synergy, (d) compatibility of individual and organizational goals, or (e) management by objectives, the theme remains the same. The long-range and continuing successful attainment of organizational objectives is in direct proportion to the degree of congruence between the goals (needs) of individuals and those of the organization.

Instructional Leader, Not Clerk

Many principals are concerned about the transitional problems which would occur if they were to move from their present role to that of a differentiated staffing principal. The new role seems to require much more time. Principals usually say "This idea of being an instructional leader and a specialist in human relations is fine, but when will I find time?"

Principals are busy now but primarily because they are entrapped by administrivia. They spend hours handling details and making decisions any high school graduate could do as well. The principal and his secretary must, out of necessity, work out many problems which arise daily. The author never kept a log of what he

---

[21]Paul Hersey and Kenneth H. Blanchard, *Management of Organizational Behavior* (Englewood Cliffs, New Jersey: Prentice-Hall, Inc., 1969), p. 117.

[22]See George S. Odiorne, *Management by Objectives* (New York: Pitman Publishing Corporation, 1965).

did as a school principal, but if he had, it would have included tasks such as:

- Checking out keys to the staff
- Sorting out mail and sending it to the proper curriculum area
- Dropping the "principal's letter to parents" off at the P.T.A. president's house
- Meeting with the school safety committee
- Getting audio-visual equipment tagged
- Ordering films, arranging for their distribution and return
- Ordering teachers' supplies
- Getting a dirty word on the wall painted over
- Having broken windows repaired
- Monitoring the school budget
- Developing room use and student assignment charts
- Charting grading practices
- Ordering printed forms, report cards, diplomas, and other office supplies

To avoid wasting the principal's expertise, differentiated staffing plans should include the employment of a school manager to take over the administrivia which inundates a school principal. Utilization of a school manager gives a principal much more time than he formerly had. The expense of a school manager (about the same as another well-compensated principal's secretary) will be minimal if one considers the value of an educational consultant (the former principal) available to the staff full time.

As the principal's role emerges from what was basically an administrative emphasis to the role of educational leader, changes will take place. In differentiated staffing, the following will be typical priorities for the principal:

1. Systematic study of the behavioral sciences
2. Meeting with curriculum specialists regarding logistical decisions
3. Assisting curriculum specialists with personnel problems
4. Chairing the school's decision-making body and being responsible for the administration of policy
5. Coordinating public, board of education, and interschool relations
6. Working for the improvement of student-staff relations
7. Providing information about the state laws (keeping the school legal)

Serve, not Supervise

As is the case with all persons in a school district, principals exist to bring one more degree of competency and service to bear upon learners. In a modern school system, they do not exist to supervise teachers. They must, in order to warrant their presence in the system, contribute to the singular cause of schools. As teachers facilitate the daily learning of students, principals are charged with a similar task, that of providing what might best be described as an "enabling environment" for teachers. Principals are to assist the staff with the problems which arise in and out of the classroom. Most will now admit the principal is unable to serve as a specialist in the sense of helping a teacher understand his content better or assisting him with the selection of instructional materials. One of his primary tasks is to demonstrate, by his actions, a willingness to serve rather than supervise. Few administrators really think of themselves as facilitators. They have tended to act out a supervisory role loaded with the traditional expectancies considered generic to the role.

This idea of supervision, of course, has developed as a result of the way the principal's role was first designed. Principals have, in the past, been considered headmasters, and as such were the pillars of experience and knowledge. Teachers literally served the principal and he was the authority symbol on campus. Some feel this situation was perpetuated (given the sexist nature of school organization) by the presence of so many female teachers. They were expected to readily acquiesce to the patriarchal role he played.

A further entrenchment of this historical role occurred when teachers were not protected by fair employment practices. The image of the principal as an authoritiarian grew. No teacher who wanted to remain employed dared openly disagree with the principal.

The modern principal must accept the responsibility of incorporating what the behavioral sciences have taught us about management principles such as: Capacities of individuals clamor to be used; people need to be able to exercise personal prerogatives, they need to be able to act creatively; people are not basically lazy; people want to be achieving and progressing.

It is the task of today's principals to operate within the parameters of current research about how people behave and what motivates or inhibits them.

No Man's Land

Principals should learn the lesson taught by expert tennis players. "One is either at the net or near the baseline. One should never get caught between those two points. That middle area is 'no man's land'."

So it should be with principals. To try to be "management" when you are uptown and "labor" back at the school site is a dangerous game. Principals are responsible to the superintendent for the operation of a school. The superintendent is responsible to the board of education. The board is "management." They alone make final decisions on policy. The superintendent and his staff, down to the last custodian, teacher, and bus driver are an employed team of people, all responsible ultimately to the board.

Principals likewise are team members working with the various staff members to achieve the goals of the organization. Somehow it has become a popular game to classify administrators as management. As the writer stated in a recent issue of *Educational Technology:*

> Teacher organizations are asking for more power in the educational decision-making process. The tug-of-war has clearly been focused as a labor-management issue. Teachers have been labeled labor, and adminstrators have been aligned with management. Adminstrators have witnessed with increasing alarm the militant, active stance of teachers' organizations. The anticipated merger of NEA and AFT has escalated management's anxiety.
>
> In an act of self-preservation and in an effort to unite the forces of management, administrators have reacted with hurried merger talks of their own.
>
> The wedge of division between teachers and administrators is being driven in deeply and with haste, for how else can the labels of "labor" and "management" take on real meaning?
>
> Mergers and exclusive associational memberships are developing on the basis that we must unite to be able to gain all of the

political leverage possible; this leverage is equated with security. The labor-management distinction becomes the Raison d' Etre of each group, so long as they must exist separately.[23]

Principals and senior teachers, under differentiated staffing, are equals. As such, they develop school policy in a collegial way. The principal is clearly not "management" any more than are the senior teachers. No man's land, or part labor, part management, is, in the author's opinion, a piece of ground no informed administrator would want to defend.

SUMMARY

Differentiated staffing is the formalization of effective leadership practices. It enables a system to institutionalize a managerial philosophy which retards ineffective leadership styles and facilitates effective leadership styles.

Effective leadership styles take into account such research and ideas as McGregor's Theory Y characteristics, Herzberg's motivational factors, Maslow's Eupsychian Management assumptions, and Likert's research on system 4, participative management.

This new leadership style requires that (a) power be shared, (b) non-normative behavior be permitted, (c) penalties and rewards as a power-based motivational device be eliminated, (d) participants assume greater degrees of responsibility and accountability for the accomplishment of personal and organizational goals, (e) the maximum growth of each participant (self-actualization) be a legitimate goal of the schools, and (f) leadership be viewed as a service function rather than one of exercising control.

Differentiated staffing recognizes that principals are generalists in respect to curriculum development, teaching methodology, and material selection. Principals are not trained, in respect to these skills, to lead teams of specialists, nor are they expected to do so.

Traditional practices of principals result in the "involvement" of teachers in leadership and decision-making, however, principals in those situations usually retain veto power and actually are able

---

[23]Bruce G. Caldwell, "Differentiated Staffing, Who is Labor and Who is Management?" *Education Technology,* December, 1970, p. 59.

to increase the potential for issuing penalties and rewards by such "involvement." Differentiated staffing, like other innovations, is suffering from courtship by well-intentioned, but uncommitted suitors. The result is a diminishment in potential for long-range, dramatic changes.

Differentiated staffing does not dismiss a principal from *a* leadership role, it simply requires him to step down from *the* leadership role. His input, charisma, leadership, and insight become a part of the whole, rather than a fixed course for the entire school. If knowledge is power, his potency is as great as his preparedness.

The principal must be expert in group relations, and be able to orchestrate the skills of others. That calls for cuing, *fortissimo* and *pianissimo* at propitious moments, recognizing that leadership entails risk taking and consistently authentic behavior.

Principals cannot expect to venture forth with the staff into unplowed ground and not receive any repercussions. Conflict is an essential part of a healthy organization. It is only the stifling of dissension which leads to catastrophic results.

The achievement of organizational goals should not be in deference to, or at the expense of personal goals. As the organization facilitates the self-actualization of its participants, they in turn propel the organization forward.

Administrivia, which takes the bulk of a principal's time, should be delegated to a school manager and the principal should begin to perform professional functions appropriate to his training and remuneration.

Principals must see themselves as service agents/facilitators. Patriarchal, benevolent dictator, big daddy roles of the past imply a degree of omniscience reserved for a deity, not a person who, too, is "becoming." The idea of staff and line relationships, bosses and bossed, oppressors and oppressed, is repugnant within a professional colleague relationship and antithetical to healthy management principles.

THREE

The Role of
the Senior Teacher

Senior Teachers Are Significant Change Agents

The positions of senior teacher in Temple City are the key roles in differentiated staffing. The quality of the changes which can be anticipated are in direct proportion to the level of skill and degree of commitment held by these people. Their effectiveness is facilitated by the degree of power and autonomy inherent within their role.

Since the senior teachers are selected and evaluated by those they serve, one of their primary tasks is to satisfy the needs of their subordinates. They are not leaders due to the beneficence of a principal or superintendent. On the contrary, in their new role they become economic, technical, and social colleagues with what was formerly regarded as the "uptown" administrative hierarchy.

Is Teaching a Profession?

The role of teacher leaders in differentiated staffing is unlike the one which prevails commonly in American education as described by Dan C. Lortie:

> Teachers, whether on term or continuing contracts, are officially employees without powers of governance. Public schools, unlike major universities, have no legally-based "senates" or similar arrangements for collective participation by faculty members in the overall operation of the organization. The formal and legal allocation of authority in school systems is monolithic, hierarchical, and concentrated; official powers are focused at the

apex of the structure. A system of this kind implies that those in
command set goals, oversee their realization, and are accountable
for outcomes.[1]

As Lortie points out, teachers at the opposite end of the apex of
power seem unwilling to take steps which are necessary to assume
a posture more closely resembling a profession. He cites a study
conducted by Sharma which indicates without explication that
teachers in his national sample did not wish to participate in
personnel decisions about other teachers.[2]

In relation to differentiated staffing, one thing appears certain:
teachers must, if they want "professional status," begin to accept
the responsibilities that status incurs. According to Conrad Briner,
professional   status   related   to   teacher   involvement   in
decision-making is not feasible given the present conditions in
education. He contends, "It is not possible to hold teachers
accountable for the quality of learning. They are too little
involved in educational management, including the allocation of
resources; and surprisingly, the pronouncements of teacher
organizations to the contrary, they do not want to be involved
greatly."[3]

A present reality, then, for a system considering differentiated
staffing is the reluctance teachers in general will have towards the
notion of self-regulation. Those same reluctant teachers are also
discontent with "outsiders" doing the regulating, so perhaps given
the alternative of being regulated by "us" or "them," teachers will
begin to move towards self-regulation. Those who do not are not
really seeking freedom gained through self-regulation but are
perpetuating "authoritarianism" as it has classically existed in
schools.

Healthy organizational principles are only applicable with
healthy, self-actualizing people. Freedom for the immature,
dependent types is not a privilege to be sought, but a liability to
be avoided. Differentiated staffing assumes that most of the
participants are eagerly *seeking* greater levels of responsibility and

---

[1] Dan C. Lortie, "The Balance of Control and Autonomy in Elementary School
Teaching," in *The Semi-Professions and Their Organizations,* ed. Amitai Etzioni, (New
York: The Free Press, 1969), p. 4.

[2] *Ibid.,* p. 25.

[3] Conrad Briner, "Administrators and Accountability," *Theory Into Practice,* a
publication of Ohio State University, Volume VIII, no. 4, October, 1969, p. 206.

autonomy and are prepared to be accountable for their exercise of discretion.

Additional evidence indicating the presence of professional hesitancy on the part of teachers is cited by Lortie. He reminds us that the licensing of teachers is not controlled by the teaching profession, that senior colleagues in education do not establish expected levels of performance from junior colleagues seeking full partnership in the profession, and that teachers are granted tenure on the basis of an administrator's judgment and not on any criteria established by teachers. Perhaps the point regarding teachers who are "semiprofessional" which is most difficult to rationalize is the one which Lortie makes regarding the vacuum in which teachers "learn their trade:"

> It is noteworthy that teachers . . . had difficulty in describing colleagues of outstanding competence; their replies frequently contained the phrase "we never see each other at work" . . .It is significant to observe that the first year of actual teaching experience—the point of full involvement in accountable teaching responsibility—is generally not accompanied by regular or intensive contact with senior colleagues. The beginning elementary teacher is, of course, "visited" by the principal and probably a central office supervisor, but the fraction of working time which is supervised is very small. (Twelve visits of two hours duration each would be high and would consist of less than 3 per cent of the teacher's first year, estimated at thirty-eight weeks of thirty hours each.) . . . Elementary teachers learn their core skills in isolation from other adults.[4]

Teaching, the Invisible Performance

Further emphasis regarding the cumulative effect of isolation is described by Lortie.

> Teaching techniques are developed and used by thousands of individuals in restricted contact with one another; there are no general expectations that individual teachers should record their experiences in such a way that it becomes the general property of the professional group. No provisions are made in the daily schedule of the teacher for such activity. . . . The successes and failures of architects are recorded in stone, wood, and steel.

---

[4] Dan C. Lortie, *The Semi-Professions*, pp. 27-28.

Experience in these professions has a cumulative quality; what teachers learn is largely lost. It is not possible for the professor of education to gain ready access to decades of "cases" for critical review and scientific testing; nor is it easy for the beginning teacher to get the feeling that she begins where predecessors left off.[5]

The role of the senior teacher requires the invisible performance of teaching to diminish, if not disappear. This is another reason it is difficult to introduce the role. Teachers, like many adults, enjoy being able to perform their duties without direct scrutiny. The presence of another adult in a teacher's classroom can be very threatening. It can be observed that teachers tighten up when an outsider watches them at work. They behave in an artificial manner and they expect their students to display "company" manners. Some excellent teachers refuse to have student teachers assigned to them or balk at the offer of a parent to come in and assist. This kind of resistance can and should be overcome, but it will have to be recognized that teachers have generally been conditioned to work in isolation from other adults.

The existence of the role of senior teacher is contingent upon interaction with staff and associate teachers. If staff and associate teachers were to continue in the independent, autonomous behavior patterns of the past, the new role would be of slight consequence and few changes of any substantive nature could be expected to occur.

Differentiated Staffing and Teacher Collaboration

Differentiated staffing requires some form of teaming. The concept will not function well if teachers are going to work in a completely independent manner. The differentiation of teaching is not able to be accomplished in self-contained units wherein a single teacher has the ultimate responsibility for all teaching-learning. The term "differentiation" connotes specialization and diversification. Isolated teachers are one personality trying to interact with and be responsive to a wide variety of students with many backgrounds. They will do well with some students and fail to develop a good relationship with others. One teacher is neither intellectually nor

---

[5]*Ibid.,* pp. 28-29.

culturally equipped to satisfy the interests and needs of a heterogeneous group of students. Teachers working in isolation are denying the value of collaboration for themselves, their students, and their colleagues.

The importance of the role of the teacher to the learning process is made explicit by Madeline Hunter, Director of the University Elementary School at the University of California in Los Angeles.

> Even when the student has selected his own learning, a teacher can markedly facilitate, impede or even arrest it. All of us have had the experience of learning very well with one teacher and only with great effort with a different teacher, even in the same subject area. We have enrolled in a course in which we had little interest but which a teacher unexpectedly made fascinating. At other times our interest in a subject has been extinguished by the instructor.[6]

Most agree that the teacher is instrumental. Differentiated staffing asserts that no teacher working as a "loner" is able to contend with all the variables present in a group of students nor able to capitalize on the teachable moments which come and go a thousand times a day as well as a teacher who collaborates regularly with a team. The old model presupposed teaching skills were inherent traits widely distributed among credential holders and that interaction was unnecessary. Each new teacher had to "discover" methods, means, and often goals as if they were the first to ever tread the path of being an educator.

In education, it is entirely possible for a teacher to violate everything which is known about the way people learn and to get away with it. Teachers are generally not evaluated on the basis of applying effective learning theory. As pointed out by Charles E. Silberman in *Crisis in the Classroom:*

> If teachers are obsessed with silence and lack of movement, therefore, it is in large part because it is the chief means by which their competence is judged. A teacher will rarely, if ever, be called on the carpet or denied tenure because his students have not learned anything; he most certainly will be rebuked if his students

---

[6]Madeline Hunter, "The Teaching Process," in *The Teacher's Handbook,* ed. Dwight W. Allen and Eli Seifman (Glenview, Ill.: Scott, Foresman and Company, 1971), p. 146.

are talking or moving about the classroom, or—even worse—found outside the room, and he may earn the censure of his colleagues as well. Nor will teachers receive suggestions from their supervisors as to how to improve their teaching methods and materials; they will receive suggestions for improving "discipline."[7]

With little or no attention given to the acquisition of teaching skills and the evaluation of student learning, we find isolation reinforced at every turn. Sarason and his associates underline this:

> Despite the continuous contact with children, moreover, teaching is a lonely profession. Teachers rarely get a chance to discuss their problems or their successes with their colleagues, nor do they, as a rule, receive any kind of meaningful help from their supervisors, not even in the first year of teaching. "When we first started working in the schools," members of the Yale University's Psycho-Educational Clinic report, "we were asked in several instances in the early weeks, not to go into several classrooms *because* the teachers were new."[8]

Differentiated staffing requires the formation and utilization of collaborative processes among teachers. A differentiated team consists of the staff and associate teachers, led by a senior teacher, serviced by a master teacher, and augmented by student teachers and paraprofessionals. These teams interact regularly, in and out of the classroom, engaging in such activities as planning curriculum, team teaching, in-service education, and evaluation.

Teachers and Accountability

It would be difficult to imagine the state of the art which would exist in medicine or architecture if neophytes were given the same degree of responsibility as seasoned journeymen. Patients would suffer and structures would collapse if all physicians and architects had "equal responsibilities." Only the field of education with its many quixotic practitioners permits professionals to function on the basis of intuition and feeling. Teachers have thus far escaped

---

[7] Charles E. Silberman, *Crisis in the Classroom* (New York: Random House, Inc., 1970), p. 144.

[8] *Ibid.*, p. 144.

the public indictment (which would surely be the lot of doctors and architects) that accompanies large degrees of failure. Educators have also been quite successful in eluding the issue of accountability which one would expect to rear its head given present conditions.

Professional organizations are trying to anticipate the accountability crisis by introducing their members to the idea of "competency-based instruction." The Association of Classroom Teachers discovered that this approach is apparently not going to be easily sold to the teachers if the headline in *Education Daily* is representative of most teachers.

> *Teachers See Competency-Based Instruction as Peril to Tenure.*
> The classroom teacher sees the wave of competency-based instruction as a threat that will wash away his tenure, force him into extra hours of lesson preparation without extra pay, and drown him in standards he had had no part in setting up. These fears recurred many times in the recommendations made by eight workshops sponsored last week by the Association of Classroom Teachers at the National Education Association headquarters in Washington, D.C.[9]

Competency-based instruction simply means teachers will have to possess measurable skills which when applied in the classroom will result in fairly predictable outcomes in the form of student changes in behavior (such as possessing new skills, knowledge, or attitudes). These teacher skills would be required for credentialing purposes and become, in a sense, a screening/evaluation tool for administration.

This movement, like Program Planning Budget Systems (PPBS) and Performance Contracts, is linked to the new surge of interest in accountability. Leon Lessinger focuses on the accountability problem when he states:

> The American education system today is experiencing the most sustained, diverse, widespread, and persistent challenge ever to confront it. Virtually everyone agrees that something has gone wrong, that corrective action is needed. Congress and state legislatures have responded to this crisis of public concern by

---

[9]*Education Daily,* published by Capital Publications, Inc., Washington, D.C., November 30, 1971, p. 6.

providing additional funds, but are increasingly dismayed that puzzling educational problems persist. Interest in some form of fiscal accountability for what the American public puts *into* the education of its young people has been with the schools for a long time. It is evident that some form of accountability for what comes *out of* the schools is required as well.[10]

The teaching profession must accept the reality that the taxpayer's demands for increased accountability are going to result in changes. A few of these anticipated changes are:

1. Transformation of the teacher's role from information-giver to the director of learning.
2. More openness and flexibility, and less group orientation in school facilities.
3. Increased relevance in the curriculum.
4. Exposal and elimination of outmoded myths and an incomplete educational tradition.[11]

The Genesis of the Senior Teacher Role

Changes of the kind called for are not easily accomplished. Collaboration and cooperation of a higher order must prevail. New specific skills are required.

The old hierarchy and rigid isolationism of the organization must give way to a more responsive system. Differentiated staffing begins with the premise that everyone can improve. It also places those who try to help others to improve in the role of service agents as opposed to supervisors. To be a service agent one must determine what services are needed from those being served. The acceptability of the senior teacher role and the ultimate benefits rendered by its incumbents depend in large part on the establishment of *mutual goals* by team participants. If an undifferentiated team can agree on broad goals it then becomes an easy task to identify the independent and interdependent needs which exist.

---

[10]Leon M. Lessenger, "Accountability: Its Implications for the Teacher," in *The Teacher's Handbook,* pp. 73, 77.

[11]*Ibid.,* p. 77.

The charge then becomes one of identifying activities which will enable team participants to achieve their goals.

Depending on the level of skill, experience and sophistication present within the group there will be various needs. Examples of needs could include the following:

1. *In-service training* in the use of media such as video and audio tape equipment, film projectors of all types, sound production equipment, etc., and media materials such as programmed tapes, phono-visual aids, student-produced films, micro-teaching films, transparencies, etc.
2. *Seminar techniques* such as inquiry training, micro-teaching skills, listening skills, and small group techniques.
3. *Flexible space utilization* including open space, multi-modal space (large, middle and small groups, labs, and tutorials) project and/or activity areas as well as facilities outside the walls of the school.
4. *Alternate forms of reporting students' progress* such as parent conferences without report cards, but with achievement indices, pass-credit-no-credit systems, or periodic individual performances sheets.

A department or team may have other less typical needs for a senior teacher to consider. It is not unlikely that the team will need to have some guidelines in the use of the team paraprofessional(s). The team may need a parent volunteer program enacted as a means of achieving their goals.

The team could ask the senior teacher to work out an alternative to the customary preservice education program for credential candidates or to consider employing interns (several at a part-time rate) instead of filling a teacher vacancy within the department.

A need may arise among the members of a senior teacher's staff to visit some demonstration schools in the area or to attend professional conferences. (It is amazing how many teachers have *never* been to a professional conference.) Visits to other districts and to conferences often lead to the development of a teacher and/or student exchange program with neighboring districts.

Staff and associate teachers may have heard of a new program or curriculum idea and want further information on it or they may want vendors of educational technology and curriculum materials to provide demonstrations at the school.

All and more of the potential needs just mentioned have been actual needs of various teams in Temple City. Sometimes the needs cut across team and district lines and inter-school training programs are developed. Needs of staff and associate teachers are the foundation of the senior teacher job description. The needs of teams differ, making it necessary to assess needs each time a job description is written. This process of establishing goals, assessing needs, and translating them into training formats embodies the crucial fundamental steps in the development of the senior teacher role.

Employing a Senior Teacher

When the first senior teacher job descriptions were written, teams which were selecting leaders established their lists of needs. On the basis of this somewhat "general needs assessment," job descriptions were developed, the new positions were advertised, and applicants were requested. Temple City has, during the first five years of the program, followed a policy that the openings for teacher leader roles are first opened within the district and if no successful applicants emerge, the positions then are advertised outside the district. They did so assuming their training program for teacher leaders was yielding fruit. Even then, they filled several leadership openings with outside applicants.

The screening of applicants is done by a team of five persons, including two elected team-member representatives, the principal, the assistant superintendent, and a representative from outside the district (often a university specialist) selected by the team. On occasion, at the request of a team, the outside representative has been eliminated and an additional team member selected.

Temple City does not involve students or parents in the selection of senior teachers at this time; however, such a development would not be surprising. In fact, the last few principals have been selected by a committee composed of senior teachers, parent representatives, student representatives, and one administrator from the central office. Once a senior teacher applicant is selected, the job description is translated into performance criteria, enabling his evaluators to more objectively judge the merits of his service.

The original task force of the steering committee which dealt with job descriptions had made estimates when the proposal of differentiated staffing was in its design state, concerning senior teacher duties. Figure 3-1 is a copy of the original senior teacher job description based upon those early estimates.

SENIOR TEACHER

General Description

The senior teacher is primarily responsible for the application of curricular innovations in the classroom. The role may be described as putting educational innovations into effect in the classroom and subjecting them to the modifications which arise from day to day experience. Out of this work should emerge refined curriculum, sound in theory and practical in the light of classroom experience.

The senior teacher is the master practitioner in his area. He is the exemplary teacher, one who possesses a great deal of experience and training and who has remained vital and imaginative. He is knowledgeable of the most recent developments in teaching and in his subject/skill area. He is the teacher's teacher.

Specific Functions

1. Three-fifths to four-fifths of the time spent in classroom instruction as staff teacher.
2. Ten- or eleven-month contract (to be arranged).
3. Salary (basic salary schedule plus factors for leadership and extra time responsibilities with a range from $11,000-$14,000).
4. Conducts in-service classes, workshops, seminars for teachers in exemplary techniques and methods in subject or skill areas.
5. Is responsible for the assignment of student teachers.
6. Develops teaching strategies (pilot programs) which can implement new curricula.
7. Serves as advisor in curriculum development and research experiments.
8. May function as a teaching team leader.
9. Plans with his team the school schedule and pupil programming.
10. Aids staff teachers in discovering and refining methods to work with individuals and subject matter/skills.
11. Develops creative techniques and materials.
12. Coordinates work of all teachers in his subject/skill area.
13. May represent his area on the school academic senate.
14. Is responsible for the selection, performance, and evaluation of educational assistants in his area.

Training and/or Experience Required

1. Valid California teacher credential.
2. M.A./M.S. or equivalent (experience, time, travel, other professional, or unit equivalents pertinent to the professional assignment).

Personal Qualities Desired

1. In-depth knowledge of subject matter/skill area.
2. Demonstrates excellence as a teacher.
3. Manifests leadership capabilities.
4. Commands the respect of pupils and colleagues.
5. Demonstrates organizational abilities.
6. Demonstrates awareness of educational trends in his area.
7. Possesses ability to communicate effectively with colleagues, students, and parents.

Figure 3-1

Balancing Responsibilities and Rewards for
Senior Teachers

This general description was used to screen the first round of senior teachers, since Temple City had not yet developed specific job descriptions for each opening. Several specifics which planners had projected failed to materialize. For instance, implementors settled on a 3/5 maximum as a formal teaching load, an 11-month work year, and a higher salary range.

In general, it could be said the expectancies increased as did the inducements. Such a development is consonant with the postulations of organizational equilibrium as described by March and Simon. They support the theory that "Each participant will continue his participation in an organization only so long as the inducements offered him are as great or greater (measured in terms of his values and in terms of the alternatives open to him) than the contributions he is asked to make."[12] In other words, they theorize that organizational equilibrium is sustained when the inducement-contribution relationship is properly taken into account. From that, one could extrapolate a thesis which indicates that when contributions (expectancies) are in excess of inducements (rewards) disequilibrium results.

That seems like common sense; however, a quick look at the reward system in public schools denies that bit of logic and would lead one to feel that low contributions are "expected" and perpetuated by low inducements, maintaining a predictable *quid pro quo* relationship. The lore says, "you get what you pay for." March and Simon refer to it as an attainment of "zero point," meaning that point at which there is a balance between inducements and contributions. As has been pointed out, the single salary schedule gives all teachers, regardless of their level of contributions, equal inducements.

Regarding this search for zero point, which goes on continually as new contributions are expected by management and new inducements are in turn sought by labor, March and Simon indicate that " . . . very few of the 'satisfied' participants leave an organization whereas some, but not all, of the 'unsatisfied' participants leave."[13]

---

[12]James G. March and Herbert A. Simon, "The Theory of Organizational Equilibrium," in *Organizations: Systems, Control and Adaption*, ed. Joseph A. Litter 2nd ed., Vol. II, (New York: John Wiley & Sons, Inc., 1963), p. 270.

[13]*Ibid.*, p. 271.

Strong evidence of dissatisfaction among teachers is available if you equate dissatisfaction with leaving the profession. Recent U.S. Office of Education statistics indicate that 100,000 teachers leave the profession each year.[14] Silberman points out that the situation is even worse in the British Infant Schools. He reports that the Plowden Committee, an English Parliamentary Commission which reported in 1967, found " . . . that two-thirds of the women who had taught in infant schools (roughly students of the same age as American primary school youngsters) during a period of two years and nine months, were no longer in those schools at the end of the period."[15]

Such data offer momentum to those pleading for professional status for teachers based on the general notion of stabilizing the work force and tends to confirm the presence of organizational disequilibrium, if one accepts the ideas proposed by March and Simon.

Taking inducements into account, the original senior teacher job description gave way to more specific statements dealing with the actual performances a team could expect from a senior teacher. Figure 3-2 presents one such statement.

THE SENIOR TEACHER OF SOCIAL STUDIES

Curriculum

1. A social studies major and advanced work beyond the B.A. to include background in at least one of the following: economics, history, sociology, geography or anthropology, political science, American history.
2. Knowledge of recent trends in social studies to include the new California State Guidelines.
3. Ability to write performance objectives.
4. Demonstrate ability in curriculum design: "Unipac" approach.
5. Knowledge of new social studies curriculums and new materials in the field.
6. Possesses a broad overview of current research.

Instruction

1. A successful teacher on the junior high school level with current experience.
2. Knowledge of methodology as it uniquely applies to large group instruction, small group study, and independent study.
3. Knowledge of instructional modes: lecture techniques, inductive methods, independent study assignments, programmed instruction, etc.
4. Knowledge of instructional materials appropriate to each of the aforementioned items in number three.

---

[14]Stanley Elam and Will P. McClure, *Educational Requirements for the 1970's* (New York: Frederick A. Praeger, 1967).

[15]Charles E. Silberman, *Crisis in the Classroom,* p. 267. (Parenthetical statement added.)

5. Recent classes and workshops in curriculum development, flexible scheduling.
6. Knowledge of techniques of pupil diagnosis.
7. Ability to produce creative teaching aids.
8. Knowledge of teacher education instruments such as Flanders Interaction Analysis.

Organizational Abilities

1. Ability to organize and be responsible for the total social studies support system: media, teachers, paraprofessionals, resource centers.
2. Knowledge of flexible scheduling and pupil programming.
3. Knowledge of current organizational trends and grouping practices.
4. Knowledge of testing: instruments (standardized and nonstandardized) construction, and procedures.
5. Knowledge of organizational problems.

Personal Qualities

1. Possesses leadership qualities and initiates action.
2. Has undergone sensitivity training and is able to recognize "people" problems.
3. Can effectively relate to adolescents.
4. Has the ability to establish rapport with colleagues.
5. Ability to effect personal/professional growth in colleagues.
6. Works effectively with parents and paraprofessionals.
7. Has "decision-making" experience similar to Academic Senate.
8. Displays evident enthusiasm for the subject.
9. Possesses mature/adult approach to problem solving with colleagues, exhibiting stable personality and a high tolerance level.

Figure 3-2

Operationalizing the Senior Teacher Job Description

In the first attempt to operationalize the job description, individual teams being served met with the project director and developed performance indicators under the separate headings of curriculum, instruction, organizational abilities, and personal qualities. Under these headings the social studies team listed the various skills shown in Figure 3-2.

Again these expectancies were vague and not sufficiently measurable and steps were taken to state them in more behavioral, measurable terms. Examples of recent attempts by the social studies teachers at Oak Avenue Intermediate School to operationalize the job description give one a more complete picture of what a senior teacher is expected to accomplish. The format incorporated a less subjective stance when it forced respondents to place a check next to each performance under the columns of "accomplished," "not accomplished," and "not applicable." The choice of "not applicable" gave teachers an opportunity to not deal in an exclusively positive or negative manner with each performance, since some performances either were deemed unimportant in the judgment of the respondent or could not have been fulfilled, due to extenuating circumstances such as prolonged absences, mid-year transfers, etc.

The new format did, for the most part, force respondents to declare that a performance was or was not accomplished. For example, responses were required to such behaviors as:

	Accomplished	*Not Accomplished*	*Not Applicable*
a. Writes or assists teachers in writing performance objectives	___	___	___
b. Reports back on Master Teacher's evaluation of Oak Social Studies Program (at least once a semester).	___	___	___
c. Performs demonstration teaching or in-service training at least two times per semester for the purpose of illustration of new content, methods or materials for either grade level (including both grade levels during the year) (At least 70 percent of the staff must agree that such demonstrations are worthwhile).	___	___	___
d. Conducts periodic consultations (not less than once per semester with each teacher of the team regarding individual teacher satisfaction with the program).	___	___	___
e. Responsible for presenting expenditure requests to the staff for its consideration prior to presentation			

	Not Accomplished	*Not* Accomplished	*Applicable*
to the school senate (at least 70 percent of the staff must agree that the proposed budget is representative of the instructional program/objectives).	——	——	——
f. Reports to the school senate concerns and proposals of his area (at least 70 percent of such items must appear in the written minutes of the senate).	——	——	——
g. Ability to act on others' ideas.	——	——	——
h. Actively seeks professional consensus.[16]	——	——	——

It is apparent these performances could be written in an even more specific manner, further delineating the conditions, criteria and time span involved, but team members at Oak Avenue School have chosen to keep them broad. The strength in this job description/evaluation instrument is that (a) it can and should be updated as new needs emerge, (b) it forces the respondents into a pencil-and-paper, periodic feedback pattern, and (c) leadership people are aware of the need to perform in specific ways.

It should be noted that as differentiated staffing has moved into all of Temple City's schools, job descriptions and evaluation instruments have not gotten more standardized. Efforts toward standardization are fruitless in that no rigid pattern of expectations can exist among different schools and different teachers. A senior teacher's job should change as the needs of the staff he serves change. Some consistencies can remain from year to year as a means of institutionalizing the change, but it is critical that the role be responsive to emerging needs vis-à-vis past needs.

---

[16]See Appendix 1 for the complete senior teacher job description/evaluation instrument of the Oak Avenue Social Studies Department.

A Case Study of a Senior Teacher

My personal experience with differentiated staffing has enabled me to observe firsthand some significant behavioral changes on the part of role incumbents at the senior teacher level. A case in point is that of William H. (Bill) Schmidt. There are other cases of equal significance; however, this particular case is an excellent example of what an outstanding teacher can do when given the opportunity.

Bill had taught at Oak Avenue Intermediate School for ten years prior to the implementation of differentiated staffing. He was a respected and loved teacher from the beginning. It is interesting but of no particular importance that he was blind and had been so since he was a child, and that he was the first blind teacher regularly employed as a teacher in the State of California. Many parents looked forward to having their child taught by Bill. He had demonstrated a sincere concern for children, outstanding ability as an instructor, and his opinion regarding personal and professional matters was frequently sought.

As an instructor at Oak, he taught math most frequently but had taught other subjects from time to time (including auto mechanics and wrestling). He was a recognized leader, having served as an officer in the Temple City Educational Association and having received a number of honors including National Defense Education Act grants for advanced study and numerous opportunities to speak to professional and civic groups.

The point that it is important to focus on is that Bill, even though he had been an outstanding citizen and educator, still remained a "teacher" with the same pall of anonymity referred to when Dwight Allen said "a teacher is a teacher, is a teacher."[17] He taught well, dealt with problems as best he could, and tried for ten years to improve the quality of his contributions to students.

Not until Bill became the senior teacher of math at Oak Intermediate did he really become a formidable influence on others, especially his teaching colleagues and *all* of the students at

---

[17]Dwight W. Allen, speech delivered in Temple City, California, March 7, 1969.

Oak Intermediate. No matter how creative, ingenious, or committed he was to improving education, he, in his former status, was
powerless to do any more than teach his own students and exhibit
"normal coping behavior" with the power structure of the schools.
As a senior teacher, Bill gained complete control over the math
program at Oak. It was truly his program to make of it what he
could.

Complete control as intended here can best be defined by
comparison. People generally regard a principal as the local power
figure. It is his program, faculty, facility, and budget. In this case
the senior teacher assumes all of the above "ownership" for his
area, math.

The Senior Teacher as a Change Agent

Bill, like others, with a new degree of autonomy and accountability, exercised his prerogative early. He completely revamped
the physical resources allotted to his team, rearranged the schedule, and began vitalizing the curriculum.

The math team gathered a wide variety of print and nonprint
resources. These resources are organized in a manner that enables a
student, as he studies any particular topic, to have access to such
learning aids as film strips, 8mm loops, audio-tapes, charts,
textbooks, transparencies and a variety of manipulative devices.
These resources are placed in a central area (resource center)
which is supervised by a paraprofessional. Each topic studied has
programmed learning activity packets (including the objectives of
the packet, a pre-test, a set of activities, and a post-test) which
integrate the resources available into the assigned activities.

The offices of the math team are adjacent to the resource center
and math teachers are either assigned and/or available to students
using the math resource center. Each teacher posts his weekly
schedule on his office door. The schedule indicates a teacher's
class and departmental meetings, and times a teacher is available to
work with an individual student. The student who wants to make
an appointment with a teacher enters his name on any open
module of time where the teacher and himself have a common
unscheduled period. Some students sign up as small groups when
they have friends who need help on the same topic themselves.

The paraprofessionals who are assigned to the resource centers and labs are screened and selected by the team. The senior teacher has supervision and evaluation responsibilities for the paraprofessionals. Most of the training of paraprofessionals occurs within the team setting; however, workshops at the school and district for paraprofessionals are conducted at several intervals.

It should be noted that other academic areas developed resource centers and practical/aesthetic skill areas (art, physical education, home economics, music, foreign language). All resource centers and laboratories (project and activity areas) are available to students during the unstructured part (40 to 50 percent) of a student's day.

Bill's team specifically changed the program for seventh and eighth grade math from separate courses of study to a two-year program which investigates topics in a spiral manner. That is, when his team deals with fractions, for instance, there are four levels of groups working simultaneously on curriculum packages of varying difficulty. Each "new topic" is pre-tested and groups are formed based on the results. If a student's pre-test places him in a "B" level packet, he is free to complete that packet quickly if he chooses and to either go on to "A" level materials or to pursue personal, related interests.

Fractions and other topics are introduced each year for a span of several grades. The math department's pre-tests and subsequent individual placement allow a student to build on previously acquired skills each year, thus the widening ascension on a spiral of math skills of which fractions are a part.

Changes of the type generated by Bill and his team have implications beyond the boundaries of the math area. One team's scheduling plans directly affect all other teams in the school. The school senate, composed of all the Oak senior teachers and the principal, spend many hours negotiating matters related to space, schedules, budgets, and community relations. Differentiated staffing has required many concurrent changes to take place.

The staff chose to adopt a flexible schedule to permit senior teachers with ideas like Bill's to function. The planning to utilize a computer-generated variable course structure was an integral part of the transition to differentiated staffing. It would be of little consequence to give senior teachers and their teams autonomy and to then lock them into a traditional school schedule.

It is noteworthy that other schools in Temple City have chosen means to loosen up the schedule other than computer-generated flexible scheduling. For example, one elementary school utilized multi-age groups of youngsters which have a team of teachers assigned to them. This team has open space (the size of three former classrooms) allotted to them. They generate their own schedule and have access to special curricular areas on the campus such as art and science labs, physical educational facilities, and the library.

To support needed improvements and to develop a viable role for senior teachers, a district must be prepared to consider such changes as the alteration of physical space (where structurally possible), relinquishment of budget controls to local schools, and the generation of new curricular offerings.

Due to the kind of autonomy Bill and his team have had in the past five years, Oak now has a mathematics program of considerable reknown and one of which the team members are proud.

It should be underscored again, that this significant set of changes took place in a relatively short time and that the prime mover was in the school for the ten preceding years. The catalytic event was that he was given the "opportunity, responsibility, and accountability" for making things better for the staff and students at Oak Avenue Intermediate.

Senior Teacher Proprietorship

Bill Schmidt's behavior is seen as somewhat predictable if one looks into the literature on productivity and proprietorship. As Saul Gellerman states, a management policy that will work is one which recognizes the power of the workers in regulating the quality of the product.[18]

A simple analogy illustrates Gellerman's point. If you were employed to work Saturdays and Sundays at a gas station down the street belonging to someone else, do you feel you would make the same effort as you would have if the gas station in fact *belonged* to you? So it is with organizations. When management (administration) plays the role of proprietor, labor (teachers) naturally is relegated to the role of workers. We generally use the

---

[18]Saul W. Gellerman, *Motivation and Productivity*, pp. 45-46.

word "committed" to convey the notion of personal involvement of teachers and ascribe to it a high place. It appears that commitment (as a result of involvement) and proprietorship are interrelated factors.

Outstanding Teaching Is Not Uniformly Defined

The proposition is not that the senior teacher role as defined by Temple City will have universal application nor is it meant to be implied that the majority of teachers are "outstanding."

In respect to the evaluation of competence, Sarason raises an important question. He reminds us that the situation in which a teacher finds himself dictates his behavior to a large degree: "Characteristics of individuals are always, to some extent, a reflection of the setting in which these characteristics are manifested."[19] This is one means of explaining the radical changes a new senior teacher can institute, in contrast to his lack of effectiveness as a change agent in his former status of "teacher." It is also a reminder that the definition of an outstanding teacher in system A will differ from that of system B due to the "teaching situation," i.e., degree of teacher autonomy, attitudes of fellow teachers, and expectancy of the students and community.

A teacher who runs a "tight ship" may be considered outstanding in one system and deemed hopeless in another. Many schools continue to measure a teacher's excellence in relationship to his tolerance for rules, regulations, and routines and the number of discipline referrals he has. The organizational setting will greatly influence the characteristics attributed to teachers who are considered outstanding; thus role descriptions and expectancies for teacher leaders will differ from system to system.

SUMMARY

No role in differentiated staffing is of greater importance than the senior teacher role. Senior teachers are the crucial variable in mobilizing a school or district for new dimensions in education. They are given power and status equivalent to that of a principal while accepting the responsibility and accountability for their

---

[19]Seymour B. Sarason, *The Culture of the School and the Problem of Change* (Boston: Allyn and Bacon, Inc., 1971), pp. 170-171.

team of teachers and their respective programs.

Differentiated staffing assumes there is strength in teacher affiliation and collaboration and that invisible performances and isolationism should be characteristics of the past.

Education in general and teachers specifically are being confronted with the accountability issue. The establishment of measurable skill levels for teachers is inevitable.

Senior teachers, if they are to serve effectively, should be selected by the team they are going to lead. The team's individual and collective needs should be the primary indicators of what a senior teacher does.

The improvement of teaching skills, methodology, curriculum, and planning is a continuing need. Senior teachers exist to fulfill that need. They must continually be adjusting their services and leadership to emerging needs. Their role is not static.

Senior teachers are rewarded at a level commensurate with their responsibilities. The inducements must be equal to or in excess of their contributions if long-range participation (continuity) is hoped for.

Job descriptions for senior teachers must be in operational terms and the evaluation instrument should reflect the specific expectancies a team has of a senior teacher in measurable ways.

The case study of William H. Schmidt exemplifies the type of changes which can be expected when an outstanding teacher is given total responsibility and accountability for a program within the school.

FOUR

The Role of
the Master Teacher

The Theory-Practice Gap

Educators have long recognized that there is a considerable time lag between what is "known" due to research, testing, and experimentation, and what goes on in the classroom. It is the author's position that this regrettable situation will persist until an intervention method is utilized which changes the organizational relationships among the professional staff. As this chapter indicates, the master teacher role is designed to fulfill this need.

Classical educational hierarchies have long had a void in the field of research and development. Research has largely been an evaluative, testing, analysis function which assesses ongoing programs. It has not been related to the concept of development.

Reasons for the lack of significant research and development programs within school systems vary. However, the primary ones are covered by Douglas Ayers in a speech presented at the California Test Bureau Institute.[1]

1. Psychologists have researched primarily with animals, not humans.
2. That there has been little money.
3. That there have been few researchers.
4. That the research has not been programmed or blocked so that concerted efforts could be made in specific areas.
5. That studies have tended to test ad hoc hypotheses rather than be theory oriented.

---

[1] Douglas G. Ayers, speech delivered in Anaheim, California, 1967.

If one were to visit the average school system in the nation and ask "Who is in charge of research and development?", he would in most cases find that the responsibility does not fall clearly on anyone. As a rule, teachers depend upon colleagues, trade magazines, journals, and the principal to gain knowledge of research findings. The number of teachers who actively display such initiative is probably limited, not necessarily due to a lack of interest, but due to a lack of responsibility to do so. One is not negatively evaluated due to his inability to seek, study, and adopt proven research findings.

In fact, according to the Ohio State University Newsletter, *Strategies for Educational Change:* "What goes on in classrooms simply does not reflect what is known about teaching and learning. In addition, a significant time lag exists between knowledge produced through research and actual school practice—all too often the two never come in contact at all."[2]

Clearly, the schools are ill equipped to effectively deal with the problem of implementing research findings. In today's schools research and development is a function seldom utilized. There exists almost no communication between the practitioner and the researcher.

If the fault lies in ineffective organizational relationships, then the role of the master teacher in differentiated staffing provides a possible solution. It is specifically the task of the master teacher to perform the research and development function. The need for such a function is manifest. The unique contribution of differentiated staffing is that the master teacher has a means of reaching the classroom teacher which facilitates his task.

It was previously mentioned that the master teacher's job description is formulated by the senior teachers in the curriculum area which he is going to serve. The senior teachers screen, interview, and select their master teacher. The master teacher then serves a team of senior teachers in a manner which they specify. In addition he is evaluated by the senior teachers. A key component of his role is research.

Contrast this arrangement to the situation present in most large districts where the administrative hierarchy selects leaders to do

---

[2]*Strategies for Educational Change,* a newsletter published by Ohio State University, Volume 2, No. 5, April 1968.

research and development and gives them titles such as curriculum coordinators, directors of research, assistant superintendents for instruction, and so on. These R&D types do not serve the teachers; they serve the system. Teachers avoid interaction with them, consider them central office adminstrators, and have no voice in their evaluation.

A similar phenomenon is now occurring in urban centers where key leaders are receiving training in "Organizational Development" (O.D.). They exist as a separate entity, apart from the classroom, and have relatively little effect on the lives of students in the classroom. Worse yet, consider what happens most frequently in districts with less than 5,000 students. There is no specialist in curriculum development. The principals and superintendents assume the responsibility but in effect are not trained for that role, have too much else to do, and thus do very little R&D work.

The Self-Renewal Feature

Few plans possesses ultimate, unchanging goals. Certainly the process by which goals are attained is constantly being adapted to emerging needs. John Gardner speaks of this renewal function when he states "In the ever-renewing society, what matures is a system or framework within which continuous innovation, re-newal and rebirth can occur."[3]

The need for continuous development, growth, analysis, and evaluation of what happens in a classroom is as persistent as the need for the growth of an individual. The master teacher's major role is to minister to that need. He is the central figure in the renewal process. Mervyn Cadwallader spoke of this function as it relates to an open system when he said "An open system, whether social or biological, in a changing environment either changes or perishes."[4]

A major task of the master teacher is the "translation" of research findings into local, usable curriculum materials. Many teachers have written to other school systems and agencies to borrow some new materials or innovation only to discover upon

---

[3]John W. Gardner, *Self-Renewal* (New York: Harper and Row, 1963), p. 5.

[4]Mervyn L. Cadwallader, "The Cybernetic Analysis of Change in Complex Social Organizations," in *Organizations: Systems, Control and Adaptation,* p. 305.

receipt of the "research" that it wasn't usable. Either the receiving teacher couldn't decipher the materials and conclusions to initiate some new action, or the receiving teacher's district didn't have the materials to implement the change.

A good example of this is the growing interest and development of Learning Activity Packets (LAPs). Most LAPs are developed by teachers in a particular setting with its unique circumstances, materials, equipment, and so on. To borrow a LAP from one system and simply insert it in another system isn't likely to work well. This is not to imply that one must "reinvent the wheel" each time progress is made; however, it is necessary to adapt materials to local conditions.

The master teacher, in conjunction with senior teachers, is to pilot new programs, work out the logistical problems, and evaluate the results before introducing new materials to staff and associate teachers. A side effect of the master teacher role is the control of the flow of new ideas and programs. He is in a position to protect the teachers in his curriculum area from a continual flow of suggestions. Most teachers are given a smorgasbord of "opportunities to test new frontiers" but little guidance on which ones. The resulting overload of information results in poor choices, no choices, and general confusion among teachers.

Master Teacher Job Description and Evaluation Instrument

Since the master teachers serve senior teachers in each school, K-12, the job description and evaluation instrument must be cooperatively developed by the participating senior teachers.

In Temple City the evaluation of the master teacher is performed each semester. The senior teachers who participated in the development of the evaluation form stated several assumptions regarding the prime importance of such concepts as the "service agent role" and the ongoing correlation of senior teacher needs and master teacher functions. One such assumption spoke disparagingly of the notion of a standard evaluation instrument. The senior teachers stated that "Evaluation instruments should reflect activities and functions of the master teachers that are ongoing in nature and not static, idealized categories."

The evaluation instrument covered such responsibilities as research, staff in-service, self-renewal, coordination/administration, evaluation, and teaching. Senior teachers are to indicate on a response sheet whether a function is needed and whether the master teacher is performing the particular function well, adequately, or inadequately.[5]

Master-Senior Teacher Relationship

The master-senior teacher relationship is basically a collegial-peer model as are most of the relationships within a differentiated staffing structure. This model avoids the undesirable side effects of an administrator to teach or change model. This would be undesirable in the sense that healthy management principles (shared power, responsibility, accountability) are not facilitated in the authoritarian model.

Katz and Kahn[6] list three advantages of producing change through the influence of the peer group which in summary are (1) associates have tremendous power over peers, (2) immediate and continuing reinforcement occurs, and (3) solutions to problems are more acceptable since the group is not inhibited by a power figure.

The nature of the organizational relationships between senior and master teachers affords them a degree of influence not commonly present between renewal or change agents and clients.

The power of a senior teacher lies in his command of resources such as the departmental budget, use of space, assignment of rooms, development of teacher schedules, evaluation of their team, and the selection and deployment of student teachers and paraprofessionals. The master teacher does not singularly control any facet of the local school operation, but does, as "a member" of the K-12 vertical curriculum committee, participate in district-wide decisions concerning sequencing curriculum, establishing base-line performance objectives, and assessing staff professional growth needs.

The master teacher is chairman of the senior teachers of his curriculum area as they meet in their vertical K-12 committee. He

---

[5] A complete copy of the evaluation instrument appears as Appendix 2.

[6] Daniel Katz and Robert L. Kahn, *The Social Psychology of Organizations* (New York: John Wiley and Sons, 1966), p. 395.

introduces ideas to the group and "agrees" with the senior teachers on district-wide directions. He has no veto power at these meetings and in effect is a member with a power base equal to that of the senior teachers.

It would be misleading to indicate there is "no" position power. The significant difference is that those who hold leadership positions are vulnerable to those they are leading.

The Leadership Role of the Master Teacher

This limitation of position power and emphasis on personal power has caused concern among some. They feel the master teacher should, in fact, have veto power over the decisions of senior teachers. To have the master teacher serve as a line officer, however, would be a key error, in this writer's opinion. The master teacher would then be returned to the status of the traditional coordinator/supervisor.

Position power is, among self-actualized motivated professionals, a bottleneck. The presence of position power perpetuates all of the ills present in any authoritarian model. It forces *key decisions* to be approved by a single person. This single person thus can exert directional control over the entire program. Again, differentiated staffing *assumes* the wielding of such power is unhealthy among motivated professionals.

Gellerman makes the case for the kind of leadership being suggested when he says:

> What was called for was someone whose own motivations were geared less to the satisfactions of controlling other people than to the rewards of facilitating group productivity. Unfortunately, having power over others is too often a seductive experience for those who wield it: It takes a remarkably self-controlled person to relinquish any of it deliberately or to realize that he has simply gone through the motions of letting it go.[7]

If change which is going to endure the test of time is expected, leaders such as the master teacher must exhibit great personal control over their egos and their hard-won conclusions.

Other independently thinking, fully functioning individuals must be able to debate the wisdom of a proposal from their

---

[7] Saul W. Gellerman, *Motivation and Productivity*, p.30.

vantage points without the disadvantage of being considered "unenlightened."

This change model relies upon knowledge as a sufficient base for change vis-à-vis coercion/manipulation. It is important to note that the master teacher is working with senior teachers who have competed successfully for the right to lead and who are accountable for the results of their leadership. The position power model would effectively allow senior teachers to pass the poor results of an innovation on to the master teacher since it was "his idea in the first place."

The lack of accountability among teachers in most districts today is relative to that set of circumstances. Teachers say: "We have no authority. How can we be held accountable for the results of our teaching? We are just implementing the programs the administration created."

Change agents such as the master teacher in differentiated staffing are selected by their peers, are fulfilling functions specified by their peers, and are evaluated relative to their performance. It is clear that their performance as a change agent is based upon the requests of the staff as laid down in the job description. The staff which employs a leader is in effect giving him a *mandate* for change.

The pivotal issue becomes one of specifying the functions of the leaders by the followers. My experience is that the expectations of followers for leadership *exceeds* the time and ability available. The followers expect more, not less, of leaders than leaders do of themselves. This is particularly true in planning stages.

The Master Teacher as a Field-Oriented Person

Frequently service agents in research and development are located in the central office (often negatively referred to as the people "uptown," "on the hill," or "downtown"). This central office location and the image it projects effectively limits the degree of interaction between research and development people and field people.

People who work in the central office tend to develop close relations due to the opportunities for communication that exist. They take coffee breaks together, go to lunch together, share ideas, and generally develop informal social relationships. Clearly, time spent with one group is at the expense of another.

For this reason the master teacher is located in a school, not centrally. Since he is a classroom teacher he should be located in the school where he is teaching. This permits his students to gain access to him and facilitates intrateam communication. It may be advisable to rotate the master teacher from one school to another each year.

John Gardner speaks of the dilemma leaders face when the organization and the communication networks grow in complexity. In such instances face-to-face communication is reduced and condensed forms of information are increasingly utilized. These condensed forms of processed data often deal with generalities, compilations and summaries. The items of information the leader in a complex central organization does not receive, due to the filtering system, are "emotion, feeling, sentiment, mood, and almost all of the irrational nuances of human situations. It filters out those intuitive judgments that are just below the level of consciousness.[8]

A study of the Illinois Gifted Program revealed that the degree of director involvement is crucial to the success of that program. They cited "actual teaching—teachers conducting training for teachers "[9] as the kind of involvement that developed positive program results. In addition, they found that directors who usually filled out forms and processed budgets to be least effective. Being a field-oriented practitioner as opposed to a central office administrator is very important to a master teacher.

The Master Teacher: Cosmopolitan or Local?

In *Patterns of Industrial Bureaucracy*, Alvin W. Gouldner reports a study he made of a factory, the General Gypsum Company, and discusses the role of the expert in that company in a way which closely parallels the role of the master teacher. He indicates the "expert" is not a member of the formal hierarchy and that he generally advises, not commands. These experts are

---

[8]John W. Gardener, *Self-Renewal*, pp. 78-79.

[9]A paper developed by Ernest R. House, Joe M. Steéle, and Thomas Kerins entitled "Development of Educational Programs: Advocacy in a Non-Rational System," supported by Office of Superintendent of Public Instruction, Illinois, Nov., 1970.

expected to persuade the power structure to accept their expert advice. The expert's peers, in terms of technical training, are in the research and development field. The experts' professional points of reference, therefore, are outside the organization. They care a great deal about issues of national importance, participate in professional associations, contribute to and receive professional journals, and are generally committed to their peers in other organizations who, in turn, are "resident experts."

The master teacher, due to his unique resource and development function, has few academic and/or technical peers within the local school system. Therefore he looks to his resource and development peers in other organizations, a cosmopolitan identity, rather than his peers within the school system, a local identity.

This distinction is by no means discrete but it does point out a role-set difficulty with which local systems must contend. To allow the master teacher to be effective in his research and development function, districts must not only permit, but they should insist, that the master teacher retain his cosmopolitan communication networks. It is the only way the district will be able to be fully effective in the self-renewal process.

The Instructional Council

Master teachers serving various curricular areas meet together and are called the Instructional Council. The superintendent is the chairman of the Instructional Council. This body shapes the direction of the district in regard to curriculum and instruction. Their members (master teachers) chair vertical committees of senior teachers who represent every school, K-12. The outreach potential of the Instructional Council is considerable.

The Instructional Council makes recommendations to the district senate. The district senate, (senior teachers, principals, elected teacher representatives, students, and superintendents) is the policy-making body and thus controls the resources necessary to implement the recommendations of the Instructional Council.

Again, as with master teachers singularly, the Instructional Council is not a formal, position power group. They are the resident experts, the research and development people. They serve the needs of senior teachers and do not "control" local school programs. Undoubtedly their influence and personal power have considerable effect on the decisions made by senior teachers.

It would be well to recall at this point that senior teachers are the power figures throughout the system and they in turn are held "most accountable" by the system. It is assumed this arrangement is better than vesting power and accountability in the hands of a few, especially those who are the greatest distance from daily school and classroom interaction.

Interdisciplinary Education

The Temple City Model has, up to this time, been developed along specific curriculum lines such as mathematics, science, language arts, and so on. Criticism regarding the unnecessary compartmentalization of academic disciplines has been offered.

It appears that the steps to integrating the curriculum will begin with the actions of master teachers. Rather than restrict master teachers to disciplines, there is an effort being made to broaden the base of their input and coordination. Indications in Temple City are that there will be five master teachers heading such areas as citizenship, communication, technology, aesthetics, and applied arts. This will enable them to branch out and deal with a broader concept of curriculum.

Experiments are now going on at the school level (K-8 up to this time) to develop either interdisciplinary units or ungraded, multi-level, self-contained teams. The latter is being implemented with success at the primary grade level. This kind of experimentation will effect the roles and type of expertise needed by senior and master teachers.

There is a strong likelihood that differentiated teams of teachers representing an interdisciplinary background, operating as autonomous units may be the optimal organizational structure. The major reasons are:

1. Interdisciplinary education can provide meaningful links between isolated ideas. Students now must often "discover" the connection.
2. Flexibility in the use of time and space is facilitated by teams having autonomously developed schedules. Lock-step scheduling could be avoided.
3. Multi-age teams provide many opportunities for student-to-student learning.
4. Curriculum could be continuous rather than fragmented.

5. A subject (ecology, politics, neighbors) could become a vehicle which is used to study technical and social skills, making it possible to integrate life with learning.

The Master Teacher and Task Relationships

It has been indicated that the master teacher has a referent problem (cosmopolitan-local) and that he must lead without authority in a manner which places him in close proximity with the "field."

In addition, given academic curriculum areas, there is the problem of isolation. As a master teacher gets to know his senior teacher colleagues and they become a closely knit productive unit, they are in danger of excluding others from a close relationship. Homans states it this way: " ... the liking of friends within a group carries with it some dislike of outsiders. The greater the inward solidarity, the greater the outward hostility."[10] Task-oriented, productive groups who see a lot of each other such as vertical committees, Instructional Councils, academic senates, and teams often lack a concern for and willingness to interact with "outsiders," and thus misunderstandings develop.

Going along with this need to belong is the proposition that t ie participants of the group may often be convening from their point of view for a reason other than the task at hand. Homans says "A great deal of social activity—dances, parties—is enjoyed less for the sake of the activity itself, which may be trivial, than for the possibilities of social interaction it affords."[11] This bit of insight is often needed by group leaders who can't wait to deal with the task when in effect the group's members are taking care of what they consider to be a higher priority.

Another problem relative to task selection is posed by Clark Kerr. This is the dilemma research and development people face as they consider the various innovations available for testing. As Kerr describes it, program administrators grope with: "How to identify the 'good' and the 'bad' and how to embrace the good and resist the bad ... to pace the rate of change, and to discover the rate of change that will do least damage to traditional processes. ... "[12]

---

[10]George C. Homans, "Social Systems," in *Organizations: Structure and Behavior,* Vol. I, p. 187.

[11]*Ibid.*, p. 188.

[12]Clark Kerr, *The Uses of the University* (Cambridge, Mass.: Harvard University Press, 1964).

The master teacher has a problem with sorting out what is available and what will be most acceptable to the system. His failure to pace his input will weaken his effectiveness.

Logistical Support for the Master Teacher

Many difficulties can be avoided if the master teacher's need for support services is anticipated. For example, to function efficiently the master teacher should have access to secretarial services. It is a tremendous waste of time and talent to have a master teacher sitting at a typewriter or operating a duplicating machine. Schools generally have not provided this kind of support and have as a result developed norms which require many professionals to do clerical work.

The master teacher also needs financial support. If he is going to retrieve prototype materials, visit other systems, attend conferences, and receive professional journals he will need to have some discretionary funds available.

The role of the master teacher is enhanced if he can develop a resource materials center—one which takes on the character of a professional library for the teachers in his curriculum area. This center could double as his office and a seminar room for team planning. Not providing such facilities often requires the master teacher to operate out of his car and can inhibit the development of a team identity.

The master teacher can be more effective if he can lend support to the ideas of senior teachers or their emerging needs. Therefore it is beneficial to allow each vertical committee (K-12 senior teachers and master teachers) a budget which they can use to do such things as employ a consultant, buy an experimental set of materials (programmed instruction, simulations, etc.), hold a weekend workshop, visit another site, or develop an exchange program.

SUMMARY

The role of research and development in the public schools is almost nonexistent; therefore, schools are well behind in the application of recent findings. Some have estimated they are always ten years behind. The role of the master teacher is to reduce the theory-practice gap and to do it as a colleague, charged with the responsibility of retrieving, translating, demonstrating and helping implement new curriculum materials and methods. He has a distinct advantage over former "central office types" who retained power and thus were unable to share accountability.

The unique function of the master teacher is to be a renewal agent. His role is perpetual in that any healthy, organic system needs to continually adjust to the conditions and requirements of the environment around them.

The master teacher does the tasks specifically required of him by the senior teachers whom he serves. He is formally and regularly evaluated by his senior teachers.

The master teacher must rely on his expertise (technical competence) and persuasiveness (personal power) to accomplish change. He should not function as a person with position power forcing his conclusions upon senior teachers.

The master teacher must physically and psychologically identify with the teachers in the schools, not the administration of the system. At the same time he is expected to retain a good relationship with the experts in his field, and thus is influenced by his cosmopolitan peers.

The master teacher is a member of the Instructional Council and can directly influence district-wide curriculum decisions. This also provides him opportunities to work on the integration of curriculum areas.

The master teacher must be aware of the dynamics of group process and exhibit sensitivity towards the needs of others. Problems with inward solidarity at the expense of external communication losses do exist, as well as problems related to the pacing of input and the establishment of tasks.

The master teacher must have logistical support in the form of clerical services, discretionary funds, and office/resource center space.

FIVE

Differentiated Staffing: What is in it for Students?

Students and Decision-Making

The following notice appeared as the lead article in a recent *Bill of Rights Newsletter:*[1]

WALKOUT   WALKOUT   WALKOUT   leave   WALKOUT   WALKOUT

Don't go to sixth (6th) period.

Walkout at 2:10

Rally on Tracy Street. Afterwards high school students from all schools are going to the Board of Education at Sunset and Grand.

What we want . . .

Abolish the dress codes . . . Open campus . . . abolish the kiddy cops . . . give the students power to get rid of lousy teachers . . FREE SPEECH (the right to petition and leaflet) . . . Stop searching lockers and student belongings . . . We want the right to determine our curriculum . . . abolish detention . . . improve the food.

We

Jefferson High School got their rights and demands.

can too.

Don't be scared: Students are more powerful than the administrators or the police.

Pass around   *Spread the word.*

---

[1] *Bill of Rights Newsletter,* published by the Constitutional Rights Foundation, Los Angeles, California, Volume III, No. 2, Fall 1969.

Situations like this one are becoming quite common across the country. Perhaps they are less dramatic and confrontation oriented in some places than others, but nonetheless the issues remain the same. Students are not willing to be passive recipients in the educational enterprise any longer. They want a voice in the policies which govern them.

The concept of differentiated staffing, if it is to actually be implemented on a comprehensive basis, requires schools to extend the right of participation and self-governance to the students. Many would quickly agree that the students certainly should be involved in setting goals, telling educators what seems to be working and what is not working, and engaging their teachers in meaningful, collegial dialogue. Of course, one would have to hold a Theory Y view of students as well as adults for this to be possible.

If schools are interested in obtaining students' opinions and feelings, there are a number of ways in which students may be enfranchised. In Temple City, the process of student involvement in decision-making has evolved slowly, but it now takes place widely. Examples of student involvement include:

- The selection of school administrators. Two high school students were included on the committee which selected the current high school and intermediate school principals. They had full voting privileges and joined with representatives of the school's academic senate, a parent representative, the director of secondary education, and the assistant superintendent of personnel. The student representatives were selected by their student council.
- The high school academic senate has two full-time student participants. They were selected by the student council. They have full voting rights and are free to express themselves on any issue. They are encouraged to introduce agenda items for the senate to consider.
- Each curriculum area in the high school has a curriculum committee which evaluates programs, recommends changes, and considers such issues as scheduling and budgets. Student representatives are on each curriculum committee.
- The Board of Education has a full-time student member, seated with the Board at each meeting, and an alternate. The student is selected by the high school student council. The student is free to express herself on any issue. (A senior girl, who has been a member of the high school academic senate, is the current representative). State laws do not yet permit the student a vote on the Board of Education. (Of course, it may not be long until an 18-year-old student does occupy a

seat on the Board of Education.)
- Each teacher at the high school and intermediate school functions as an advisor to students. (The role is explained in detail on page 112.) The students select their advisor.
- The district senate, composed of representatives from each school, includes a high school student with full voting privileges. This body deals with district-wide policy.

There are other less dramatic ways in which the students of Temple City are involved; however, the issue is the tone which underlies the process. If students feel and see evidence of the school system's willingness to allow them to participate in decision-making, they become eager constitutents and will seek constructive means of expressing their opinions. This is not to say there is instant harmony. Harmony is not the most important goal in participative decision-making. The goal is to give the students a formal voice in the decisions which effect them. There is no one in an academic senate meeting or a Board of Education meeting who can speak with authority on how a student feels except a student.

The involvement of students in decision-making has worked well in Temple City. However, that involvement has been incremental, not in the form of a sweeping, dramatic innovation.

Freedom has to be more than rhetoric. According to Donald Arnstine the essence of freedom is closely related to the achievement of power: "Like the hole in a doughnut, freedom can never be created directly. It only appears when something else is achieved. That something else is *power:* the capacity to deliberately make decisions of educational policy and practice and to act on those decisions."[2]

Current movements relative to freedom, creativity, autonomy, individualization, and the distribution of power have resulted in some school systems developing "involvement plans." However, there are many indications that this "involvement" is petty and unreal. When it comes to matters which threaten traditional procedures or are of educational importance, the students' voice is ignored. It is a dangerous move to plan to involve students without providing them a legitimate role, one which may cause the system

---

[2]Donald Arnstine, "Freedom and Bureaucracy in the Schools," in *Freedom, Bureaucracy, and Schooling,* ASCD Yearbook (Washington, D.C.: The National Education Association, 1971), p. 28.

to reconsider many of its traditional practices. Educators must learn to listen to student criticism without casually dismissing it as the response of an unenlightened child.

Student Prerogatives in Education

If one is to embrace a comprehensive view of differentiated staffing, it is necessary to see the student as something other than a recipient in the process of education. It seems trite to say that without students there would be no schools, teachers, administrators, or educational systems, but that is the situation. First come the needs, prerogatives, and concerns of students, and second comes the delivery system. The regrettable part is that the delivery system has become central and the student secondary.

John Gardner places this concept in perspective when he states: "Quite as important as the tradition of dispersed power is the tradition of tolerance and intellectual freedom. This permits a pluralism of beliefs, a tolerance of differing traditions and a diversity of intellectual positions that have contributed greatly to the vitality of our national life."[3] The concept of pluralism does not lend itself to a well-defined, tidy set of organizational circumstances. Quite to the contrary, it will force people to be flexible and open, not necessarily without commitment to any set of values, but committed to permitting others to seek to become what they will based on their feelings, experiences, and intellect. Pluralism, then, is not going to be well developed in an authoritarian environment. Differentiated staffing is a participative, non-authoritarian concept, and will foster pluralism. A nonauthoritarian environment, by nature, requires flexibility. Gardner offers two cogent thoughts about flexibility. He defines flexibility as a trait that permits a man to "try it [an idea] on for size," and to "argue to himself that it is true and then argue that it is untrue." A man like this " . . . can give up his initial perception of a problem and redefine it." Secondly, Gardner argues that flexibility " . . . is a trait of the creative person that psychologists have called a 'tolerance for ambiguity'."[4]

Educators must be flexible, then, in testing new ideas and being

---

[3] John W. Gardner, *Self-Renewal,* p. 70.
[4]*Ibid.,* pp. 37-38.

patient with the confusion which nearly always occurs as a result of abandoning comfortable and administratively convenient processes. New ideas will not be comfortable, as a rule, and will cause some anxiety.

Again Gardner offers timely advice as he says, "One of the reasons why mature people are apt to learn less than young people is that they are willing to risk less." This unwillingness, especially on the part of educational leaders, has created unnecessary rigidities and perpetuated the status quo. Gardner goes on to say, "We pay a heavy price for our fear of failure. It is a powerful obstacle to growth."[5]

Obstacles to growth among our students are largely present in the form of rules. In order to create order, rules are imposed. These rules do make it possible to control large numbers of people and to be able to predict their behavior. The problem is that rules are at the same time encumbering.

It is difficult to generalize about the nature of the learner, the needs of students, or the personality of the teacher, yet rules must do just that. They force students and teachers alike to fall into routinized, predictable patterns. Philip Jackson has observed there are two curriculums for teachers, " . . . the official curriculum, the three Rs, and the curriculum of three other Rs known as rules, regulations and routines . . . and . . . the reward system is tied to both."[6] It becomes the task of the schools to reduce the number of rules and yet maintain some semblance of order.

Temple City has approached this problem conservatively, but with increasing enthusiasm and success. The specific ways they have tried to reduce structure are not really innovative in the sense of being new; they simply give substance to their intentions and are considered essential if the philosophical rationale for differentiated staffing is to retain consistency. A few examples are:

> *Unstructured time.* Students throughout the system, although it varies from school to school and within schools, are given significant amounts of time, 30 to 50 percent, to pursue interests and assignments of their own choosing. At this time, the majority of the students' unstructured time is spent on the campus, although the secondary students are being

---

[5]John W. Gardner, *Self-Renewal,* pp. 14-15.

[6]Philip W. Jackson, "The Student's World," *The Elementary School Journal,* April 1966.

encouraged to develop off-campus learning opportunities. It is necessary to have some type of flexible schedule to permit this condition to exist.

New Electives and Courses. Many schools have tried to force-fit their existing curriculum, old facilities, and comfortable routines into a new flexible schedule. Hopefully, they can be more daring than that and rethink the goals and objectives of the school and come up with some new, relevant opportunities for students. Flexible scheduling, where students and teachers have an average of 40 percent unstructured time (this exists in three of Temple City's schools under a computer-generated format and in other forms through the use of multi-age teams) permits staff members and students to develop new relationships, courses, and alternatives. Tutoring, counseling, and new electives are easily implemented. It is possible for students with particular skills to develop new courses, for community members to come to the school and offer electives, or for short seminars on current topics to be offered. These electives or ad hoc experiences may or may not be for credit or receive grades. They may last for an hour, several weeks, or for the entire year. It is possible for a student to negotiate his program with any one teacher, enabling him to seek alternate means of "covering the required course."

Student Study Stations. Schools which wish to offer options for students must consider the need for development of "stations" for students who want to learn independently. Resources such as teachers, media, software, paraprofessionals, and self-directed study materials must be provided if a student is going to exercise his prerogatives. Many who have offered students unstructured time have not given them meaningful opportunities to utilize their time and then have been upset when the students failed to meet the expectations of planners. Stations as a term is meant to include such areas as the lab facilities (science, physical education, art, music, shops, and so on), resource centers, and the library media center which are available to students on an unstructured basis; that is, the students can freely come and go.

Self-Initiated Curriculum. Students come to schools with a wide variety of interests. Most educators realize the "required curriculum" represents only a small part of that interest. In addition, most are willing to admit that the content of a course, given the fact that the student is competent in the basic skills the course requires (reading, writing, etc.), is not as important as the concepts the content is able to be used to transmit. Content is then classified as a vehicle and the concept, skill, and/or attitude becomes the goal. Given this mind-set, a teacher can readily agree with a student on alternative vehicles, that is, alternate forms of content, to arrive at the agreed-upon destination. The shortcoming has been that teachers have too long considered content the issue and they are not skilled at stating the goals of the course. When goals are stated, students can be encouraged to initiate various means of accomplishing the goals. One function of differentiated staffing is to provide the mechanism to operationalize course goals into meaningful objectives which deal with much more than simple recall.

Credit-No Credit Courses. There is abundant evidence that grades, A, B, C, D and F, are of questionable value. Removing the negative motivational value of grades is long overdue. For students who are good achievers, some feel grades provide incentive. If that is true, what will be the incentive to continue learning when grades are no longer the reward? It could be effectively argued that grades, red stars, and M and Ms are all extrinsic motivators which cause many students to focus on the reward rather than the value of the knowledge, skill, and/or attitude. It promotes a very competitive environment, results in untold misery between parents and children, and places an emphasis on the wrong value. Alternatives to grades have been slow in coming; however, there is an increased tolerance for systems which give "credit" for objectives accomplished and "no credit" for the failure to accomplish an objective. A student's prerogatives are enlarged when a teacher will specify what the objectives for a lesson or unit of study are and then will play the role of "legitimizer," giving credit when earned, rather than a person who is threatening to withhold the reward if the objective is not accomplished. If a student desperately needs some successful encounters with life, an "individualized" set of performance objectives will permit that success to be attained. This will enable some to get credit for different objectives and at different rates than others, which is the beginning of individualized instruction. Improvements such as these require time, expertise, and considerable staff in-service education. Again, differentiated staffing is a plan that helps phase in new structures which represent a changing philosophy.

Why Can't Schools Be Enjoyable?

The term "school" is derived from the Greek word *skolé*, meaning "leisure." There was a time when learning was not meant to be considered work. It was meant to be a pleasurable experience, recreational in nature. People who manned the *skolé* were considered resources, available and willing. Learning took place informally in a congenial atmosphere. Times have changed!

Schools are generally considered places of work in America. You go there to learn. The school environment of today evokes such images as grades (paychecks), homework, task orientation, paddling, detention, and other authoritarian devices. This circumstance is due in part to the historical setting in which school has evolved. Not too many years ago one could get a sense that (a) " . . . children are perceived as sinners or 'savages' . . . in which human impulse or desire is not to be trusted and must therefore be constrained or 'trained' " or (b) they came from such diverse backgrounds they must be "Americanized" or (c) our society needs well-trained technical expertise.[7] None of these reasons for schooling deals with the nature and needs of the individual.

The result of the emphasis on work is time clocks for teachers, impersonal education for the masses, state-imposed courses of study (textbooks), endless rules, teachers with "standard training and credentials," predictable patterns of schools (nationwide), carnegie units, grade cards, year-long courses, and so on.

If schools are going to grow in value to individuals and the society, they must become more humane, flexible places where students are viewed as patrons and educators are viewed as service agents. The schools could then become a resource center with offerings as diversified as possible. Its task would be to serve, not manipulate and control. One goal of the schools then would become "making them an enjoyable place."

A recent survey[8] of summer schools and their diminishing programs led one administrator to conclude "There isn't too much interest in learning anything new." Such statements should motivate educators to look behind the problem and try and discover what has caused students to appear to be apathetic toward schools and their programs.

It would be well for a school to consider implementing some of the following ideas, if they wish to make schools a more enjoyable place.

1. Organize the school in a manner that permits instructors to summon variable-size learning groups. Don't make them always have 25 to 35 students in a class.
2. Allow students to receive information through as many mediums as possible. Don't force all students to receive input via a lecture or a

---

[7] Peter Marin, "The Open Truth and Fiery Vehemence of Youth," in *This Book Is About Schools,* ed. Satu Repo, (New York: Random House, Inc., 1971), p. 144.

[8] "Educational Summary," Croft Educational Service, Inc., August 6, 1971.

film strip. Offer the student a number of alternatives, rather than forging ahead and suggesting "The kids ought to get with it." Some just can't learn by listening alone.

3. Allow students and teachers to develop "contracts" individually or in small groups. The contracts can be in lieu of or in addition to the regular curriculum.

4. Integrate learning with life. Deal with current, relevant issues. If a boy hates math and loves cars, then use the medium of cars to teach him the basic skills of mathematics.

5. Give attention to the aesthetic dimension of the learning environment. Provide colorful, comfortable places for the students to learn.

6. Employ teachers who are primarily excited about "learning" rather than "teaching."

7. Avoid rules, lessons, materials, and expectancies which are for the "good of the group" at the expense of the individual. Individualize everything possible.

8. Develop opportunities for teams of teachers and learners to function cooperatively on projects of common interest. Abandon the idea of an isolated teacher and a captive group of learners.

9. Refrain from the traditional practice of assigning the most imaginative teachers to "advanced students" and average teachers to average students and most of all, avoid giving problem students to teachers who themselves are problems.

The relationship of differentiated staffing to changes such as these is simply a matter of conveyance. Differentiated staffing provides students and teachers with a means to: (a) communicate needs, (b) request services, (c) participate as colleagues in the implementation of change, and (d) evaluate progress. Responsibility and accountability—thus power and prerogatives—are available to a greater degree than customary. Instant success is not a guarantee or a realistic prospect. However, in-service education, peer-to-peer dialogue, and the absence of authoritarianism do provide hopeful signs.

The Relevance of Curriculum

Differentiated staffing gives specific staff members the task of evaluating curriculum, methods, and materials. An expected outcome is a distinction between subject matter/teaching and education/learning. The schools have been preoccupied with training of students and less concerned with their growth as individuals. As

Peter Wagschal puts it, "We must stop confusing the teaching of subject matter and skills with the development of human potential."[9]

Schools have a dual responsibility. They must be concerned with the training aspect which transmits skills and develops technologists but they must also offer a general education program designed to improve a student's chances of becoming a better citizen, a happier person, and more mature and highly developed as an individual. Alfred North Whitehead gets at the issue of relevancy as he says, "I am urging [you] to eradicate the fatal disconnection of subjects which kills the vitality of the modern curriculum . . . The students have got to be made to feel that they are studying something, and are not merely executing intellectual minuets."[10]

In the traditional school setting, few are expected to deal with the dual responsibility of creating a curriculum which emphasizes the acquisition of skills as well as developing the broad human potential of the individual. Schools adopting a program of differentiated staffing are assumed to have already agreed philosophically that a change of emphasis from training to education is essential. This change is a necessity if schools are concerned with the "maximum growth of each learner." The methods employed will vary from developing a formal feedback system to charging service agents who have resources with the task of making the transition.

Is a Trained Teacher Important to Students?

A glance at history reveals that the art of teaching has not always required extensive training. In 1895 most elementary school teachers had less than a high school education, and even as late as 1922 more than 25 percent of the elementary teachers in the United States had not finished high school. In fact, in 1926 only four states required teachers to have two years of post-high school education.[11]

---

[9]Peter H. Wagschal, "Students, Teachers and Subjects: On Condensing the Trilogy," in *The Teacher's Handbook*, p. 790.

[10]Alfred North Whitehead, "The Aims of Education," in *Studying Teaching*, ed. James Raths, (Englewood Cliffs, New Jersey: Prentice-Hall, Inc., 1967), pp. 92-94.

[11]Robert Holmes Beck, *A Social History of Education* (Englewood Cliffs, New Jersey: Prentice-Hall, Inc., 1965), pp. 116, 120.

Some argue that most teacher behavior is determined by the experiences they had as students. The average teacher today has been a "student" observing teaching for 10,000 hours before being licensed to teach. This first-hand observation, coupled with imperfect teacher training programs, results in the average teachers relying heavily upon their own backgrounds and resources as they make teaching decisions.

Students have been the unfortunate recipients of this condition. Their teachers come to them ill prepared and function as isolates from their teaching peers. Training for teachers beyond the credential and their first teaching position is largely voluntary. Where in-service is required, it often is "night school" oriented and considered a task rather than an opportunity by teachers.

Madeline Hunter says, "The professional skill of teaching is transmittable. Teachers are made, not born."[12] The concept of differentiated staffing is in agreement with this principle and thus embodies a commitment to continuous in-service training for teachers. The trainers are most frequently experienced colleagues and the location is the school itself, not the university. Technical experts are sought, including some from the university, but the training is tailored to the needs of the individual teachers. Training in differentiated staffing is considered a requirement and worth incorporating as an integral part of a teacher's job-description and work year.

In addition, differentiated staffing makes it desirable and possible to have an on-site intern program for credential candidates who are finishing their last year of college. In this way, the school district is able to play a large role in the training of prospective teachers and the professors from the university become clinicians rather than theorists as they work on site with the school discrict.

Exposing Students to a Wider Variety of Human Resources

Schools should give attention to the opportunities they have to expose students to a wide variety of human resources. It is regrettable when a student is assigned to a single teacher in an

---

[12]Madeline Hunter, "The Teaching Process," in *The Teacher's Handbook*, p. 146.

elementary school, especially when the teacher and the student do not get along well. According to the Equality of Educational Opportunity Study, commonly known as the Coleman Report, " . . . it is clear that variations in teacher's characteristics account for more variation in children's standardized performance in cognitive skills than do variations in any other characteristics of the school."[13]

The school should be organized to allow students "easy access" to a wide variety of human resources. This requires some form of teaming, flexible scheduling, and freedom of movement. Schools must abandon forced-fit relationships between students and teachers. If a teacher cannot cope with or appreciate the life-style of a particular student, the student should not be forced to adjust his behavior to fit the needs of the teacher. The school should seek to place the student with someone who does appreciate his behavior. Schools tend to develop stereotyped images of what a "normal" teacher is and to socialize its constituency to a point of acceptability or sameness. This homogeneity fails to meet the needs of a diverse student population and those students who fall out of the "normal range" are considered "problems."

Teachers are only a portion of the human resources available. Many of the noncredentialed participants are capable of offering excellent advice to students. Many schools have found custodians, secretaries, clerks, instructional aides, and maintenance men to be valuable teaching assets. They are able in many cases to effectively motivate students who were unable to be reached by teachers. The school's task is to provide the environment and expectation for such relationships to develop.

A conclusion the author would draw, concerning the overwhelming value of teachers in the learning process, is not that we must concentrate on raising the verbal ability or humaneness of teachers (although those things would help), but to realize that learning is strongly related to "relating." That is, schools should concentrate on developing programs which foster human interaction—not limited interaction of the sort that takes place in a classroom with one teacher and 30 students, but expanded interaction where students learn from and teach students, where

---

[13]John Chaffee, Jr. and Patricia Wagner, "Teachers Do Make A Difference," *American Education*, May 1970.

all teachers are resources to all students, and where the broad community of involved persons are encouraged to interact with students.

The term differentiated staffing in itself is a statement of philosophy. Differentiated staffing is a refutation of the "exclusive" role of the teacher as a resource and forces adherents to recognize that "different" staffing patterns are possible. New patterns must, of economic as well as practical necessity, include participants other than "teachers."

Students as Colleagues

A recurring theme of differentiated staffing is collegiality as evidenced by shared power and the concept of leaders being service agents. This collegiality is not intended to be limited to adults. The school should extend itself to become a more humane, responsive place for all of the participants. This concern for people cannot be merely verbal or a statement of intentions. It must be evidenced by actions. As Hall T. Sprague states:

> The only way for good human relations to exist in a school is for there to be a situation in which the kids and everyone else behold a situation in which a high value is placed on people generally, definitely including them. Again, to try to connect with the analogy to blacks and whites in America, the black man can't be conned by people who want to like him and want him to like them; he *can* be persuaded by situations, activities, and events which, between the lines, say "you are a worthy human being, like me." Actions speak louder than words; the medium is the message; don't talk, do; and so on.[14]

Differentiated staffing is the formalization of intentions. It lends structure and continuity to the "organizational conscience of a school." It will force participants to display manifestations of their beliefs.

A large part of the collegiality issue, aside from the formal sharing of decision-making (power) is the issue of expectancies. To clarify the meaning intended, recall McGregor's Theory Y-Theory X ideas. If a person expects another person to be eager, involved,

---

[14]Hall T. Sprague, "Human Relations School Model," unpublished paper, Western Behavioral Sciences Institute, La Jolla, Cal.

worthy of "equalness" and so on, it could be said he has a Theory Y view of people; that is, he wears those kind of glasses. He is viewing the world in that manner. On the other hand, if he expects people to be lazy, passive and untrustworthy, he holds a Theory X view of people. That is his expectancy.

To apply this in the classroom Rosenthal and Jacobson quote the authors of *Youth In the Ghetto* as they summarily state, "When teachers and principals have a low opinion of the children's learning ability, the children seldom exceed those expectations."[15] They also quote a study by Gordon and Durea (1948) which found " . . . when . . . examiners behaved more warmly toward their eighth-grade subjects, the IQ scores obtained were over six points higher than when they behaved more cooly toward their adolescent subjects."[16] In another experiment of the same nature, Larrabee and Kleinsasser (1967) had five examiners administer the Wechsler Intelligence Scale for Children (WISC) to sixth graders of average intelligence.

> Each subject was tested by two different examiners; one examiner administering the even-numbered items and the other examiner administering the odd-numbered items. For each subject, one of the examiners was told the child was of above-average intelligence while the other examiner was told the child was of below-average intelligence. When the child's examiner expected superior performance the total IQ earned was 7.5 points higher on the average than when the child's examiner expected inferior performance. . . . When only the verbal subtests of the WISC were considered, the advantage of having been expected to do well . . . exceeded ten IQ points $(p < .05)$.[17]

The meaning is clear. The expectancies one holds for another are related to the outcomes achieved. Differentiated staffing will function best when students are viewed as colleagues, not beneficiaries, in the learning process.

A model such as differentiated staffing is necessary to aid teachers in understanding the ramifications of *Pygmalion in the*

---

[15]Robert Rosenthal and Lenore Jacobson, *Pygmalion in the Classroom* (New York: Holt, Rinehart and Winston, Inc., 1968), p. 53.

[16]*Ibid.,* p. 33.

[17]*Ibid.,* p. 34.

Classroom. Traditional evaluation and in-service models have been largely ineffective in changing teacher behavior. Differentiated staffing considers the teacher's view of and attitude toward the student as crucial. Therefore, with differentiated staffing students evaluate their teachers, participate in decision-making activities and select their own advisor.

Teachers as Advisors

With or without differentiated staffing, schools must address themselves to the problem of increasing communication with youngsters in a format other than the formal classroom situation. The role of the counselor is a vital role; however, present conditions prevent the vast majority of youngsters from ever receiving any personal counseling. A quarter of our secondary schools have no counselors, and the average counselor load in the remaining 75 percent is 400 to 500 counselees. Worse yet, 33 percent of our elementary schools employ only one counselor for every 1,000 pupils.[18]

The counseling needs of students are accelerated in a flexible program which gives them many decisions to make. Flexible programs also reduce teacher-pupil continuity since it isn't probable that a student will be with a single teacher for extended lengths of time every day.

In Temple City, advisory groups were formed to provide students with a daily advisory contact. The primary task of this contact (advisor) is to aid the student in gaining maximum benefit from the educational program.

It is very important that students select their own advisor. The advisor they select will see them briefly each day. In Temple City's secondary schools, students meet with their advisor each morning. Advisory group meetings also serve as the master attendance period. During advisory group meetings, general information is shared, roll is taken, and appointments are made by either the advisees or the advisor for personal conferences which may be needed.

The advisor is the initial contact between the system and the student. If a student is having academic difficulties or personal

---

[18]John W.M. Rothney, "Who Gets Counseled and for What?" in *Freedom, Bureaucracy and Schooling,* p. 175.

adjustment problems, the advisor is notified first. In this way, the advisor who was selected by the student gets an opportunity to assist the student before the situation worsens.

The advisor should establish a personal, caring relationship for his advisees and make every effort to get to know them as a people. Since all credentialed persons serve as advisors, the average group size is limited to 20 to 25 students. Students can change advisors any time they wish providing they can find another advisor who will accept them. In some cases, special interest groups such as a choral group and their teacher form an advisory group.

Counselors still exist and provide special assistance when called upon. In Temple City High School, the counseling staff developed a training course for teacher advisors relative to the skills of personal counseling. Other specific advisor needs, such as college admittance requirements, merit tests, and scholarship information are shared with advisors by the counseling staff. The counselors are prepared to offer any advisor assistance on problems which develop.

The advisory role permits teachers to relate to students in an informal, helping manner. Since the teacher is selected by the student, it is assumed that the assistance will be valued and well received. It is particularly important in a flexible schedule where students have an average of 40 percent unstructured time, that some adult is working with a student on a continuing, cooperative basis. One side effect of flexible scheduling is that students get lost in the shuffle of IBM cards and they have difficulty getting quick, friendly assistance. Advisors help solve this problem.

In elementary modular scheduling or multi-age teams, similar disjointedness can occur and there is also a need to provide a method of assistance which gives the youngsters who need it a sense of stability and continuity. The counseling/relating role of elementary teachers generally is a role they value. Incorporating a degree of choice for students or paying attention to match-mis-match personalities would generally improve the situation.

Not to have a student-selected advisor or some counterpart doesn't mean one can't be "doing differentiated staffing." It just is an indication that the model is lacking a dimension which probably would be helpful to students.

Students as Teachers

One of the richest untapped resources of any school tends to be the students. Schools have not fully utilized their talents. Students have been considered patrons, not participants.

A number of studies have been conducted in the past decade which indicate that students who teach other students learn at increased rates themselves. Ron and Peggy Lippitt of the University of Michigan's Institute for Social Research have been involved in carefully controlled research of older students as teachers. Arthur Pearl reports that the Lippitts specifically recommend " . . . that students who have difficulty in school be appointed as tutors. Weekly seminars are recommended for older helpers . . . and . . . that older children functioning as teacher aides require supervision, support, and training. The professional teacher who functions as supporter is the crucial ingredient."[19]

The use of students as teachers isn't intended to be in lieu of the services of a teacher but should be considered as a supplementary source of manpower. Students who teach others are contributing to their education as well as the person they are teaching. Teachers have long felt that the best way to learn something well is to try to teach it to others.

Student tutoring can have several facets. It may be used to motivate an older student, to create smaller learning groups, to improve peer relations, to teach skills, or to enrich the curriculum. The last use mentioned provides motivated students an opportunity to share their knolwledge and enthusiasm.

Differentiated staffing provides for the delegation of responsibility to all levels. Responsibility should be withheld from no one who is prepared to accept it. If time, space, and the curriculum are flexible, students can be valuable teaching assets.

The United States Army, training hetero-aptitudinal populations, has devised a unique form of peer instruction they call the APSTRAT model. Their trainers now train trainees who train other trainees in a cycle which includes observation, learning, job-performance, and teaching. They claim that the system has the following advantages:

— there is a one-to-one student-teacher ratio which provides flexibility for self-pacing and a rapid feedback.

[19] Arthur Pearl, "Teacher Aides: Paraprofessionals, Tutors, and Volunteers," in *The Teacher's Handbook*, pp. 43-44.

- there is less fear of failure compared to superior-subordinate relationships.
- they are aware their "teacher" just learned the skill himself and thus are less shy to display ignorance or uncertainty and are more free to ask questions.
- an individual is more eager to learn when he knows he is going to have to teach someone else what he is learning.

The researchers make it clear that "The system relies on the regular instructors to maintain rigorous quality control, through spot-checks of instruction and tests of proficiency." They also indicate that in the planning stage " ... the instructors ... have the major responsibility for redefining course objectives in performance terms."[20]

Schools could use similar peer teaching models to accomplish many of their tasks; but before steps along that line can be taken, teachers must define in performance terms what the objectives are. Once the objectives are operational students could profit from peer-teaching models.

Accountability from a Student's Perspective

Differentiated staffing is accountability oriented. Power is decentralized (along with accountability), job descriptions are in performance terms, and self-paced learning materials with specific objectives are used by students.

This increased emphasis on accountability is in the interest of students. Almost every recent edition of a professional journal or newsletter mentions the increased degree of national concern with the accountability issue. For instance, the *Education Turnkey News* reports:

> The Washington, D.C. School Board has asked Professor Kenneth B. Clark, President of Metropolitan Applied Research Center, to develop a plan for measuring teacher and administrator performance throughout the city's school system ... it would appear that specific standards for what children in different grades should learn will be established and teachers and supervisors would then be held accountable if student results do not measure up ... The plan has already drawn fire from the Washington Teachers Union.[21]

---

[20]"The Development of a Low-Cost Performance-Oriented Training Model" (Alexandria, Va.: Human Resources Research Organization, 1970), pp. 4, 6.

[21]*Education Turnkey News*, Volume 1, No. 2, (Washington D.C.: Education Turnkey Systems Inc., 1970), p. 1.

And the same edition cites a study commissioned by former Associate Commissioner of Education, Leon Lessinger, on "Educational Engineering:"

> The Report cites the current low status of performance of our public education system and the problems that have been mounting over the past few years. Costs have increased astronomically while performance levels have remained the same, or in some cases, declined. Taxpayers are removing their support through bond issue defeats. Parents who can afford to are taking their children's educational future out of the hands of the public schools.[22]

Students will eventually suffer the loss which comes when the public loses faith in an educational system not capable of specifying its outcomes and the dollars needed to produce those outcomes. If the education profession continues to balk at getting accountability oriented, the outcome may be that industry will have to be called upon to teach basic skills.[23] A differentiated staffing program that ignores the accountability issue would be neglecting a need which is central to the evaluation of programs and personnel.

The Standardized Test Syndrome

As Joseph L. Dionne recently stated, "Although we spend millions of dollars every year on standardized testing, it is not relevant for instruction today."[24] Yet the schools methodically test the students on a regular basis. The tests are required and are one of the strongest factors used to determine if a school is succeeding. Joseph Featherstone reminds us, "Far too many of our school systems have emphasized conventional measurement and ignored children's learning: forgetting the principle that children and teachers do not get any heavier for being weighed."[25]

---

[22]*Ibid.*, p. 5.

[23]*The Educational Marketer,* Volume 2, No. 18 (New York: Knowledge Industries Publications, Inc. 1970), p. 2.

[24]Joseph L. Dionne, "The Outlook for the Future in Testing and Evaluation," a speech made to the Los Angeles County Research Council, in Los Angeles, April, 1970.

[25]Joseph Featherstone in *The New Republic,* in *Education Summary,* (Washington, D.C.: Croft Educational Services, Volume 24, No. 21, November, 1971).

Four major limitations of existing standardized tests have been pointed out by Stephen Klein:

1. likelihood of poor overlap between the test's and the school's objectives and the priorities associated with these objectives.
2. inappropriate test designs and formats for the target populations.
3. difficult and confusing test instructions and adminstration procedures that introduce irrelevant factors into a student's score.
4. low test validity in the sense that the tests do not really assess the kinds of student skills and abilities that their titles imply they do.[26]

In spite of the lack of relevance and the degree of accuracy which standardized tests yield, they remain the essential "payoff" in American education. They are used to determine where students should be placed in a tracking system, for determining who should be encouraged to go to college, and to measure the "value" of the local school system.

The presence of differentiated staffing cannot eliminate standardized tests; however, it will force schools to place them in perspective. It is most difficult to be concerned about individualization and mass testing programs simultaneously. They run at cross purposes. One should be most cautious in the selection of tests and should certainly regard the inferences gained from standardized data as tentative rather than conclusive.

Rather than focus on standardized testing, schools will seek to evaluate their services to students based on objectives such as these:

– Learning how to learn—how to acquire new knowledge—for knowledge will be constantly changing.
– Understanding concepts and generalizations.
– Using the various processes of thinking.
– Developing basic skills—how to study and read.[27]

In addition, schools will not penalize students for using their imagination and intuition, which are keys to creativity, by demanding "right" answers. The preoccupation of teachers with

---

[26]Stephen P. Klein, "The Uses and Limitations of Standardized Tests in Meeting the Demands for Accountability," (University of California: Center for the Study of Evaluation, Volume 2, No. 4, January, 1971).

[27]"Developing Thinking Skills," Department of School Services and Publications, Wesleyan University, Middletown, Connecticut, Curriculum Letter No. 58.

right and wrong will be replaced by a concern for nurturing a student's successful involvement in the search for answers. The school will be less concerned with testing and more concerned with self-concept and involvement. The new processes are consistent with the rationale for differentiated staffing which, in part, assumes there is much more to an educational program than that which can be measured with a test.

The use of test data by teachers turns out to be the critical factor. If the data limit one's expectations and hopes for students, they are of negative value to have it reported. If, on the contrary, a teacher views a student's score on a particular test as one thread in the complex fabric determining a child's potential and/or achievement, then it can be useful. Perhaps Solomon said it best, "The wicked man's fears will all come true and so will the good man's hopes."[28]

If the role of the school is to promote the maximum educational growth of the individual learner, as it has been declared by many, a considerable part of that promotion must deal with the concept of life-long learning. Surely tests, standardized and others, will endure. However, in a differentiated staff the teachers no longer can legitimately blame the power structure for the measurement program. They have the opportunity to state their objectives in a manner which allows for individualized instruction and measurement. When the measurement program has the interest of the individual learner at its center the student will profit.

SUMMARY

Any educational plan must, at its heart, be practical and of conspicuous value to students. Differentiated staffing establishes a framework in which students can achieve status and gain considerable ongoing leverage in the process.

Political and personal leverage for students is fast becoming a national issue. The recurring theme of student activists is the issue of power. The students want to be heard. They want to feel that they as recipients of policy have a voice in its formulation and evaluation.

Educators are philosophically prepared, now more than ever

---

[28] *The Living Bible,* (Wheaton, Illinois; Tyndale House Publishers, 1971), p. 507.

before, to involve students in the policy decisions of the school. Youth commissions and student delegates to what were formerly all-adult decision-making bodies are emerging rapidly. Eighteen-year-olds can now vote. The time for student participation in decision-making is now.

The focus of education has shifted from teaching to learning, from content to concepts, and from singular modes to multiple modes of instruction. In addition, schools are expanding the prerogatives of students permitting them to have unstructured time, a choice of learning activities, and a choice of teachers. Schools are becoming concerned with the self-concept of the student and with the teacher's attitude towards the student. Teachers are thinking in terms of teaming, peer instruction, teacher-student match-ups, using all of the human resources available, and offering advisory roles to students.

Aside from the humane concerns of schools is the increasing demand for accountability. To teachers, this will mean quantifying and objectifying the curriculum. To students, it means knowing what is expected, being able to work at individual rates, and being evaluated on the basis of skills, knowledge, and attitudes achieved rather than on what is not achieved.

The trends in modern education need efficient delivery systems. Differentiated staffing from the student's point of view offers significant structure and capability as a process to lend impetus to such intentions.

SIX

Differentiated Staffing
and the Process of Change

Change is Inevitable: Differentiated Staffing
is a Strategy

Assuming, in a dialectical sense, that human systems are zig-zagging in an upward spiral toward a more ideal condition, it follows that change is not an unanticipated phenomenon. Change becomes a variable which contributes to or detracts from the general health of an organization.

Differentiated staffing is a plan which accommodates change. It provides for the orderly assimilation of new leaders, policies, physical arrangements, curriculum materials, instructional methods, and external variables. Differentiated staffing is in itself a process, not a product. The process assumes that renewal is a constant variable. This is evidenced by such practices as changing job descriptions and evaluation instruments (based on changing needs), the research and retrieval function of the master teacher, the provision for systematic feedback to service agents, and the commitment to shared power (resulting in widespread creative input).

Change must be approached systematically. Without a well-conceived strategy of change, carried out by informed advocates, the change process can be circuitous and inefficient. Observers, who themselves are leaders in what should be change situations, often get very conservative as they view the amount of energy and degree of frustration which accompany change. They see change as risky and difficult.

Why Change?

If a school seems to be stable in terms of its economic, social, and academic relationships, why change? Change admittedly carries risks, takes more energy, and upsets tradition. Should a system change just so it can embrace the latest fads or in order to gain visibility? That is unfortunately the motive behind many "innovations." The innovation is considered a goal, not a process. In this situation one would typically hear an administrator say, "If we just had flexible scheduling, we would have a much better school."

Change must be directed towards goals, not towards projects or innovations. If a school system's program and policies are completely congruent with their goals, so long as their goals remain stable, they need not change. Since goals provide a means of assessing the present condition of an organization, no organization should function without goals. The presence of goals stated in fairly specific terms provides a yardstick enabling an organization to mark its progress in relation to a particular goal. The establishment of goals then becomes a critical step in determining the activities, programs, organization structure, and policies of a system.

Entry into any new program or change, including differentiated staffing, then, becomes a goal-oriented decision. If the new program accelerates the system toward its goals, it then is worthy of consideration. Practical problems, such as can we afford it; will it upset tradition or personal relationships; will it reduce our effectiveness in athletics, drama, music, or art; is it too radical; and so on, are secondary to the question of congruity with goals.

Change then becomes a "life-maintenance" function. It is used to propel the system towards its goals. If it is disrupting, it is primarily because previous practices were preventing goal attainment. The disruptions become healthy, caring interventions rather than negatively inspired disloyal acts. In effect, perpetuators of status quo, when the system is incongruent with goal attainment, become the disloyal parties.

Goals: Ours or Theirs?

Schools generally have established goal statements. Many have "adopted" them from professional associations or from nationally recognized authorities. When a person seeks to unite with a school district in an employment or service relationship, they generally accept the existing conditions of the system (salaries, policies, goals, etc.). At the outset they are subscribing to the existing relationships. They are joining with a coalition. They receive "side-payments" from the organization such as money, personal treatment, and authority. In exchange for these side-payments, they "adopt" the organization's goals.

As new members join an organization they bring with them personal philosophies, objectives, and needs. These new members often influence the eventual direction of the organization by helping modify its goals until there is a better match between personal and organizational goals. This process can be considered healthy by policy makers or can be seen as a threat. If the latter is the case, the power structure limits and/or disregards suggestions for modification. They operate autocratically.

Differentiated staffing as a concept facilitates the modification of goals by extending policy-making power to the participants. As goals become the product and property of the participants in the organization, a degree of homogeneity develops which permits continued decentralization of power and authority. This is due to the general compatibility of the goals of the organization and the goals of the individual. It is assumed that as power is shared, goals and policies will remain responsive to the organization's participants.

This is not to imply that the inputs of the external forces (legislators, taxpayers, political groups, national needs) will not be taken into consideration. Under differentiated staffing, the expectations of external forces become a lever on the general body of participants (Board, staff and students), not just the Board and administration. This partially neutralizes the fear some have of "turning the organization over to the common people" in that the "people" become as accountable as the former power structure and thus must contend with the realities of the external forces as well as the needs of the internal forces.

Relative to any discussion of joint goals is the growing interest in Management by Objectives (MBO). This is a process whose central theme is built upon the notion of jointly established goals which have been agreed upon by all of the participants. Common support of these agreed-upon goals enables the organization to state them in measurable performance terms and thus permits progress to be systematically monitored and reported. Districts which have tried this system find it less threatening and imposing since goals are "jointly owned" by line and staff. MBO as a system addresses itself to the accountability issue very well.

The Goals of Temple City

The Temple City Unified School District Board of Education has adopted the following set of goals. These goals were originally developed by the Education Testing Service for the State of Pennsylvania.

1. Quality education should help every child acquire the greatest possible understanding of himself and an appreciation of his worthiness as a member of society.
2. Quality education should help every child acquire understanding and appreciation of persons belonging to social, cultural, and ethnic groups different from his own through an understanding of his own culture.
3. Quality education should help every child acquire, to the fullest extent possible for him, mastery of the basic skills in the use of words and numbers.
4. Quality education should help every child acquire a positive attitude toward school and toward the learning process.
5. Quality education should help every child acquire the habits and attitudes associated with responsible citizenship.
6. Quality education should help every child acquire good health habits and understanding of the conditions necessary for the maintenance of physical and emotional well-being.
7. Quality education should give every child opportunity and encouragement to be creative in one or more fields of endeavor.
8. Quality education should help every child understand the opportunities open to him for preparing himself for a productive life and should enable him to take full advantage of these opportunities.
9. Quality education should help every child to understand and appreciate as much as he can of human achievement in the natural sciences, the social sciences, the humanities, and the arts.
10. Quality education should help every child to prepare for a world of rapid change and unforeseeable demands in which continuing education throughout his adult life should be a normal expectation. [1]

[1]"Relevant Change and Educational Direction," a Temple City Unified School District Publication, July 1968.

Goals such as these represent broad statements of intent. Frequently they never become a focal point for change. They get adopted and shelved. Operationalizing the goals and stating them in performance terms is a much more difficult task. It requires a degree of specificity that will provide considerable debate. Where people readily agree on goals, they often disagree on the best routes for achieving them. It is one matter to state as a goal that a child should acquire an understanding and appreciation of persons belonging to other ethnic groups, but quite a different one to *adopt a program* which makes it possible to achieve the particular goal. It is the same old problem. Intentions are useless; action is what counts. Games are not won at the chalkboard, but on the field.

The Temple City leadership group (senior teachers, master teachers and administrators) attempted to operationalize the ten general goals of the district. They did so by holding a post-school workshop in June, 1971. The group reevaluated and established priorities for a list of objectives which the district steering committee and district senate had approved as part of the district's application data in pursuit of federal funds. Some of these objectives had been fully implemented in Temple City's schools. The task of the workshop was to decide if the leadership group still supported the objectives, and for those which were supported, to assess the stage of implementation for each objective in each school. The purpose of the workshop was to congeal the thinking and energy of the district's leaders (43 are "leaders" out of 200) in regard to operationalizing the goals of the district. It had become obvious that schools were progressing at different rates with different degrees of enthusiasm. The task, stated another way, was to determine if anyone was philosophically in discord with the direction of the district, and if not, then to develop plans for assisting schools to implement the objectives. (As might have been predicted, leaders generally agreed on the objectives. After all, who can in good conscience denounce an objective such as "to have teachers evaluate the quality of services rendered by leaders?")

The objectives were listed and individual school senates were given time to evaluate their progress in terms of each objective. They then convened with other senates and discussed their self-assessments. Following the self-assessment, task forces (interdistrict) were developed to address themselves to common problems within the district which were inhibiting progress.

The goals which were agreed upon were presented to the Board of Education as "Educational Directions" (see Fig. 6-1) for their approval and support. It was originally hoped by the administration that each school's progress in terms of implementing each objective could be included in a presentation to the Board of Education. This did not take place mainly due to the fact that each school viewed themselves as having "fully implemented" some objectives, yet as one compared the programs and means of implementation it was apparent they were at very different stages of sophistication and efficiency.

The superintendent decided it was unwise to push the issue of what was and was not a fully implemented objective and that the self-assessment process and the school's commitment to the objectives were sufficient for the present.

EDUCATIONAL DIRECTIONS

Temple City Unified School District

At the close of the school year, the Board of Education, the Citizen Curriculum Committee, and the professional staff identified terminal learner objectives in the various curricular areas. Subsequently, school district leaders, administrators, and senior teachers specified 25 educational objectives that in their opinion were either crucial or desirable for future program development and full implementation. The objectives were unanimously agreed to by the district leaders as encompassing the best available methods and programs to achieve the citizen-established terminal objectives.

The chart below depicts the stage of implementation of the 25 objectives at the various district schools. This compilation is the result of a rating collectively reached by the district's administrative staff during a recent training session.

The chart suggests the challenges to be met by each school's staff during the upcoming year. The reaffirmation of support by the Board of Education for the objectives listed below will encourage the professional staff to further the progress made to date.

STAGES OF IMPLEMENTATION

EDUCATIONAL GOALS	NOT YET PLANNED	PLANNED	PARTIALLY IMPLEMENTED	FULLY IMPLEMENTED
1.To provide for the flexible use of time and space within school programs				
2.To eliminate artificial constraints such as grade levels and traditional report cards				

EDUCATIONAL GOALS	NOT YET PLANNED	PLANNED	PARTIALLY IMPLEMENTED	FULLY IMPLEMENTED
3.To develop educational objectives in performance terms with every learner which may be modified				
4.To develop a curriculum that focuses on the process of learning as well as the content				
5.To organize time and curriculum that allows students to learn from other students				
6.To provide for the differentiation of staff roles and responsibilities in performance terms				
7.To have teachers evaluate the quality of services rendered by leaders				
8.To provide for the systematic training of all credentialed persons				
9.To develop opportunities for self-instruction and independent learning by students				
10.To have students accept personal responsibility for their actions				
11.To have students involved in the selection or development of curriculum or materials				

EDUCATIONAL GOALS	NOT YET PLANNED	PLANNED	PARTIALLY IMPLEMENTED	FULLY IMPLEMENTED
12.To formalize teacher involvement in decision-making				
13.To allow teachers to play a major role in the screening and selection of their leaders				
14.To establish an evaluation system that provides for the teaming of instructional specialist and general administrators in assessing the quality of instruction performed by individual staff members				
15.To provide for curriculum vitalization by retrieving the latest research data, utilizing current curriculum materials, and providing for continual input from students, teachers, and the community				
16.To develop media centers, resource centers and labs for self-directed learning				
17.To maximize multimedia instruction				
18.To provide increased autonomy with accountability for professionals				
19.To make school a more enjoyable experience by eliminating fear as a motivator				

EDUCATIONAL GOALS	NOT YET PLANNED	PLANNED	PARTIALLY IMPLEMENTED	FULLY IMPLEMENTED
20. To allow students to receive multiple inputs in terms of teaching personalities				
21. To establish a counseling and/or advisory system which permits students to choose the adult to whom they wish to relate				
22. To involve students and citizens in educational planning and goal setting				
23. To provide for "on-site" teacher training programs (precredential)				
24. To increase the effectiveness of paraprofessionals				
25. To maximize the involvement of professional associations in the development of district goals and programs				

Figure 6-1

Translating Objectives into Curriculum

The Temple City Unified School District's Board of Education formed a citizens' advisory group to make a study of the district's curriculum. The major intent was to survey the parents in regard to their views of program priorities. The Board appointed a steering committee of parents to work with district personnel on study. The group, known as the Citizens Curriculum Study Committee, spent many hours discussing what the priorities in curriculum were. They eventually dealt with grading, learning theory, and other related issues. In order to assess the wider community's point of view, the committee developed a survey instrument. Figure 6-2 is a copy of the instrument. This survey gave the Board of Education some sense of the community's expectations but provided no surprises (consistent with most internally generated surveys).

The citizens' group felt the next step was to attempt to define what the base-line objectives were for the graduates of Temple City's schools. To accomplish this the citizens' group divided itself into five general areas: (a) communications, (b) citizenship, (c) technology, (d) aesthetics and (e) occupational education. Each area had its own citizens' committee. The senior teachers in each area (vertical curriculum committee) then met with their citizen-counterparts and began to develop base-line objectives for graduates. The objectives became known as terminal objectives for Temple City High School graduates.

DEAR CITIZEN:

One of the responsibilities of local control of education is the opportunity and advantage of the citizens to have a major voice in the operation of the school system.

We would like to know what you would like to have taught in our schools; what emphasis you feel whould be placed on the content; and what priority you would like placed on the various items in relation to the entire curriculum.

We are, therefore, asking your help in improving education in Temple City by filling out this questionnaire and adding any suggestions, comments, or evaluations you may have. A report will be published when the questionnaire information has been summarized.

Your assistance will be greatly appreciated.

Thank you very much.

Dave Wood, Chairman
Citizens Curriculum Study Group   PLEASE RETURN WITHIN TWO WEEKS

PLEASE DO NOT PUT YOUR NAME ON THIS QUESTIONNAIRE.

Check each of the items you think are important in describing yourself.

□ Parent with one or more children in Temple City public schools. In grades

      K-3 _____
      4-6 _____
      7-8 _____
      9-12 _____

□ Parent with one or more children in private schools. In grades

      K-3 _____
      4-6 _____
      7-8 _____
      9-12 _____

□ Parent with no children in school
□ Retired
□ Educator
□ Employer
□ Employee

□ Student in Temple City public school
□ Student in private school
□ Renter
□ Homeowner
□ Other–Specify

INSTRUCTIONS

Rate each item 1 to 5 by circling your choice of numbers. This will show the importance you place on each item in relation to entire curriculum (Kindergarten to 12th grade).

EXAMPLE:

Physical fitness

Weightlifting	1 2 3 4 5
Acrobatics	1 2 3 4 5
Team Sports	1 2 3 4 5
Basketweaving	1 2 3 4 5

QUESTIONNAIRE ON EDUCATIONAL GOALS

	Greatest Emphasis	*Secondary Emphasis*	*Moderate Emphasis*	*Minimum Emphasis*	*Omit*

AREA 1–CITIZENSHIP PREPARATION

UPON GRADUATION THE TEMPLE CITY HIGH SCHOOL STUDENT SHOULD HAVE:

A knowledge of the responsibilities and rights of an American Citizen	1	2	3	4	5
A clear perspective of the culture of Temple City	1	2	3	4	5
An awareness of the varieties of cultures in the United States	1	2	3	4	5
A knowledge of American Heritage	1	2	3	4	5
A knowledge of America's relationships with other countries	1	2	3	4	5

AREA II–OCCUPATIONAL PREPARATION

UPON GRADUATION, THE STUDENT SHOULD HAVE HAD:

Opportunities for vocational training for direct employment	1	2	3	4	5
Appropriate course work to meet public and private university entrance requirements	1	2	3	4	5
A broad choice of electives	1	2	3	4	5
Career Counseling	1	2	3	4	5
Academic Counseling	1	2	3	4	5

AREA III–BASIC KNOWLEDGE

UPON GRADUATION, HIGH SCHOOL STUDENTS SHOULD BE PROFICIENT IN:

English	1	2	3	4	5
Reading	1	2	3	4	5
Composition	1	2	3	4	5
Arithmetic	1	2	3	4	5
Science	1	2	3	4	5

AREA IV–CURRENT ISSUES

THE TEMPLE CITY STUDENT SHOULD HAVE THE OPPORTUNITY TO INVESTIGATE CURRENT ISSUES AND TRENDS IN SUCH AREAS AS:

	Greatest Emphasis	Secondary Emphasis	Moderate Emphasis	Minimum Emphasis	Omit
Moral Values	1	2	3	4	5
World Religions	1	2	3	4	5
Political Systems	1	2	3	4	5
Economic Systems	1	2	3	4	5
Human problems	1	2	3	4	5

(e.g., labor, pollution, technology, race, social changes).

AREA V–SELF UNDERSTANDING

THE TEMPLE CITY STUDENT SHOULD HAVE A KNOWLEDGE OF:

Getting along with people	1	2	3	4	5
His academic potentials	1	2	3	4	5
His emotional strengths and weaknesses	1	2	3	4	5
The physical body	1	2	3	4	5
The importance of family life	1	2	3	4	5
The importance of continuing education in a changing society	1	2	3	4	5

AREA VI–EXTRACURRICULAR ACTIVITIES

ALL TEMPLE CITY STUDENTS SHOULD HAVE THE OPPORTUNITY TO PARTICIPATE IN:

Competitive athletics	1	2	3	4	5

(e.g., intramural, interscholastic sports)

Performing arts	1	2	3	4	5

(e.g., band, chorus, theatre)

Student activities	1	2	3	4	5

(e.g., student government, newspaper, clubs)

RANK THE FOLLOWING AREAS FROM THE MOST IMPORTANT "1" TO THE LEAST IMPORTANT "6". This will show the relative importance you place on each AREA of curriculum.

Example: Physical fitness   2 (next most important)

     Art   3 (least important)

     History   1 (most important)

AREA 1   CITIZENSHIP PREPARATION   ____

AREA II   OCCUPATIONAL PREPARATION   ____

AREA III   BASIC KNOWLEDGE   ——
AREA IV   CURRENT ISSUES   ——
AREA V   SELF UNDERSTANDING   ——
AREA VI   EXTRA-CURRICULAR ACTIVITIES   ——

YOUR COMMENTS ARE APPRECIATED:

(please write on other side)

Figure 6-2

This effort to define terminal objectives is in accord with the continuing movement toward Program Planning Budget Systems (PPBS). PPBS will require schools to specify expected outcomes and to place a dollar value on the cost of achieving a particular objective.

As the citizens' curriculum groups and the senior teachers worked together they had difficulties such as (a) should a terminal objective be stated in terms of *all* students being able to achieve it—such as, swim 200 feet in 95 seconds using any stroke, (b) should a terminal objective be stated at a percentage rate—that is, 75 percent of all the graduates will be able to read at the twelfth grade level, or (c) should the objective be stated so that all are expected to achieve the goal but the goal is modified—100 percent of all the graduates will be able to read at the eighth grade level or better.

A different approach from any of those listed was taken by the Citizenship goals group. They did not state expected outcomes in typical behavioral terms. They stated their goals in three categories: (1) decision-making skills and processes, (2) base-line knowledges, (3) self-concept attitudes and behavior. Under the first category, decision-making skills and processes, their first goal is "The student must be able to recognize a problem and be able to identify why it is a problem to society and/or to themselves."

The remaining goals under that section are incrementally more difficult and built upon the satisfactory achievement of the first goal. The rationale offered by the joint citizens and teachers group for not specifying the goal in behavioral terms is that the social sciences do not deal with content as an entity, but with concepts and processes as a whole. They claimed one could not limit the goal to a statement, such as, "Given a list of the five major subcultures in America (black, Indian, Mexican, Oriental and Appalachian), the student shall be able, with 90 percent accuracy, to state the 'major' religious, economic and social beliefs of those subcultures as judged by his teacher." Aside from being racist and fraught with gross generalizations, this goal would be more acceptable stated: "The student must know that the practice of judging other cultures on the basis of one's own cultural standards may distort one's perception of that culture." The citizens-teachers group indicated that the goal was less specific and limiting than the objective which "each team" would develop to achieve the goal.

Although the goals derived from the citizens-teachers groups are in tentative condition and have had only brief attention, they are points of departure for future program priorities and planning. A list of the citizenship and communication (one section, English) goals appears as Appendix 3.

Getting Change into the Classroom

The teachers of America are the critical ingredient in determining the eventual effectiveness of any change strategy. Change can take place at the level of the Board of Education and administration and have virtually no effect in the classroom. It is likely that some of the best-stated goals in the country by schools with good intentions do not significantly affect what goes on in the classroom.

A new program, recently announced by the U.S. Office of Education, has committed $363 million to a project which supports the notion of directing change at the classroom teacher. The new program is known as the National Education Renewal Center plan (NERC). The bulk of the investment will be aimed at getting training resources to local teachers. Sidney Marland, U.S. Commissioner of Education, justifies this investment by stating,

"It has been found that the teacher is often the key to success of educational reform."[2]

Behavioral research has been telling people for some time that policy change at the top of an organization can be effectively resisted by the "implementors" at the bottom. Arnstine points out that:

> When an institution is bureaucratically organized, a hierarchy of control has the effect of creating increasing amounts of apathy, passivity, and ineffectiveness. This is increasingly true the further one descends from the higher, directive positions to the lower, directed positions. . . . Teachers will act immaturely in direct proportion to the extent that their behavior is directed from above. The immaturity of teachers . . . may be mitigated—and sometimes simply masked—by their advanced education and its residual benefits, and by a school administration which either distributes or effectively pretends to distribute decision-making power more widely."[3]

This author suspects the 363 million dollar expenditure in Educational Renewal funds may be money largely wasted unless (a) the distribution of power, rewards, and incentives in schools is changed and (b) there is some device which provides for the retention, sharing, and eventual institutionalization of the changes the individual teachers make.

To explain point (a), there is no question that there is a national power struggle occurring between teachers and administration. It will not be reduced by change agents (a role the U.S. Office of Education is now playing) directing their attention to one faction or the other. Just as teachers are effectively able to resist change which is imposed, administrators are able, given the present power structure, to inhibit the role of the teacher as change agent. Even the most casual observers have noted that administrators, especially in smaller towns and cities, have tremendous power to retard or accelerate change. Changing a teacher's attitude towards education will not give him the base of leverage necessary to implement his new ideas if there is an administrator present who views the teacher's action as inappropriate.

---

[2]*Education Daily,* published by Capital Publications, Inc., Washington, D.C., January 26, 1972, p. 4.

[3]Donald Arnstine, "Freedom and Bureaucracy in the Schools," in *Freedom, Bureaucracy, and Schooling,* p. 16.

Although categorical, restricted federal aid to schools is not wanted by school administrators, it seems appropriate to suggest that the "seed money for change" should be limited to those school districts who are prepared to restructure the system in terms of power, rewards, and incentives.

In regard to point (b), it is of questionable value to change one teacher's view of education if that teacher (1) does not remain in the classroom (gets promoted by leaving it), (2) operates as an isolate, not "infecting" others and (3) has no responsibility or opportunity to train aspiring teachers in new methods.

Differentiated staffing, if it has any uniquely inherent value, does address itself to the organizational structure of a school district, and in so doing builds in a base for renewal in the classroom consonant with research from the behavioral sciences.

Resistance to Change

There are many reasons participants resist change. Any change strategy such as differentiated staffing is subject to these forces and should be prepared to encounter them.

The Change Is the "Property of the Leader." When a person considers an idea his "baby," most people are reluctant to become foster parents. Until an idea or a change is viewed as useful and of personal value by others, it will receive timid support. The task of a change agent is to release ownership of an idea so others may possess it as their own.

People Have Immediate Needs Which the Change Ignores. It is unwise for a school principal or senior teacher to try to have a teacher focus on some ethereal educational notion, when that teacher needs a broken window repaired, paper for her students, and time to call a parent. Maslow refers to this situation when he speaks of the hierarchy of needs among people, pointing out that needs are arranged incrementally beginning with physiological and moving up through safety, belongingness, esteem and finally self-actualization.[4] Others refer to the same basic idea: "Every individual has many hundreds of needs. All of these needs compete for his behavior. What then determines which of these motives a person will attempt to satisfy through activity? The need with the *greatest strength* at a particular moment in time

[4]Abraham H. Maslow, *Motivation and Personality*, pp. 35-36.

leads to activity. . . . Thus, activity is the result of the need with the highest potency."[5]

In short, don't be surprised if the staff is more concerned with a functional coffee pot than with an in-service program on "advanced technology in the classroom." Fix the coffee pot and then discuss issues of greater substance.

Change Upsets Social Relationships. Frequently a change agent will see a problem, consider how it might best be solved, and propose a solution. Paul Lawrence reminds us concerning that simple change situation that " . . . it would be useful to . . . think of change as having both a technical and social aspect."[6] The point he makes is that technical change is a relatively easy circumstance. Everyone would seem pleased to have a good technical solution to a problem. However, what often happens is that the technical change, proper as it might have been, upsets social relationships and is either cooly received or not implemented.

Examples of change situations which would render the social relationships inadequate could include (1) the personal style of the change agent: people such as teachers may not like the change agent, therefore his ideas are not valued; (2) upsetting the normal routine for change; that is, have change agents in the past "usually consulted" with those affected by the change; (3) changes which upset personal routines and habits such as with whom one can go on a coffee break or who teaches next door; (4) a lack of appreciation by the change agent for his predecessor who may have been highly valued as a person. Teachers will not easily forgive the change agent for belittling the former leader's efforts.

Change Agents Are Enamored with "Technical" Change. One of the most rapid ways to reduce the interest of a staff in a new idea is to overwhelm them with the technical jargon and rationale which supports the change. It would be far better to clearly define, in nontechnical terms, the anticipated benefits of the change. As Alexis de Tocqueville once said, "A false notion that is clear and precise will have more power than a true principle that is obscure and involved." The change agent must control his natural

---

[5]Paul Hersey and Kenneth H. Blanchard, *Management of Organizational Behavior*, p. 11.

[6]Paul R. Lawrence, "How to Deal with Resistance to Change," *Harvard Business Review*, January-February 1969.

tendency to espouse the intriguing and often recently learned technical terms which may accompany the change. His challenge is not to impress his peers with his expertise but to gain their support for a needed improvement.

Change Agents Assume That Logic and Rationality Are Sufficient Motivators. Much to the chagrin of some change agents, they find that a clear, logical exhortation to improve the organization does not always receive immediate support. Change agents are so perplexed by this that they are often heard reiterating the same logical rationale for the change over and over again only to find continued resistance.

The reasons vary in each situation but generally are attributable to the nonrational circumstances of the case. If only rationality was needed as a condition for change, many of the traditions and rules of society would be viewed as irrational. Schools provide some of the best examples. Is it logical and rational to close educational facilities one quarter of each year? Or to enclose the playgrounds of schools with fences and locked gates except during school hours? Or to air-condition and carpet churches, stores and offices, but not schools? Or to offer algebra for nine months, fifty minutes a day, in groups of thirty, for every "individual?"

Change agents cannot ignore the nonrational attitudes that often exist and which serve to perpetuate many of man's illogical traditions. Increasing the flow of logical reasons against an avalanche of irrationality is not usually a fruitful endeavor. It will only increase the resistance.

Change Agents Want Immediate Results. New ideas and procedures take time to be learned. It is unusual, for instance, to find teachers quickly mastering a new technique such as use of the video tape recorder in monitoring and assessing teacher behavior. The technical equipment in itself represents a considerable challenge, even to the mechanically minded. Achieving mastery over the equipment will take time and then developing skills which will allow it to be a useful evaluation tool will take additional time.

If the change agent views the teacher who is having difficulty learning and effectively using the technique as recalcitrant and resisting change, when in fact the teacher is trying and wants to make it work, then the teacher will become upset. As Lawrence expresses it, " . . . there are few things that irritate people more than to be blamed for resisting change when actually they are doing their best to learn a difficult new procedure."[7]

The Change Agent Is on an Ego Trip. Those who have observed change processes have undoubtedly seen instances where the change agent was so excited about the ramifications of an anticipated change that his peers questioned his motivation. Change is often accompanied by visibility, especially in schools. Local newspapers are likely to treat an innovation in the schools as front page material. Continued innovation results in schools becoming demonstration centers, widely heralded and visited.

Change agents must be sensitive to the possibility that they are becoming too ego-involved and are considered by staff members to be seeking only self-agrandizement. The staff has to sense that they and the general system may gain as much from the change as the person who proposed it.

One indication of poor judgment in this area is suggested by Lawrence when he says " . . . the [change agent's] very identification with his ideas tends to make him unreceptive to any suggestions for modifications."[8] In other words, when an innovator's plan takes on a note of infallibility, it indeed is possible that people working with him will resist all or at least parts of the plan. He has gotten too ego-involved with his plan.

Change Agents Expect and Therefore Receive Resistance. Just as teachers cue the behavior of students, leaders often cue the behavior of followers. If a leader acts and speaks as though he anticipates resistance it will become a self-fulfilling prophecy.

Examples of this include instances where leaders have been heard to say (1) "You people may not like the change we are about to make, but it is a needed change," or (2) "Although this idea isn't easily understood by most of you, I have thought it through and it will work," or (3) "I know change is difficult. It upsets routines and takes time to get adjusted to, but it has to come."

Leaders must avoid the overt as well as subtle types of communication that suggest they expect resistance to change lest their expectations be fulfilled.

---

[7]Paul R. Lawrence, "How to Deal with Resistance to Change," *Harvard Business Review,* January - February 1969.

[8]*Ibid.*

The Motivation Problem

Since differentiated staffing is a comprehensive model of change, few participants within a system are unaffected by its presence. Motivation becomes a prime area of concern. The question which must be dealt with is how, given what is known about resistance to change, can systems smoothly bring about change?

Physical factors have been mentioned before; however, to be more specific, leaders would do well to realize that wide-range needs, including low-level needs, exist in every person. Failure to overcome these needs will often result in motivational losses.

Leaders can accomplish two important objectives by satisfying low-level needs. First, it establishes the leader as a person who can accomplish tangible tasks. People can see and be recipients of the benefits of the change. Secondly, it removes an excuse for not focusing on higher-level needs by members of the organization. People frequently reduce their output due to their unhappiness over some minor environmental (physical) factors, such as inadequate heating, lighting, parking space, or quantity of food served at lunch. When the problems are solved, the excuses for not considering more important issues are weakened.

Creating a situation that enables an organization to embark upon and sustain change is a pivotal concern within differentiated staffing. It is largely made possible by restructuring the distribution of power. This distribution of power results in many members of the organization having a personal investment in its productivity: " . . . one of the most basic satisfactions to be obtained from work is the feeling of pride and achievement at having accomplished something . . . the instinct of craftsmanship."[9] The wielding of formal power which restricts personal, intuitive (albeit accountable) responses, greatly reduces the potential for sustained motivation. If pride in the product, craftsmanship, is to be desired, artisans must be regarded as experts, capable of self-direction.

Differentiated staffing as a model must not only broaden the base of power within schools, emphasizing the integrity and worth of each individual, but the specifics of the model itself should emerge from the teachers, not the administration. Motivation to

---

[9] J.A.C. Brown, *The Social Psychology of Industry,* p. 205.

support the administration's model will generally be lacking, as a number of superintendents could attest. The model must belong to those most affected by it if they are expected to expend energy and have pride in their craftsmanship.

Rules Are Inhibiting

Rules within an organization are necessary; however, they have a considerable influence on motivation. Rules such as stop signs, paying for merchandise, taking care of public property, and not harming others are all meant to facilitate human interaction. Rules should be considered as helpful and useful. They should lend order to a pluralistic society. Rules should not be established to reckon with the errors of exceptional people.

The motivational problem in schools relative to rules is that there are too many rules which generate corporate restrictions rather than enhance personal freedoms. Rules should exist to aid in the orderly flow of human interaction—not to restrict it. Gerald D. Bell found that the number of rules present within an organization was a good predictor of the type of supervision which was present. His study concludes, "The analysis indicated . . . as closeness of supervision increases, the extent of rule-usage also increases."[10]

To apply that to schools, it seems apparent that a proliferation of rules requires a large amount of time and attention to be devoted to rule enforcement. Many of the enforcement activities are counterproductive in terms of motivation. Minimizing the number of formal rules and regulations forces responsibility for the effective operation of the system upon the individuals within it.

Incentives for Change

Temple City's model of differentiated staffing originally had a serious flaw which has since been partially corrected. Master and senior teachers were given power, rewards, and status for assuming greater responsibilities in the educational system. The problem was that they constituted only 20 percent of the teaching staff. That

---

[10]Gerald D. Bell, "The Influence of Technological Components of Work Upon Management Control," in *Organizations: Structure and Behavior*, p. 445.

left 80 percent of the staff in their former status regarding personal incentives for change. It could be argued that the 80 percent have more power and control over the system, and work in a psychologically healthier environment. The point is, however, that they remain without incentives to be change agents themselves.

Temple City has attempted to cope with this problem by initiating a plan which allows staff and associate teachers to develop change proposals of their own. Figure 6-3 is a copy of the bulletin distributed to all staff and associate teachers explaining the intent of the plan.

TEMPLE CITY UNIFIED SCHOOL DISTRICT

March 2, 19___

TO: All Staff and Associate Teachers
FROM: Bruce Caldwell
SUBJECT: *Staff and Associate Teacher Initiated Proposals*

Differentiated Staffing provides an opportunity for some teachers (Senior and Master) to exercise increased initiative and to receive greater recognition and rewards than others.

An opportunity to broaden this opportunity for staff and associates is now at hand. The U.S. Office of Education is supporting Temple City's efforts to improve education for children this year as they did last year, which enables us to develop creative ways to encourage teachers to utilize their full potential.

One way to involve more people in the improvement of education in Temple City is to set aside a portion of the federal money we receive to encourage staff and associate teachers to initiate proposals they feel will improve education. For the sake of convenience, let's refer to the idea of *Staff and Associate Teacher Instituted Proposals* with the acronym "SATIP."

SATIPs are ideas which are to be implemented by staff and associate teachers to improve education. Hopefully, the ideas belong to the staff and associate teachers; however, it may be that proposals are developed collectively by a senior teacher and a staff or associate, or by an entire department, grade level, or team.

Since the goal is to improve education, SATIPs can be very diversified. The SATIP will be a proposal or offer to accomplish some specific task for a set number of dollars.

It has been suggested a committee of staff and associate teachers be formed (two representatives from each school) to work out details such as: (A) the format for applying for funds, (B) The screening of proposals and granting of funds, (C) The evaluation of completed tasks.

School senates are to select their representatives as soon as possible.

It is possible to pilot the idea between now and June 30 with some remaining 1970-71 U.S.O.E. funds.

SATIPs probably will be funded to do such things as: (A) Prepare a new unit in a curriculum area, (B) Prepare curriculum materials, (C) Develop audio-visual materials, (D) Develop an alternate educational experience for a group of students who don't respond to normal offerings, (E) Purchase a sample of commercially developed materials to be tested locally, (F) Develop a teacher training experience for a select group of staff members, (G) Employ a consultant to work with students or staff on a specific task.

Find out who your staff and associate teachers representatives are and keep in contact with them regarding deadlines and procedures for filing proposals.

Figure 6-3

Although the author introduced this idea in Temple City, the impetus came from Mesa, Arizona, Public Schools. They essentially base their entire differentiated staffing concept on the SATIP format. Its greatest strength appears to be the extension of incentives to a broad number of participants.

SATIPs in Temple City and RFPs (Requests For Proposals) in Mesa both were made possible through the use of outside funds. Neither district has yet built in a local base of funds to perpetuate the concept. Temple City may find it necessary to take a portion of its associate teacher trade-off funds (funds generated by the differentiation of the staff) to continue to offer SATIPs. An alternative is to consider the added cost of SATIPs an investment in teacher in-service education and professional development and to fund it as part of the general budget.

It it the author's opinion that the SATIP concept is an excellent point of entry for a system considering an eventual comprehensive differentiated staffing model. The major problem would be to prevent the traditional power structure from stifling the creative flow of new ideas, programs, projects, and processes. If that could be accomplished it would only be a matter of time until the creative members of the staff began to pilot new ideas.

Dramatic Changes Versus Small Changes

One can find proponents of change styles which are dramatic and sweeping as well as those favoring planned entry on a pilot basis. Each may be correct given local conditions and situational variables. Differentiated staffing as a model requires considerable comprehensiveness; therefore, rationale will be offered for dramatic change.

A typical change strategy is to phase in a school at a time on a pilot basis. When a school becomes a demonstration school or a pilot study, several disadvantages accrue. Some of them are:

— Non-demonstration school personnel, such as the principals of nearby schools, do not receive the attention, support, and advantages of being "experimental" that the prototype receives. This often results in petty jealousies as well as subtle undermining.

— Demonstration schools stand for a "new program" which in effect de-values the traditional program. If the rationale for the new program is sound and persuasive enough, then the personnel of the old program are not engaged in educationally up-to-date practices. The author has observed considerable anxiety among "nonparticipating" schools when the justification for the "participating" schools was largely irrefutable.

— Parents of the model school are worried about their children being experimented with and non-model school parents want to know why their children are not able to receive the advantages of the model school.

— Personnel who are unsure of and/or in opposition to the goals of the demonstration school will be waiting for weaknesses of any kind to emerge in the "innovation" so that it, like other changes, can be laid to rest, permitting business as usual.

— A minor amount of the district's resources (personnel and finances) is committed to the pilot study. Since the majority of personnel and finances continue to support the traditional program, the pilot is often relegated the status of a stepchild. When funds become scarce the innovation (minor number affected) is "postponed" for the sake of perpetuating the "regular program" which affects the majority of the staff.

Most of the preceding arguments apply with even greater intensity when a team and/or department representing a *minor* portion of a school deviates from the norm. When the demonstration center is within the same school, differences are more quickly and frequently compared. The participating and nonparticipating personnel (students and teachers) are continually exposed to one another. In addition, logistical constraints regarding schedules, use of space, buses, and school policy complicate matters. For instance, a multi-age, interdisciplinary team may not want to use the library, playground, or lunch area at consistent times. They may not want to follow a structured schedule which the rest of the school (the majority) follows. The result is nonparticipants become nonsupportive of the experimental team's needs.

Of equal importance is the need for a school to enact changes which reinforce each other. Some schools have attempted to initiate a single change such as flexible scheduling and naively expected that change to be an educational panacea. If all one did was institute flexible scheduling without paying attention to the needed support systems such as resource centers, labs, teachers' offices, independent study as an instructional mode, and so on, one would have gone from bad to worse. Singular changes such as the development of sophisticated multi-media-oriented libraries are a needed improvement in education. The materials and their availability are certainly of benefit; however, it seems incredible to deny students easy access to this wealth of materials by scheduling them in such a manner which prohibits any in-depth, daily use.

Minor changes bring one back to the theory of equilibrium. If an input (change) in a system occurs, it upsets equilibrium. The system, attempting to restore itself to a state of equilibrium, reacts to the input. One form the reaction could take, if the conditions permit, is rejection. An indication of this reaction was found in a study conducted by Robert Bales: "The Idea man is the one most prone to equilibrium disturbing acts through his constant movement toward the instrumental goal, and hence he is most likely to arouse hostility."[11] In the same manner, an "idea" pushed by a minority is likely to arouse hostility, or at the very least, upset equilibrium.

It seems so much must be done and it all is so interrelated that the timid will have difficulty succeeding. As Dwight Allen says, "A little change hurts but a lot of change doesn't hurt much more."[12] Bold, sweeping changes seem best able to withstand society's urge to retain the status quo. Half-hearted attempts to introduce a change are very unlikely to achieve the intended goal.

This writer believes that in today's schools, a commitment to a broad set of goals should precede gross structural changes, and that change, whether comprehensive or not, succeeds best only when goals do exist which are clearly defined and agreed upon by

---

[11]Robert F. Bales, "The Equilibrium Problem in Small Groups," in *Organizations: Systems, Control and Adaptation*, p. 180.

[12]Dwight W. Allen, from the University of Massachusetts School of Education Catalogue, 1972.

the majority. Otherwise, dramatic changes tend to simply be dramatic. They lack a relationship to goals and certainly could not be considered to be the property of the people expected to implement the changes.

ESEA as a Change Strategy

The Elementary and Secondary Education Act provided large sums of money under Title III to encourage educators to try unique ideas. One strong requirement for funding was that the proposal be exemplary and innovative in nature. The U.S. Office of Education was not interested in funding old ideas that were already operating. The key concept was *change.*

One problem with ESEA, Title III, was that when funding terminated, innovations it had generated tended to expire too. It seems many projects were appendages to the total district program. They were not an integral part of the whole. The existing organism was successful in its resistance to the well-aimed innoculations of the U.S. Office of Education. As Sidney Marland, U.S. Commissioner of Education put it:

> More than $1 billion in Federal research and development expenditures have produced so little in the way of tangible results in our schools. We have sprinkled our R & D dollars like seeds, hopefully but thinly, enthusiastically but improvidently, not so much working systematically for a new order of educational efficiency as wishing one might suddenly burst into luxuriant blossom. . . . It hasn't happened.[13]

In the past, many districts feared using ESEA monies due to the threat of impending federal control. Many of those who did develop programs carefully established a project director, offices and staff as a separate entity. They frequently housed them in portable, temporary facilities. Projects of this nature were doomed in terms of residual long-lasting values prior to their inception.

It seems safe to suggest that a central theme can be extrapolated from an assessment of these various probes which were often singular in scope and narrow in terms of objectives. The probes represented a David and Goliath situation without the benefit of divine support. The giant (traditionally organized schools) just did

---

[13]*Education Daily,* Capital Publications, Inc., November 24, 1971, p. 2.

not make a hospitable host for the lightly armed U.S. Office of Education.

A substantial difference in the U.S.O.E.-public school relationship may be in the offing since the President of the United States has indicated a strong interest in having the federal government assume a greater share of the financial support for public schools. This, coupled with an NEA request which suggests that the federal government pay for one-third of the cost of public education, appears to indicate that the program priorities of U.S.O.E. may yet become realities, particularly if the old adage "money is power" holds true.

Those without a model of their own, consistent with what is known about organizational theory and the behavioral sciences, may find themselves "pressured" to consider alternative structures. Differentiated staffing provides a means to accomplish that task as a local priority, which in the long run is an improvement over being co-opted by external forces.

Momentum and Change

One often hears it said of a winning team that they have momentum. Loosely interpreted, this means they expect to keep winning and thus have a psychological advantage over their opponents. In the change process a similar phenomonon occurs. When organizations have made many changes, more changes can be easily made as contrasted to an organization which has not made any major changes.

Sarason indicates the importance of momentum when he states that: " . . . the fate of any single proposal for change will be determined in part by the number of changes that have been proposed but never implemented."[14] In other words, if people hear a great deal of talk about change (or winning) and yet nothing substantive occurs, they begin developing an insulation to such unfruitful dialogue and are negatively impressed with further talk about change. (This is made manifest in the cultural revolutions of today.)

The people (oppressed) often become so cynical when people speak of change that they actually move to oppose that for which

---

[14]Seymour B. Sarason, *The Culture of the School and the Problem of Change*, p. 221.

they once had hoped. It becomes the task of the change agent to avoid talking about change until he is sure it is possible to implement it. In addition, he should understand that having successfully implemented some change, others will come more easily.

Feedback as a Change Strategy

There are a number of techniques which are intended to raise levels of self-awareness and self-understanding. The general incentive to do so rests on the theory of *imbalance*. This term was used by Heider to describe a condition which exists whenever a person finds that he holds a different attitude toward something (his behavior) from what he believes is held by another person or group to whom he is positively oriented. Heider theorized that a person in such a state of imbalance is motivated to do something about it—that is, to restore balance.

Heider's theory was tested by N.L. Gage, who found that teachers in his study indeed did want to behave in a manner consistent with their pupil's expectations. He had sixth-grade pupils rate their teacher and rate an "ideal" teacher. Gage reported that "Teachers who received feedback did seem to change in the direction of pupils' "ideals" more than did teachers from whom feedback was withheld. . . . The feedback not only produced changes in behavior: it also produced corresponding changes in the accuracy of teachers' perceptions of their pupils' perception of them."[15]

In a parallel study conducted with elementary principals, R.W. Daw and Gage attempted to determine whether the teachers' feedback to a principal indicating how his performance is viewed, as contrasted to that of an ideal principal, would yield a similar outcome. They found "All in all, the results indicate that the feedback affected changes in the principal's behavior."[16]

Differentiated staffing is feedback oriented. Provisions are made throughout the model for leaders (service agents) to receive periodic formal feedback. This feedback process occurs when

---

[15]N.L. Gage, "A Method for 'Improving' Teacher Behavior," *Journal of Teacher Education,* 1963, pp. 261-266.

[16]Robert W. Daw and N..L. Gage, "Effect of Feedback from Teachers to Principals," unpublished dissertation, Stanford University.

students select their advisors, evaluate their teachers, and participate in the decision-making process as well as when teachers select
their leaders and evaluate them.

It is assumed that providing feedback for leaders is in itself a
change strategy. Differentiated staffing introduces variables not
present in the Gage studies such as (1) the persons giving the
feedback have power to act as well as the opportunity to advise,
(2) persons receiving feedback were selected and are kept in
leadership positions by those giving them feedback. The hypothesis is the same. It is of positive value to allow a person to see
himself as others see him; both parties tend to benefit.

Change, a Tool of Survival

Though organizations are generally considered to be resistant to
change, it is important to remember that they usually have a
number of forces which encourage them to change. These forces,
some internal, such as teachers, administrators, and state laws, and
some external, such as taxpayers, student activists, and potential
employers, cause organizations to adjust periodically. The potency
of the forces, at least in terms of schools, varies considerably. A
city-wide teacher's strike can be a powerful force as can a
taxpayer's revolt.

When organizations respond to such forces, they are doing so in
what becomes a quest for survival. The process of remaining viable
(homeostasis) or adjusting to the pressures in a manner which
perpetuates productivity and maintenance of life is known as
cybernetics. It is essentially making use of feedback for the
purpose of accomplishing the system's goals in an unstable
environment.

Systems which make use of feedback to adjust their direction
are known as "open" or "organic" systems. Cadwallader suggests
that "an open system, whether social or biological, in a changing
environment either changes or perishes."[17] He goes on to say that
organizations which do change their structure and behavior based
on input from the forces from without and within are known as
ultrastable organizations.

Schools certainly are having to adjust to a changing environment. They must, as Cadwallader puts it, do so or perish. The

---

[17]Mervyn L. Cadwallader, "The Cybernetic Analysis of Change in Complex Social
Organizations," *American Journal of Sociology,* Vol. LXV, Sept 1959, p. 155.

reluctance to change creates organizational disequilibrium; that is, the structure of the organization (output) is inconsistent with the needs of the patrons (input). When the needs of the patrons (internal and external forces) are inconsistent with the structure of the system, the life of the system (organism) is threatened. As an organism, it must either adjust to new needs or cease to function.

One reason schools have been slow to change and to simultaneously avoid extinction is that they have enjoyed a franchise monopoly. There were few alternative structures about to replace the schools; thus, their patrons were not able to effectively remove themselves to a new, more responsive organism. Recent trends have tended to awaken the slumbering schools (which have acted as closed rather than open systems) and forced them to consider change. These trends include (1) rewards from foundations and state and federal grants for "experimenting with change," (2) denial of support for what exists by decreasing available revenue to the schools, (3) passing laws, such as new credential requirements for teachers, which force the schools to change, (4) the development of alternative schools, store-front academies, free schools, and the burgeoning interest in publicly funded private schools (voucher plan), (5) the interest in performance contracting, a format which turns the education of students over to industry on a cost per pupil (per objective) basis.

Given the organic nature of schools, the problem is not whether to change, but how, in what direction and with what kind of structure. System theory provides some of the direction as it points us towards the use of feedback as a crucial variable in decision-making. Though this has been limited and rather simplistic introduction of system theory, the general notion is clear. Schools as open, organic systems must consider change as a tool of survival. To do so requires a restructuring of schools. Differentiated staffing offers one means towards the end goal of making schools viable and responsive to the needs of their patrons through the use of systematic feedback as well as systematic forecasting.

Change Strategies for Leaders

Differentiated staffing places many people who were not previously formal leaders in roles of leadership. Many points of view exist concerning proper styles for leaders. This section will review some of them and discuss those that have worked well in Temple City.

The classical argument concerning leadership is the contrast between the authoritarian and human relations styles. Some feel authoritarianism is best, that it is task oriented and efficient. Others feel various forms of human relations styles are better because they foster cooperation and understanding and gain grass-roots commitment.

Hersey and Blanchard advance a different theory. They suggest that " . . . different leadership situations require different leader styles," and that "An effective leader is able to adapt his style of leader behavior to the needs of the situation and the followers."[18] The key to adapting one's style to the situation, according to Hersey and Blanchard, is to assess the level of maturity of the people you are leading. The factors they suggest you use are the "ability to take responsibility and achievement-motivation."[19] They also indicate that one's task-relevant level of education and amount of experience may influence maturity levels. Since maturity levels change progressively on a continuum from immature to mature at various rates, the leader's style must change accordingly. For this reason Hersey and Blanchard's model is called "The Life Cycle Theory." Their central theme seems to indicate that one should individualize his particular style based on the situation. Authoritarian behavior may be appropriate or inappropriate, and the same could be true of other behaviors.

It appears that leaders who depend on a consistent style of leadership with all followers in all situations are not likely to enjoy overwhelming success. For example, considerate, human relations styles of leadership won't get results if you are dealing with authoritarians: "Authoritarian characters confronted with human relations principles of management would consider the manager weak in the head and at the very least sentimentally unrealistic."[20] Maslow suggests that such individuals be dealt with authoritatively until they grow to a level of maturity permitting you to do otherwise.

Peter Blau adds a dimension to notions of leadership style when he suggests ". . . [the] leader, like the prudent, bureaucratic

---

[18]Paul Hersey and Kenneth H. Blanchard, *Management of Organizational Behavior*, pp. 89, 71.

[19]Paul Hersey and Kenneth H. Blanchard, "Life Cycle Theory of Leadership," *Training and Development Journal*, May 1969.

[20]Abraham H. Maslow, *Eupsychian Management*, p. 34.

superior, establishes his authority over his followers by creating *social obligations.*"[21] Blau's examples of this include leaders not enforcing minor rules, adjusting work schedules to suit the needs of the followers and leaders making the "organization a scapegoat" for personal failures. His point is that the followers, having gained personal favors, are then obligated to the leader.

In education more of this persists than one would like to admit. It generally takes the form of penalties and rewards. The leaders are in a position to "dangle carrots" to followers such as granting them a leadership position, giving them the best rooms, best students, good schedules, praise, etc., in exchange for personal support. The threat exists to use the "stick" if support is not in evidence by removing followers from leadership roles, taking away the best rooms, and so on.

Differentiated staffing is designed to neutralize this force and to create checks and balances which deny leaders continuing access to penalties and rewards they misuse. The senior teacher can be removed from his position by his team and the administrative leaders can be outvoted on policy decisions.

R.H. Tawney links authoritarianism to manipulation as he states:

> Insofar as a man's livelihood is at the mercy of an irresponsible superior ... who can compel his reluctant obedience ... whose actions he is unable to modify or resist, save at the cost of grave personal injury to himself and his dependents ... he may possess a profusion of more tangible blessings, from beer to motorbicycles but he can hardly be said to be in possession of freedom.[22]

The author would add a few leadership suggestions of his own based on experiences gained in Temple City.

1. An effective leader does not avoid the accountability issue. He actively helps identify goals and holds himself and others accountable for reaching them.
2. Once a goal is established and a person or team is attempting to reach the goal, the leader must allow them to pursue the goal, exercising their own prerogatives without his interference. He should be

---

[21]Peter M. Blau, *Bureaucracy in Modern Society* (New York: Random House, Inc., 1956), p. 74.

[22]R.H. Tawney, "Teaching the Children: Does the System Help or Hinder?" in *Freedom, Bureaucracy and Schooling*, pp. 153-4.

available to assist but should not attempt to pre-empt their authority.

3. Effective leaders should not convey an attitude of paternalism, using expressions such as *my* staff, team, goal, or school. He must not only allow others to receive the credit for their accomplishments, but must by design see that they receive credit.

4. Timing is an essential skill of change agents. To know when to press or when to retreat is critical. Therefore, a leader must be totally involved in the change process and be close enough to the action to identify the current mind-sets of informal or formal power structures.

5. Effective leaders should exert strong influence on the decision-making process only at turnkey points. He should know the difference between a decision that means losing a battle and one which means winning a war.

6. Change agents enjoy crests of popularity but in the final analysis are considered an irritant rather than a salve. Machiavelli warns, "Nothing is more difficult and risky than change."

SUMMARY

Schools, like other organizations which successfully perpetuate themselves, must always be prepared to encounter change. Change should not be considered a rejection of all previous structures and values. Change is the organization's way of renewing itself. Differentiated staffing is, in effect, a process which facilitates growth.

Change is a natural occurrence given shifting priorities, objectives, and goals. The impetus to change springs from a desire to more effectively accomplish new outcomes.

Change processes which depend upon coercion rather than cooperation often enjoy short-range, brief success. Long-range effectiveness is best gained by broadening the base of participation in the change process. Goals must become the property of the team, not of individuals.

Goals are more easily agreed upon than the programs which make the goals operational. The task of specifying activities to accomplish goals should be undertaken by a representative cross section of the system's patrons (teachers, students, parents, and administration).

Change strategies which focus their attention only on the needs of classroom teachers (National Educational Renewal Centers), or to the other extreme, ignore teachers and address themselves to the power structure, are both inadequate. Change should be introduced in a manner which forces cooperation and joint planning where power, rewards, and incentives are available to as many participants as possible.

Resistance to change is predictable when (a) a leader considers an idea his property, (b) people's basic and immediate needs are ignored, (c) stable social relationships are made unstable, (d) change agents are enamored with technical jargon rather than clear communication, (e) change agents assume rationality is sufficient as a motivator, (f) when the leaders want immediate results, (g) when the change agent is too ego-involved in his idea.

Motivational success is closely related to change processes. People who get involved and are consulted on matters tend to be much more motivated than those who are directed in their behavior. The incentive system of an organization should reward creativity and encourage craftsmanship. Physical factors should be considered before more advanced motivational needs are focused upon.

Momentum serves the change agent in two basic ways. First, changes come easier to those who expect and are accustomed to change, and second, change which seems to interminably be talked about rather than implemented eventually develops negative momentum (antipathy).

In part, differentiated staffing is a feedback model, relying heavily on the notion that people are able to successfully change their behavior. This change is accomplished by having peers whom they value (due to reciprocal relations) give them performance feedback.

Schools are organizations which are subject to change pressures from internal and external forces. These pressures are a form of feedback. The feedback is used to modify present structures, plans, etc. This process (cybernetics) is a natural, life-maintenance function. Proper corrections maintain organizational equilibrium (homeostasis); conversely, the failure of organisms to effectively read and use feedback results in disequilibrium. Differentiated staffing as a model facilitates the renewal function by providing systematic feedback.

Since differentiated staffing, as defined in Temple City, is a comprehensive change model, it avoids the problems which pilot projects and demonstration schools frequently encounter such as (1) nonparticipants being envious of participants, (2) one school in the system basing its program on one set of rationale and others on a different set, (3) parents not wanting their children to be "guinea pigs" and (4) the withdrawal of financial support from the pilot study when local funds are scarce.

A significant change in the source of funds for public schools seems imminent. The likelihood of this development bringing pressure to bear on schools to do "a better job" is strong. Differentiated staffing generates internal force to accomplish this task as a "local" priority rather than waiting for the external force of the federal government.

Leadership styles can be critical in the accomplishment of goals. No one leadership style is consistently correct. Situational variables, particularly the maturity levels of the participants, are indices of appropriate styles.

Leaders need to possess a combination of strengths from expertise to charisma and are not likely to do well if they are strong in one and weak in the other.

Leaders should value accountability, let others have the credit for their efforts, avoid paternalism, exercise discretion in exerting their strongest influence, and expect to be considered disloyal and irreverent by people resisting change.

SEVEN

Self-Actualization in
the Public Schools

The Transition from Training to Education

Schools have been very concerned, particularly in the last two decades, with the development of students' skills. Technical competence has become an overriding goal. Schools have focused on "training" during this era rather than providing a "liberal arts education," with the result that measurable skills have become the major criterion for evaluating the success of the schools.

Satisfied observers, interested mainly in the training aspect of schools, note that reading and math scores are up, the number attending college has increased, and that the evidence of the success of our schools is found in our country's technological victories. Dissatisfied observers, who are concerned primarily with the development of a broad base of competencies including human relations, maximum personal growth, and social maturity, point to alienation between schools and students, number of dropouts, and nationwide social problems as indices that the schools are failing.

Differentiated staffing is a format which offers access to the continuing need for knowledge and skills, an important and eternal concern of schools, but in addition provides a framework for education to display as great an awareness for process as it does for product. Given the notion that schools are institutions which owe more to their constituents than diplomas, test scores, and letters of recommendation, it is appropriate to organize the school in ways which facilitate "improved processes of education."

The traditional system of school organization, by its inherent nature, inhibits the optimal performance of the students and professional staff, if one accepts the premise that participants are generally more constrained than released by the current structure. This chapter will analyze the forces within schools which foster or impede personal development. The thesis is that the constraint of individuals retards their potential for self-actualization and that self-actualization is a legitimate goal of education. The definition of self-actualization relied upon by this author is set forth by Maslow:

> Self-actualization is defined in various ways, but a solid core of agreement is perceptible. All definitions accept or imply (a) acceptance and expression of the inner core of self, i.e., actualization of these latent capacities and potentialities, full functioning, availability of the human and personal essence; and (b) minimal presence of ill health, neurosis, psychosis, or loss or diminution of the basic human and personal capacities.[1]

Figure 7-1 is a model which illustrates some of the possible ways in which self-actualization facilitates or limits personal growth. The paradigm represents the theory that certain characteristics of schools provide greater potential for self-actualization than others. The characteristics (manifest properties of a school system) are represented at either end of a continuum. The postulation is that as actual practices of a school district approach the right-hand side of the continuum, more potential among participants for self-actualization will occur; and as practices approach the characteristics on the left, less potential for self-actualization will occur.

Some might argue that schools should not focus on the development of "fully functioning" individuals but should be about the business of training students in skills which will equip them to contribute to society, get a good job and maintain self-respect.

Rather than take an opposite position, which it seems is no more correct than its counterpart, it would be better to develop a set of goals for schools which incorporate the needs of both

---

[1] Abraham H. Maslow, *Toward a Psychology of Being,* (New York: Van Nostrand Reinhold Company, 1968), p. 197.

viewpoints. Certainly schools have some training responsibilities which are technical in nature yet rather easily defined, and it has educational responsibilities which are less "skill oriented" and more difficult to define. The latter deals with the development of human potential. The 1962 ASCD Yearbook Committee has strongly stated its feelings about human development: "The fullest possible flowering of human potentiality is the business of education. It is our reason for being. Whatever we decide is the nature of the fully functioning, self-actualizing individual must become at once the goal of education."[2]

A PROCESS FOR SELF-ACTUALIZATION IN THE PUBLIC SCHOOLS

Less Potential for Self-Actualization	More Potential for Self-Actualization
From:	To:
. . . external regulation	. . . self-regulation
. . . an exclusively social self	. . . a personal and social self
. . . a preoccupation with harmony	. . . a tolerance for social conflict
. . . rigid scheduling	. . . flexible scheduling
. . . conformity as a goal	. . . diversity as a value
. . . coercion	. . . cooperation
. . . "other person" directed	. . . "inner person" directed
. . . maximum formal rules	. . . minimum formal rules
. . . passion for structure	. . . capacity for ambiguity
. . . selfishness	. . . synergy
. . . authoritarianism	. . . democracy
. . . their goals	. . . our goals
. . . group-oriented instruction	. . . individualized instruction
. . . vague expectations	. . . clear responsibilities
. . . hierarchical decision making	. . . shared decision making
. . . fixed goals	. . . emerging goals
. . . training	. . . education
. . . normative behavioral patterns	. . . individualized behavior patterns

Figure 7-1

The goals and foci of education have shifted through history with the needs of society. The shift has often been belated and

---

[2]*Perceiving, Behaving, Becoming,* ASCD Yearbook, 1962, p. 2.

with reluctance. Rather than trace the social history of education, let us attempt to assess the present needs of society and assume the schools must be responsive to those needs.

The society is in social disarray. Old values are being challenged, youth are rebelling, minority cultures want identity and freedom, and world-wide differences concerning ideological values are causing international tension. The list could go on.

In the midst of these difficulties one finds America's conscience being awakened to moral truth, human needs and suffering, and the individual responsibilities of men to one another. In addition, mass media have raised levels of awareness, and a widespread amount of prosperity has caused men to focus on the higher needs of individuals and society. In less prosperous times, men were content to gain physical needs and a degree of security as "returns for their personal and social investments," but currently men are seeking to fulfill higher needs and are concerned with self-esteem and individuality.

Schools in this era must adjust to the realities of the social environment. The realities are too widespread and too widely communicated for schools to ignore them and to secretly hope they will pass by without changing the institution. It may have been inappropriate, given past realities, to develop school systems as committed to education as they were to training. However, the legitimacy of the current need is in great evidence.

It must be emphasized that the state of readiness in schools for a transition from an authoritarian model, where the intellectual elite guide the lives and destiny of the less mature, to a shared, broader base of participation has been increased due to the heightened maturity level of the participants. Not only are the participants more informed, better trained, and generally more mature as individuals, but they now sense a need to declare and express their individuality. Those who feel they can maintain supremacy and power from elitist positions by continuing to treat the masses as immature are not working toward a "self-actualizing society" but instead are attempting to perpetuate a self-actualizing elite.

Teachers in particular are recoiling from a passive, normative stance. They want to be involved in shaping the destiny of their professional futures and are demanding a voice in policy-making. They are establishing a power-base which will give them increased leverage.

Those who attempt to restrain them are not seeking collegiality, shared power, shared accountability, or to establish the individuality of teachers. Professional, mature, well-trained, and educated teachers should be allowed to expand their degrees of control over the organization's goals. In doing so, they are permitted and expected to grow to greater maturity.

The fulfillment of potentialities depends upon the exercise of personal prerogatives. As Maslow has indicated, capacities are needs. Unused capacities (potential) either atrophy or become disease centers. Schools, especially in a democratic society, must facilitate the development of individual capacities if they are concerned with the maximum growth of each participant.

The specific types of adjustments schools must make in order to enhance the potential for the full development of the individual are indicated in Figure 7-1. A comprehensive differentiated staffing plan can greatly aid a school in making these adjustments.

From External to Self-Regulation

Teachers are customarily evaluated by administrators. These evaluations generally occur in the form of scheduled or unscheduled "visits" and follow-up conferences. Elaborate check sheets and forms have been developed for the evaluator's use. Teachers have retaliated by creating intricate warning systems to let each other know, "The principal has his clipboard and pencil and is on his way," or if surprised, fall immediately into a comfortable routine such as the always reliable, "Let's review that material once more to be sure you all have it," or "Turn to page 85 and answer questions 1, 2 and 3." In any event the principal is an external agent. He would be classified as an outsider. It is a case of a visiting generalist evaluating a specialist. The potential value of this kind of control is pegged by B.H. Raven: "That coercive power becomes ineffective as soon as the subject's behavior is no longer observable."[3]

In differentiated staffing, specialists evaluate specialists and they cooperatively establish individual professional growth plans. The evaluation process becomes internal. The profession is then

---

[3]Bertram H. Raven, "The Dynamics of Groups," *Review of Educational Research,* 29, No. IV, 332.

setting its own standards and administering the evaluation of its own colleagues. It is self-regulating. To the degree that institutions and participants are self-regulating, it is proposed they are more capable of self-actualization.

This same line of reasoning applied to students. The current evaluation system places the teacher in the position of setting the goals for the student and then rewarding attainment with extrinsic motivators (grades). Kirschenbaum, Simon and Napier list eight reasons why grades are poor motivators.

> (1) We believe grades have become more important to students than learning. (2) Grades encourage cheating. (3) Grades divide teachers and students into warring camps. (4) Grades discourage students from developing their own goals. (5) Grading stifles creativity. (6) Grades are not applied fairly. (7) Grades create an unhealthy atmosphere in the school. (8) Grades support the other problems in schools.[4]

The authors offer extensive rationale for their position. It is evident that external regulation (extrinsic in the case of students) does not facilitate self-actualization.

As students begin to put forth efforts based on intrinsic motivation, the factor of self-directedness increases. Extrinsic motivation is most valued by immature people. Self-regulation is a function of maturity and a goal of differentiated staffing.

From an Exclusively Social Self to a Personal and Social Self

"The self which is shaped by social forces is not the whole self,"[5] states Harry Broudy. He contends man should be as much an actor as a reactor; that one discovers his identity and selfhood through individual decisions as well as corporate decisions.

Schools must allow for, and encourage, individuality as well as social integration. Students should not be forced to compromise their beliefs and intuitions in an effort to gain harmony with the group. Traditionally organized classrooms, with class sizes of 25 to 35 students, do not logistically lend themselves to the preservation

---

[4]Howard Kirschenbaum, Sidney B. Simon and Rodney W. Napier, *WAD-JA-GET?* (New York: Hart Publishing Company, Inc., 1971), pp. 137-140.

[5]Harry S. Broudy, "New Problems and Old Solutions," *Philosophy of Education,* October 1969, p. 221.

of divergent thinking. Seldom do more than a dozen students actually present their views on an issue and even less often do teachers "plan" to have a discussion that terminates without a convergent conclusion.

This preoccupation of schools with the development of a purely social self—one who has discovered society's expectation of him— has been accelerated by the diminishment of an educational system which focuses on thinking and the rise of a system which places too great a value on training.

Differentiated staffing fosters small-group instruction which permits the maximum use of inquiry techniques. In addition, independent study, programmed materials, contracts, and tutorial arrangements aid in developing self-reliance in students.

From a Preoccupation with Harmony to a Tolerance for Social Conflict

Schools frequently are so concerned with harmony that they are unreceptive to disagreements. If someone does not agree with the majority, it is incumbent upon them to yield and accept the group's decision. The result of this kind of thinking renders a minority point of view not only impotent, but tends to declare a tenacious proponent of a minority view as disloyal.

Healthy organizations must provide a channel for dissent if they expect personal but not popular views to be espoused. To the contrary, autocratically administered institutions avoid input from the followers and would probably be indignant towards individuals who disagreed with the ideas of the leaders. It is an environment such as this that Simmel describes when he writes: "If we did not even have the power and the right to rebel against tyranny, arbitrariness, moodiness, tactlessness, we could not bear to have any relation to people from whose characters we thus suffer."[6]

Since schools hold most of their participants captive, they must present individuals with "safe" channels for dissent. It is the absence of safety valves which generates explosive, revolutionary situations. If a goal of the school system is to develop self-actualizing experiences for its participants, the school cannot be preoccupied with harmony to the extent that is unreceptive to minority points of view.

---

[6]George Simmel, *Conflict, The Web of Group Affiliations*, (New York: Free Press, 1956), p. 39.

Differentiated staffing provides for the formal participation of teachers and students in decision-making. In addition, in situations where a decision must be reached, veto power is denied anyone except the board of education. This permits decisions to be achieved by utilizing a problem-solving method rather than resorting to the use of coercion.

From Rigid Scheduling to Flexible Scheduling

"Schedules" probably must persist in some form in schools of any size, but should be considered an alien rather than an ally to an educational institution seeking to meet the needs of individuals. Schedules which must abide should be as flexible as possible. Rigidity in scheduling represents an artificial constraint to the intellectually inquisitive, motivated student. Inflexible scheduling is due largely to the needs of some teachers and students who require structure. To impose a rigid schedule on *all* teachers and students severely limits the experiences which the school could offer.

Schools presently are too confining and military. Students are shuttled in squads through hoops which are appropriate for a few and required of all on a time line which is largely irrelevant. If a student is not "ready" for Algebra I (nine months of it, 50 minutes a day in a group of 30) at 14½ years of age, there are few alternatives. The same structure is true, of course, for most of the classes offered. The capitals of all the states are memorized in the fifth grade and so on.

Schedules should serve the needs of individuals, not groups, if one is concerned about self-actualization, and they should be as flexible as possible.

From Other Person Directed to Inner Person Directed

A person who is "other person directed" takes his cues for behavior mainly from his environment. His pattern is one of adaptability. A large part of this kind of behavior is conditioned and reinforced by the schools. Students are taught to respond with the answer the teacher wants. As John Holt puts it, "We adults destroy most of the intellectual and creative capacity of children by the things we do to them or make them do. We destroy this capacity above all by making them afraid, afraid of not doing what other people want, of not pleasing, of making mistakes, of failing, or being *wrong.*"[7] The same situation has been found to be true of graduate students where there is " . . . an almost pathological fear in the students of their own ideas and particularly their imaginations. Apparently most students by this time have been by some process so beaten down that they do not dare present their own ideas."[8]

Inner-directed persons are risk takers. They tend to value their own intuition and intellect. Actions and ideas spring from within. The schools must allow participants to be expressive in this manner. As E. V. Pullias has said, "Talent involves the inconvenience of responsibility or it dies." It seems inner-directedness is a key factor in the self-actualization process.

Differentiated staffing encourages inner-directedness by accentuating intrinsic motivators, allowing students to select their own advisors, giving students many decision-making opportunities, and permitting teachers to regulate their own procedures for such matters as evaluation, selection, curriculum and budget.

From Maximum Rules to Minimum Rules

Insecure, wavering institutions are rule bound. They do not trust people and make rules which apply to a few but inhibit everyone. Healthy organizations depend less on rules and more on understandings. They consider rules as an encumbrance and feel there should be just enough rules to maintain viability but not so many as to ensure a great deal of predictability.

A differentiated staffing environment encourages flexible, cooperative decision-making. Excessive numbers of rules are antithetical to an organization which is attempting to be non-authoritarian and which is concerned with individuals. Fewer rules increases the need for personal responsibility.

From a Passion for Structure to a Capacity for Ambiguity

Organizations which encourage divergency and individuality will naturally become less structured. Structure itself, like rules, tends to limit the boundaries of an organization's potential.

---

[7] John Holt, *How Children Fail,* (New York: Pitman Publishing Company, Inc., 1964), p. 167.

[8] Earl V. Pullias and James D. Young, *A Teacher is Many Things,* (Bloomington: Indiana University Press, 1969), p. 95.

As Hersey and Blanchard point out, "It seems that as an individual moves to a more responsible job ... expectations become less structured."[9] Delegating responsibility and broadening the base of meaningful participation is one means of safely reducing structure. Participants are more involved and independent. They are expected to be self-starting, self-regulating people.

Leaders who insist on much structure and yet want to delegate responsibility are working at cross purposes. Reducing structure increases ambiguity. Differentiated staffing, as an open system, provides for and perpetuates organizational adjustments.

From Selfishness to Synergy

Synergy is a form of selfishness. The difference between pure selfishness and synergy is that as one invests himself in various tasks and relationships purely because they are *self-enhancing* (he manipulates the culture to gratify only his needs), that is selfishness. If, however, one can make personal investments which help fulfill a personal need as well as fulfilling someone else's need—that is synergy.

When people collaborate with their culture rather than competing with it, they move away from selfishness towards synergy. Differentiated staffing does not insure participants will be more synergistic but it does make it difficult for selfish leaders to succeed.

From Authoritarianism to Democracy

"A child's individuality, curiosity, and assertiveness which has been respected has greater confidence and self-respect than those raised in authoritarian families,"[10] states Paul Landis, based on a study completed by himself and Carol Stone. Transferring this to schools, it seems obvious that authoritarian environments reduce the possibility for self-actualization.

Many behavioral scientists agree that involving people in decision-making, particularly when they are directly affected by

---

[9] Paul Hersey and Kenneth H. Blanchard, *Management of Organizational Behavior*, p. 95.

[10] Paul H. Landis, *Social Control*, (New York: J.P. Lippincott Company, 1956), p. 440.

the outcome, is one means of increasing their commitment to the decision. They will internalize the decision and "own it." Under these conditions, which are basically democratic, participants feel independent and in a position of influence which permits them to exercise initiative and to be assertive.

From "Their Goals" to "Our Goals"

Goals must be created in cooperation with and belong to the people who have to implement activities to reach the goals. With differentiated staffing, it is possible for goals to become joint goals because teachers and students are in a policy-making position and can control the development and modification of goals.

Participants such as teachers, who generally design the activities which are intended to achieve the organization's goals, are more likely to select goal-oriented activities if they understand and support the goals. If a teacher doesn't feel a particular goal, such as "The development of the maximum potential of each learner" is a good goal or simply does not understand what it means, then that goal for all intents and purposes may as well not exist. A person is not likely to be "fully functioning" if he is expected to fulfill goals which he does not agree with and/or understand.

From Group-Oriented Instruction to Individualized Instruction

The American culture, according to W.W. Whyte, has fallen victim to an ailment he describes as "groupthink." It has occurred due to the preoccupation of society with harmony, convergent thinking, sensitivity training, and other "group thinking" mechanisms. Whyte states, "The new values would incline us to the easy harmony of the group view—where the whole *is* greater than the parts."[11]

Schools perpetuate this on a different level by organizing themselves to deal almost exclusively with groups. Group-oriented instruction doesn't provide the time nor permit teachers to be concerned with individuals. Teachers constantly are having to regulate their input and establish their goals to suit the needs of

---

[11]William H. Whyte, Jr., "Groupthink," in *Selected Educational Heresies,* ed. William F. O'Neill, (Glenview, Illinois: Scott, Foresman and Company, 1969), p. 42.

the majority. All students receive the same input (media, printed page or lecture) on a particular subject even though there are several in each group who need an individualized treatment. Some people do not learn well simply hearing (audio input)—they must be able to see and handle (visual and tactile input)—yet they are frequently all given identical instruction. The presence of a variable-course structure which is designed to meet individual needs is an important element in a comprehensive model of differentiated staffing.

From Vague Expectations to Clear Responsibilities

Differentiated staffing is a performance-oriented concept. Job descriptions are written in behavioral terms; curriculum is written in evaluative, measurable terms; and the goals of the district are operationalized. The intent of these thrusts is to depart from generalized, vague descriptions and practices, and to move towards a greater degree of specificity and accountability.

This movement is referred to by Glasser when he emphasizes the need for personal responsibility, and the need to be held accountable for decision-making and the exercise of responsible behavior. According to Glasser, "The more responsible a person, the healthier he is—The less responsible, the less healthy."[12] This is another way of saying self-actualization relies in part on responsible, accountable behavior. Irresponsibility needs to be responded to honestly. One means of reducing irresponsibility is to clearly communicate the basic expectations of the organization.

From Hierarchical Decision-Making to Shared Decision-Making

It becomes redundant at this point to belabor the issue of involvement as a criterion for determining organizational health. Suffice it to say freedom is a variable most greatly affected by power or the lack of it. For one to grow to his full potential requires him to have the freedom (power) to exercise his intellect and intuition. Hierarchical decision-making is antithetical to personal growth and development. It is a means of a few keeping the ideas and potential of many in a diminutive state.

---

[12]William Glasser, M.D., *Cure for Crisis,* (Pasadena: Thomas Jefferson Research Center, 1969), p. 6.

From Fixed Goals to Emerging Goals

The goals of schools are relative to the needs of society. Unlike churches, factories or stores, which serve a limited spectrum of patrons and are able to establish relatively fixed goals, schools serve everyone. This forces them to be responsive to a variety of emerging needs and thus to have at least some goals which are in transition.

The notion of emerging goals places the organization in a more fluid state. Rogers applied this concept to individuals as he indicates "I find such a person to be a human being in flow, in process, rather than having achieved some state."[13] Schools should strive to be like other organisms: growing, changing, and becoming. They should provide an environment which encourages participants to do the same. Self-actualization is a process, a journey—not a goal.

It is especially true that the operationalization of goals must remain fluid. Means (methods) should always be subject to examination and constantly be reviewed. Ends (goals) are more like the United States Constitution. It is subject to amendment, but only after great debate and slow, deliberate actions. In schools it is probable that new means will bring greater pressure to bear and instigate the revision of the goals of education. It will be easier to change means than goals and it may be possible to modify goals by utilizing new means.

The master teacher role is intended to be a major source of system renewal, although the organizational structure of differentiated staffing does encourage creative input to emerge from any level.

From Training to Education

"Man is the only educable being. The horse, the dog—the lower animals, are trained, not educated,"[14] says H.H. Horne. Froebel adds meaning to the definition of "education" as he says " . . . all one can become lies within and that the purpose of an agent of change is to bring more out of man, not put more into him."[15]

---

[13]Carl R. Rogers, "Towards Becoming a Fully Functioning Person" in *Perceiving, Behaving, Becoming,* ASCD Yearbook, 1962, p. 31.

[14]Herman Harrell Horne, *Idealism in Education,* (New York: The Macmillan Company, 1910), p. 176.

[15]Friedrick Froebel, *The Education of Man,* (New York: D. Appleton Co., 1887).

Given this view of education which is alien to "training" as a central purpose, it is difficult to accept what goes on in most of our classrooms. In one study, based on more than 1,300 classroom observations, it was found that just nine percent of the classroom time was spent on analyzing, synthesizing, reasoning, questioning conclusions, or creative thinking—and less than two percent of classroom time was devoted to the teacher's deliberately helping students to improve their thinking.[16] These findings are explained somewhat by a study completed by Richard Weintraub in which he reports:

> ... the paramount concerns of the beginning teacher—and possibly many an experienced teacher, too—focus more on the teacher's sense of adequacy and ability to maintain interest and control in the classroom, than on the needs and accomplishments of his pupils. [Teachers] use subject matter to sustain themselves in the role of the principal source of knowledge in the classroom; the more knowledge the more security.[17]

One is inclined to sympathize with the teachers who worry most about being considered "interesting" (their need) and who must maintain "classroom control" (a key factor in their evaluation by administration). Their inclination to behave as though they are the "principal source of knowledge" is very regrettable given the diverse needs and personalities of the students. The self-actualization of the individual student is not a central goal of a training institution but should be the goal of an educational institution.

From Normative to Individualized Behavior Patterns

The term normative is intended to communicate the idea that a role exists which has been developed over time and which the lore of education perpetuates with such statements as (a) good teachers assign a lot of homework, (b) students should respect you: it isn't important whether they like you or not, (c) new teachers in the system naturally get the worst room and the slow learners,

---

[16]Donald M. Sharpe, "Studying Teacher Classroom Behavior to Determine How Paraprofessionals Can Help in the Classroom," TEPS Write-in Paper on Flexible Staffing Patterns, No. 3, NEA Publications, p. 9.

[17]Richard Weintraub, in *Education Daily*, Capital Publications, Inc., January 14, 1972, p. 6.

(d) good teachers never need assistance from anyone in dealing with a troublesome student, (e) no master's degree—no advancement, (f) a quiet room of students is a productive one, (g) you must balance out your high and low letter grades, (h) good bulletin boards and neat rooms equal a good evaluation, (i) good teachers don't make waves, (j) good teachers think of new ideas that don't cost money, (k) always complete the textbook. Expectancies such as these cannot withstand a rational analysis; however, their existence to varying degrees is quite real.

The concept of normative implies mediocrity and a pursuit of being average in contrast to being considered avant-garde. Routinization might well be called a prime product of normative behavior. Schools perpetuate much of what they do on the basis of orderliness. Orderliness can best be acquired through establishing group norms. Such norms result in predictable behavior from the participants.

Normative behavior typically seeks precedent before deciding on action and seeks to apply *the* solution as opposed to *a* solution. The pursuit of alternatives is not valued. Some of the results of normative behavior are (1) conformity, (2) inauthentic behavior, (3) structured roles, and (4) a lack of potential for self-actualization.

Teachers and students must be allowed to perform in individualized ways. A climate should be created that considers diversity a strength and encourages the pursuit of alternatives.

Differentiated staffing allows a teacher to establish practices that are not normative by securing the endorsement of a professional colleague (senior teacher) rather than trying to convince an administrator that the deviation is worthwhile. While there is no doubt that diverse routes to a solution are unpredictable in many ways, requiring a single route as a solution to a complex problem is sure to stifle the development of improved methods and exciting alternatives.

SUMMARY

Schools which are classically organized are well prepared to "train" students. The development of a fully functioning individual has only recently become a primary concern of educators. Differentiated staffing is a vehicle capable of assisting schools who are attempting to make the transition from a training emphasis to the development of a comprehensive educational program.

Traditional systems tend to organize themselves in such a manner as to centralize authority, withhold responsibility from individuals, worry about harmony, have too many rules, expect normative behavior, and so on. These characteristics do not accelerate one towards maximum personal development nor do they allow the system to take on the mantle of a growing, becoming, actualizing organism.

Less traditional organizational patterns which are intended to foster self-actualization and organizational renewal include a trend towards a tolerance for ambiguity and unpredictability, democratic decision-making, flexible scheduling, increased personal prerogatives, etc.

The emerging needs of society and particularly the diverse needs of individuals, requires schools to be responsive. In order to respond to the needs of "developing each individual's full potential," schools will have to shift from rigid, bureaucratic training structures to flexible, democratic educational institutions. Doing so will make it possible for the exhortation of Maslow to be a reality for each individual; "What a man can be, he must be."[18]

---

[18] Abraham H. Maslow, *Motivation and Personality*, p. 46.

EIGHT

Problems With Differentiated Staffing

Any idea as dramatic and comprehensive as differentiated staffing will create some problems for those who intend to implement it. When existing practices are challenged, protectors of the present who are anxious about what the future holds will seize upon every opportunity to divulge weaknesses in the new practice. There are weaknesses. The purpose of this chapter is to present those weaknesses as objectively as possible and at times to suggest ways of avoiding some of the problems. What some would view as a problem may be viewed by others as an opportunity. As Whitehead has put it, "The clash of doctrines is not a disaster, it is an opportunity."[1]

Slower Decisions and "Administrivia"

Any form of shared decision-making is inherently slower than an authoritarian model. A new department head can be appointed tomorrow by the principal, but the establishment of a job description by the recipients of the intended services and their participation in selection takes more time. Participation is greater; commitment is improved, but it is a slower process.

Aside from this consideration, it is also likely, at least at the outset, that those participating in decision-making (many for the first time) will reserve *all* decisions for the group. They will delegate little or nothing to the chairman (principal) for his own study and action. The chairman is the former authority-oriented principal whom many teachers may not trust. Thus, in an effort to

---

[1] Alfred North Whitehead, *Science and the Modern World,* New York: The Macmillan Co., 1925, p. 259.

show everyone that the new corporate decision-making body has power, the total group deals with all problems.

The difficulty this presents is that many hours are wasted debating problems which are often of minor significance. An example in a typical junior high school would be the time spent discussing logistical problems such as procedures in the cafeteria or bus schedules on shortened days. Such subjects, although interesting and needing attention, should not be prime concerns of an academic senate. The senate should be concerned with "policy making" and direct their chairman to administer the policies. Their expertise is in curriculum development and instructional methodology, not administration.

Principals probably perpetuate the situation by trying at first not to assume they have any authority to do anything without senate approval. Thus they bring "administrivia" to the senate for consideration. A perceptive senate should delegate administration of senate policy to the administrator and insist he not waste their time.

D.S. Blurs the Clear-Cut Distinction
Between Labor and Management

Shared decision-making, teacher participation in the selection and evaluation of leaders, and the decentralization of responsibility and accountability are conditions for which teacher's associations have long bargained. When they gain such conditions without a struggle with management, but as a result of a differentiated staffing structure, the distinctions between teachers and administrators are less clear.

In differentiated staffing, administrators teach, teachers administer, and policy is a matter of consensus among decision-makers, of whom teachers comprise the majority. The teachers' union is opposed to any organizational pattern which "divides the ranks" of teachers. The union wants teacher-power but only if the classical labor (teachers)-management (administration) distinction can be preserved.

The National Education Association, having adopted union strategies, is proud of its recent efforts to "out-organize" the union. According to NEA president Donald Morrison, " . . . the NEA and others feel that we have not only out-organized them, but we have out-negotiated them. And the threat of a private industrial union, especially taking over the teachers, I think, has passed."[2]

Richard Mason, President of the newly formed National Association of Professional Educators (NAPE), apparently feels the NEA and AFT are both inappropriately representing teachers, as he indicates his organization is opposed to "NEA policies of 'militancy' in advocating strikes and agency shops, unified dues to 'force membership,' and thrusts toward 'political force,' not educational action."[3]

Meanwhile administrators, librarians, counselors, nurses, and others who have belonged to associations which were always NEA affiliates, formed their own new association, the Alliance of Associations for the Advancement of Education (AAAE). They did so in order to remain autonomous and to function as a professional group in opposition to trends in NEA policy. As W.L. Pharis, President of the National Association of Elementary School Principals puts it, the new NEA constitution " . . . would, in effect, turn NEA into a teacher's union . . . since NEA membership is mandatory for a member 'of an NEA affiliate.' This provision would destroy the NEA as we have known it." He characterized the new constitution as "an attempted 'power grab' by a biased group of shortsighted individuals."[4]

Since differentiated staffing largely reduces the "issues" between labor and management to ineffectual matters, those who feel the differences must be perpetuated in order to "maintain polarity" will oppose differentiated staffing, even if it does unify educators. This associational opposition, which usually represents "external forces" and their vested interests, can inhibit a district's movement to differentiated staffing.

Lags in Colleges, Laws and Association

It will be some time before the organizational constraints provided by those who perform a collaborative function with public education gain a commitment to the flexibility that

---

[2]*Education Daily*, Capital Publications, Inc., February 15, 1972, p. 4.

[3]*Ibid.*, February 28, 1972, p. 6.

[4]*Ibid.*, December 22, 1971, p. 1.

differentiated staffing requires. Until they do, the rapid development of the program will be inhibited.

Teacher-training institutions must revamp their programs to establish new roles for teachers. It is no longer adequate to provide a general background where teachers will be required to perform specific tasks. It is unnecessary to keep teacher trainees away from teachers and students until they are in their last phase of training. Teacher trainees should spend a full year on the public school site, prior to credentialing, working closely with teachers and teacher trainers.

The state legislatures must relax their comprehensive teacher certification laws to enable several categories of training to be considered for teachers. Laws governing teacher-pupil ratios are not meaningful in a flexibly scheduled, differentiated staffing school. Requirements regulating the percentage of dollars of the total budget to be spent for certificated salaries are not relevant when a large number of paraprofessionals are employed.

Professional associations are unsure of their official position on differentiated staffing, and as such, their point of view remains skeptical and too parochial. Distinctions such as who is a teacher are unclear as administrators change their roles and instructional aides are introduced into the program.

The lag will exist for some time and is a disadvantage. The challenge of a system developing a differentiated staffing model is to work closely with training institutions, state departments of education, and professional associations, and to include their representatives in the planning and implementation of the model.

Comprehensive Change and Transitional Costs

It is inadvisable to consider differentiated staffing without being prepared to accept the multiple changes which it will generate. The act of creating job descriptions for hierarchical service agents such as senior teachers offers some clue that changes will not only be forthcoming, but are demanded. The new job descriptions may require the senior teachers to introduce new modes of instruction or to develop self-directed learning materials. It is not possible to do either without some form of flexible scheduling, small group areas, large group rooms, resource centers, and independent study arrangements.

Differentiated staffing is a springboard to comprehensive improvements. It is a method to quickly upgrade many facets of the program simultaneously. Such changes cost money and require a commitment to the improvement of the total school program. The conversion costs of flexible scheduling and its attendant paraprofessional costs must be considered before deciding to accept differentiated staffing. Remodeling and the purchase of additional instructional equipment and materials also accompany the costs of flexible scheduling. It becomes clear that differentiated staffing develops a multiplier effect in terms of change.

In addition to the costs of improving the curriculum and physical plant and adding paraprofessionals, there is the problem of "grandfathering" existing teachers. When a district moves to differentiated staffing all teachers previously employed are protected. That is, they will remain on the traditional salary schedule or be eligible to compete for leadership positions and only new teachers to the system will be placed on associate teacher status. It may take 10 to 15 years for the existing staff to turn over enough times to have all teachers on the differentiated schedules. The problem lies in the fact that some on the old schedule will continue to progress to the top of the traditional schedule whether they are willing to accept increased responsibilities or not. Consequently, until the entire staff is on the differentiated schedules, the savings effected through associate teachers which can be used to pay for the cost of senior and master teachers is limited.

Action Research Promises Some Failures

Differentiated staffing has not been broadly explored nor widely implemented. Results, in the form of "hard data," are not available to justify its existence. The plan, by nature, then, constitutes action research. Action research is not as safe as some would like it to be. As Dwight Allen has said, "In the first race between the horse and the steam engine, the horse won."[5] Some mistakes are probable when one explores new concepts. Continual adjustments will have to be made as the plan is implemented.

Many forms of differentiated staffing will be developed in the

---

[5]Dwight W. Allen, speech delivered in Temple City, California, March 8, 1968.

next decade and, it is assumed, the models and their processes will evolve rather than being instantly created. It should be emphasized that the art is in a stage of design and refinement, even though many of the long-range goals remain constant. Action research, a condition typical of new ventures, requires more tolerance for ambiguity than is commonly present among educational leaders.

Role Orientation for New Decision-Makers

Teachers are unaccustomed to leading. Their potential to creatively lead has always existed; however, when given initial opportunities to lead, the need for an adjustment period does occur.

Much self-doubt and actual learning occurs during the first year of their new role. The specific tasks (services) their teams demand of them raise anxieties. It takes time to build a base of experience and competency in decision-making.

Participation in school and district academic senates is a new role too. New members must become accustomed to the process and peculiarities of group decision-making and group dynamics. The degree of their involvement will accelerate with experience.

As Landis points out, leading is a form of risk taking. "Throughout history the innovator has more often been shot, stabbed, stoned or mobbed than blessed."[6] Senior and master teachers who are given the power to accomplish major changes in what has admittedly been a tradition-bound institution can be expected to exhibit some hesitancy in decision-making. In short, followers become leaders and there is an adjustment period to allow the transition to actually occur.

Patriarchal Force Neutralized

Schools, as traditionally organized, vest power and status in a single leader (the principal), which in many cases results in his being viewed as a father image, or in the mind of the contemporary critic, "big daddy."

Teachers have been conditioned to discover the principal's expectations and to be aware of his idiosyncratic tendencies. Of course, in doing so, they often forfeit the privilege of being

---

[6]Paul H. Landis, *Social Control,* p. 100.

inner-directed, self-actualizing individuals. In the process, a dependency relationship evolves which places the staff and their behavior in close proximity to the principal's expectations. All major decisions, penalties and rewards emanate from his office or at least have his blessing.

Differentiated staffing upsets this relationship, and many staff members may have difficulty in making the adjustment. They resent the senior teacher being very close to the former patri- archal figure and between them and that figure. Many liked having access to the principal on an "equal time" basis. There are some who will try to circumvent the teacher leader to get directly to what they still consider the power. If the principal is seduced by flattery and acts upon a request from a staff or associate teacher, which in fact belongs in the domain of a senior teacher, many problems will occur. Principals must actively assist in the shift of power from themselves to the senior teachers.

Female elementary teachers tend to have the most difficult time with this situation, perhaps due to the magnanimous role fre- quently portrayed by male elementary principals. Historically, male elementary principals have been the only visible source of authority the teachers have known and as such have wielded tremendous influence with their predominately female staffs.

Differentiated staffing disrupts that role and some are slow to adjust to the new structure. It is of some value to hold more school-wide faculty meetings than one might deem necessary during the first year, simply to placate those who have this need.

Some Compete and Lose

After a staff has philosophically accepted the salient character- istics of differentiated staffing, it requires that competition for the right to occupy leadership positions occur.

Naturally, not all who compete will succeed in winning a position. In some instances, the losers suffer a setback which lingers longer than desirable. The problem is that schools never have had distinctions among teachers and they have no experience at vying for positions. When 20 teachers compete for five leader- ship positions there will be 15 losers. Some display more resiliency than others. Maslow describes this condition and some of its anticipated outcomes as he speaks of the "continental divide" principle. He states: "I use this principle to describe the fact that stress will either break people altogether if they are in the beginning too weak to stand distress, or else, if they are already strong enough to take the stress in the first place, that same stress, if they come through it, will strengthen them, temper them, and make them stronger."[7]

Displacement of Generalist Coordinators

People who hold school or district level positions that are coordinative or directive in nature are displaced with the advent of differentiated staffing since their former position is no longer needed. They must, if they wish to continue to lead, compete for positions in differentiated staffing.

Predictably, it would be better from their point of view to have been appointed to leadership roles in differentiated staffing, but to do so would destroy a key component of differentiated staffing, that of the selection process. Basically, leadership cannot be appointive nor evaluated from the top for either senior or master teacher positions and, as has been indicated, each of these perform roles formerly provided by generalists who were administrative appointees.

It is especially true and worth noting, that in large school districts, directors, coordinators, and administrative assistants of various types exist in sufficient quantity to finance a considerable portion of the cost involved in establishing a teaching hierarchy. Smaller districts generally have no curriculum specialists and must generate the cost of a teaching hierarchy from within their system, as Temple City did.

Coordinators who are very effective in their role probably would be relieved by a transition to differentiated staffing. They could return to a meaningful role in the classroom without loss in compensation and be responsive to the needs of teachers, not the expectations of administrators.

Senior and Master Teachers Do Not Teach
100 Percent of the Time

One frequent criticism of differentiated staffing is that the senior and master teachers do not teach students 100 percent of the time. If they are the best teachers, it is argued, how can one

[7]Abraham H. Maslow, *Eupsychian Management*, p. 76.

justify removing them from as much direct contact with students as possible?

To illustrate the point, Figure 1-1 (page 36) indicates that master teachers teach 20 percent of the time and senior teachers teach 60 percent of the time. As one views the limited time a master teacher spends in the classroom, it must be recalled that he has not been characterized as an expert in multiple modes of instruction. His expertise is primarily in the field of research related to curriculum design and. learning theory. The master teacher may be an outstanding teacher in the classroom but if so, it is simply a fringe benefit to the system. It should be clarified that only the senior teacher is to have it required of him to be an artist in group process, that is, working closely with students and teachers. It is significant to recall that only three percent of the total staff will occupy the position of master teacher.

Some of the criticism regarding the master teacher's classroom role might have been avoided if Temple City had retained the original title given to this position. It was once called the Teaching Curriculum Research Associate, which is a much more accurate description of the functions of the position. That title was abandoned for the briefer though less accurately descriptive title of master teacher. The author has encountered many people who dislike differentiated staffing due to the names used to designate the positions. The titles are misleading.

The primary concern of critics should be with the removal of the senior teacher from student contact. This concern is legitimate in terms of the senior teacher role. The senior teacher is expected to be an outstanding classroom teacher. The Temple City rationale for limiting the senior teacher to a 60 percent classroom load takes three directions. First, up to this time there has been no effective means of holding teachers of the caliber of a senior teacher in the classroom and still rewarding them for their outstanding contributions to students. To reward them and not change their responsibilities from those of their colleagues would be a merit pay plan (paying teachers different rates for doing the same tasks), and no merit pay plan has ever been able to endure the test of time. (Teachers' associations and unions dislike merit pay for several reasons including: (a) How does one define outstanding teaching? (b) How does one determine whether it is occurring? (c) *Who* says it is or is not occurring? They feel merit pay for outstanding teaching is not feasible because no one has been able to identify it on a consistent and accurate basis acceptable to teachers.)

Secondly, aside from being able to hold senior teachers in the classroom, is the condition that in a differentiated staffing structure the best teachers are given responsibility for the direction of a total curriculum area. Their influence will be felt by every student in the department, not just those they personally have in class.

Finally, leadership takes time. To expect a teacher to accept greater responsibilities than his peers and yet to also teach a full load is unrealistic and impractical.

The D.S. Environment is Too Authentic for Some

When teachers are asked to be creative, inner-directed individuals, and to produce or be criticized, there is a natural tendency on the part of some to be dismayed by the openness of the climate. Dependent, other-person-centered individuals may not value their new freedom to be independent and yet accountable to a professional peer. Conformity and routinization are safe if not productive, and diversified approaches which are non-normative are threatening even if productive. Honesty in communications requires a degree of ego strength not present in sufficient quantities in all participants.

It appears that authenticity is a valued practice by the healthy, resilient individuals of society who can withstand the shock of discovering how they are really viewed by their subordinates, peers, or superiors.

Performance-oriented job descriptions result in a concrete measure of whether tasks are being accomplished or not. Leaders in differentiated staffing are evaluated by those they serve on specific behaviors. This is in contrast to leaders traditionally being evaluated by those hierarchical figures who placed them there and on much less specific criteria.

Any time one operates on performance criteria in evaluation, the necessity for "honest feedback" is increased and consequently the likelihood of direct confrontations is heightened. Differentiated staffing provides for and the procedures actually require an authentic environment. More than a few people are not prepared for such honesty in interpersonal relations.

One way to approach this problem is to provide the staff with in-service opportunities in human interaction. This "communication training" may help the participants as they move from a system with limited—even stilted—communication to open interaction.

Administrators Must Change

There are many places in the country where differentiated staffing will never receive serious consideration because the concept requires the formal sharing of power. More than a few people are enamored with the idea of possessing power. Once they have attained it, the temptation to wield it is great. It is this writer's opinion that unless administrators are willing to actually share power, differentiated staffing is not a desirable alternative.

Temple City had relatively little trouble with this problem due to the presence of a superintendent, Dr. Rand, who himself was able to release power. His example, as well as expectation for others, was an important factor.

Does D.S. Create a New Elite?

Differentiated staffing places power in the hands of an academic senate and as a result may create a division between associate and staff teachers and the senior teachers. Where power was previously in the hands of a few administrators, it now is in the hands of several teachers and an administrator at the school level. The ratio of participation by teachers is greatly increased and yet the majority of teachers do not sit in the inner circle. Some of their peers do and formerly did not. As a result, an adjustment in the perspective of associate and staff teachers becomes necessary. The author's experience indicates that this adjustment will take a year or two.

Differentiated staffing assumes that decisions cannot best be made by a majority vote and thus does not claim to be a completely democratic process. It is a process that enables some teachers to compete for the right to make decisions and to share in the responsibility of standing behind those decisions.

The problem has been somewhat ameliorated in Temple City by holding open senate meetings after school when any staff member can come and observe the proceedings. The staff can individually submit agenda items and observe the action taken.

Another positive step is to have pre- and/or post-senate team meetings to discuss the agenda and the attitude the team holds concerning the decisions being considered or that were made. The intent is to have senior teachers in good communication with the opinions and attitude of the entire staff. The challenge remains to avoid the formation of a "new elite."

Reinforcement of Departmental Isolation

Differentiated staffing has, for the most part, been developed along departmental lines. There is a senior teacher of math, social studies, English, etc. This results in curriculum specialization and compartmentalized learning. Educational leaders are dismayed by such practices and are advocating the integration, not isolation of curriculum areas. The model this writer has experienced has not yet successfully met that need, although at least one of the Temple City schools is experimenting with it.

Elementary and intermediate school models need not emulate secondary curriculum programs which accentuate segregation of specialists. The author strongly advocates interdisciplinary, multi-age teams or families of learners and teachers utilizing open-space, open-schedule concepts. It offers many more alternatives and is a more realistic learning environment. An alternative to the curriculum specialist model is presented for your consideration.

Figure 8-1 represents an interdisciplinary, multi-age model. Assuming a school had 16 teachers (or other multiples of four), they could be differentiated into four families (teams), each family serving one-fourth of the student body. Each family would be led by a senior teacher who is a curriculum specialist in one of four major areas: Technology, Communications, Human Relations, or Aesthetics. Each team would function autonomously, particularly regarding the use of time, space, and budget. The senior teachers would serve as a school curriculum planning committee, developing school-wide themes, inter-family projects and programs and school budget priorities.

The senior teachers would each be given a block of discretionary personnel funds to either employ paraprofessionals, augment the teaching team with interns, or to hire the assistance of specialists from the community, including older students.

Space other than regular team areas (area of four former

classrooms) would be scheduled for use by the school senate. This would include outdoor areas and special art, music, or craft areas.

Senior teachers, with remaining team members, would hire teacher replacements and make decisions concerning advancement, as in the specialist model.

AN INTERDISCIPLINARY, MULTI-AGE MODEL

	TECHNOLOGY	COMMUNICATIONS	HUMAN RELATIONS	AESTHETICS
Family #1	senior	staff	staff	associate
Family #2	staff	senior	associate	staff
Family #3	associate	associate	senior	staff
Family #4	associate	staff	associate	senior

    4 senior teachers
    6 staff teachers
    6 associate teachers

Note:
Each senior teacher would serve two functions. First, they would coordinate an interdisciplinary, multi-age team on a daily basis, and secondly they would serve each of the curriculum specialists who teach on the other team. For example, the senior teacher of technology would meet regularly with all of the staff and associate teachers who are in charge of technology on the other teams. Each senior teacher would perform the following basic responsibilities.

Team Leader	Curriculum Specialist
— Personal and social maturation and adjustment of students	— Curriculum renewal and development
— Coordination of team activities:	— Articulation and sequencing of curriculum
1. Use of space	— Evaluation of subject matter teaching competence
2. Scheduling of students and staff	
3. Instructional strategies	
—Evaluation, of teaching methods	
—Home to school communicaitons	

Figure 8-1

Secondary schools have been most reluctant to explore the "family of learners" model, mainly due to the logistical problems of scheduling. One hundred high school students, if grouped heterogeneously, have a wide range of subject matter needs requiring considerable teacher specialization. An alternative is to provide a portion of each day for basic subjects which can be integrated and the remainder for specialization. Homogeneous groupings, which could permit appropriate subject matter coverage (advanced courses in any field), create a number of ill effects on the learning process and do not seem to be a viable alternative.

The Effects of Visibility

Differentiated staffing and flexible scheduling increase the degree and frequency of visibility for staff and students. It has often been said that under this plan a school's problems become very apparent.

Flexible scheduling, a necessary component of differentiated staffing, makes visible what always existed but wasn't obvious—the recalcitrant and/or unmotivated student. This student was formerly subdued by the system which kept him a captive from 8:00 A.M. to 3:00 P.M. and gave him few, if any decisions to make. He could often be seen sitting outside a room or in the counselor's office. The new system gives him many opportunities to visibly fail. If he makes poor decisions it may negatively effect the entire campus. Therefore, plans must be made to cope with this type of student and his needs prior to entry into flexible scheduling. The plans generally include alternative instructional modes, structuring his time for him, and reducing his opportunities to make inappropriate decision.

Differentiated staffing, when fully implemented, will necessitate a performance-oriented system of evaluation for staff and students. As this occurs, subjectivity and all of its attendant ambiguity is replaced by objectivity and its attendant specificity. No longer can one place an "X" in the satisfactory column next to "Communicates well with students" when evaluating a teacher. The probability is that the evaluator will be marking "accomplished" or "not accomplished" next to a statement like "Demonstrates the use of at least four small group interaction techniques during the first semester of school as measured by an evaluation of a preplanned video tape recording by a senior teacher during a selected small group session."

Leaders, as they move towards increased expectancies, would do well to heed the findings of Rensis Likert. He cites research that indicates that high production is frequently achieved at the cost of placing stress of the organization's human relations.[8]

---

[8]Rensis Likert, "Measuring Organization Performance," *Harvard Business Review*, March-April 1958, pp. 41-50.

Teachers will require an adjustment period and an ample degree of in-service education in order to fulfill new expectancies.

Differentiated staffing places teachers in a continuing relationship with their evaluators on a daily basis. Flexible scheduling allows the evaluator easy access to a teacher's classes. Teaming frequently accompanies flexible scheduling: this virtually eliminates conjecture from evaluation.

A transitional visibility factor is the deluge of visitors which are attracted to a school which is involved in the innovative process. The Oak Avenue Intermediate School had 720 visitors from 22 states and three countries during 1968-69 and continues to have more requests than it is possible to honor.

Temple City was forced to reduce opportunities for visitors to come to the district to two specific days a week. Temple City High School, which moved into a comprehensive program of differentiated staffing in the fall of 1971, permitted no visitors during their first semester and limited visits to one day a month the second semester. The flow of visitors prompted the school district to establish guidelines for visitors and develop pre-visit orientation materials.[9]

As visibility increases, both internally and externally, anxiety is heightened in many of the participants. Aside from time being a "conditioning factor," plans must be made to effect as many controls as necessary, especially at the outset of a new program.

SUMMARY

Differentiated staffing is not a panacea. Schools which adopt a comprehensive differentiated staffing plan will undergo what would be called systematic improvements by some and radical changes by others. Changes will occur and routines and social relationships will be upset.

Shared decision-making will be slower than autocratic decision-making. It will take time for people with new power to learn to delegate it appropriately.

As the school moves toward a collegial operation, the distinction between administrators and teachers will diminish, yet the labor-management expectation will persist.

Comprehensive changes at the school level can be greatly

---

[9]See Appendix 4 for copies of the visitation materials.

inhibited by technical requirements imposed by teacher-training institutions, state departments of education, and professional associations.

A multi-faceted change strategy costs more, requires better planning, and greatly taxes the energy of staff. It also increases the number of uncontrolled variables to a point which reduces the predictability of outcomes.

Staff members who are unaccustomed to accepting responsibility and who are content to work under the supervision of a patriarchal-type principal will be unlikely to value their new freedom as independent professionals. They also may be unprepared to cope with personal accountability relative to teaching skills and methodology.

In differentiated staffing former "district-level" positions are phased out as the "teaching hierarchy" is phased in. Some will oppose the transition, others will value it.

New members of the teaching hierarchy are given school-wide and district-wide responsibilities and the power to significantly affect the learning environment for every student, but they also teach fewer students personally than they did previously.

Communication and visibility are increased in differentiated staffing. Staff members will need assistance in improving their "human interaction skills."

Curriculum areas have tended to develop as discrete parts rather than integral parts of the whole, forcing students to deal with subjects, not learning. An interdisciplinary, multi-age approach is recommended.

The performance of students and teachers is very visible in differentiated staffing. Due to the visibility, problems which previously went unnoticed become apparent.

NINE

Financial Implications of Differentiated Staffing

Public Attitudes Toward the Cost of Education

Differentiated staffing costs money. Money comes or doesn't come from the public. Thus, districts seeking to embark on differentiated staffing must contend with public attitudes. This section will present some of the current public perspective.

The spiraling cost of education continues to result in confrontations between educators and those who finance education. Evidence of this is offered in a recent NEA report which indicates that during 1970-71, "90,000 teachers participated in strikes, or one out of every 25 teachers . . . . In 1969-70, a total of 119,000 teachers went out for 911,000 man-days."[1]

The public, especially working parents of small children, has been very inconvenienced by school closings and is often angry about it. On other occasions parents have joined the teachers' picket lines. Strikes declined in number from 181 in 1969-70 to 131 in 1970-71.[2] The militant posture of the NEA and AFT makes it difficult to draw any conclusions concerning this decline, since during the previous ten years the number of strikes ascended annually.

Although strikes occur for reasons other than financial ones, money is usually the significant bargaining factor. The general paucity of funds prevents boards of education from meeting teachers' demands and also limits the scope of program improve-

---

[1] *Education Daily,* January 3, 1972, p. 3.

[2] *Ibid.,* p. 3.

ment which can be planned. Innovations such as differentiated staffing will generally lack support if they mean spending more money.

The lack of support for the financial needs of schools in an era of affluence is noted by historian Arthur Schlesinger as he points out what he calls the "greatest present anomaly," which is that "the richest country in the history of the world cannot build an educational system worthy of its children . . . This condition of private opulence and public squalor has always led to the fall of empires."[3]

An indication of the low-priority view our government has had towards education is provided by comparing the cost of maintaining and training one soldier for one year to the cost of educating one student for a year. "It costs $10,000 per soldier for each year and $839 (national average) for each student."[4]

There are trends which indicate education is going to be given a higher national status. One example is the willingness of the federal government to provide a substantial share of the total cost. The demands of teachers, the revolutionary spirit of students, and the concern for equal educational opportunities are forces which have preceded the reform trends and which will probably sustain them.

Some feel that the interest of legislators in education emerges more from political and economic interests than it does from a concern for social needs. Critics of the current legislative intervention programs point to the increased activities of the federal and state governments in areas such as performance contracting, Program Planning Budget Systems, and voucher systems. They feel there is greater concern for personal visibility and fiscal austerity than for the basic needs of students.

Fiscal concerns can be explained in part as one notes that the cost of underwriting education is increasing at a rate disproportionate with productivity. Many citizens feel if education is going to cost more, they should see reading scores ascend, the number of drop-outs decrease and the general climate of schools improve.

Educators claim that burgeoning budgets are a result of infla-

---

[3]*St. Louis Post-Dispatch,* August 9, 1959.
[4]"Report on School Staffing," April 21, 1971.

tion and that they still must operate the school with the same personnel, material resources, and physical facilities which were previously present. They indicate that personnel costs represent approximately 80 percent of the annual budget. Annual cost-of-living raises and increments for experience and training account for an increase of from seven to ten percent in each new budget. Given this condition, if last year's budget was $10 million, next year's budget could be $11 million and the resources would remain constant.

There are many cases where meeting next year's budget means decreasing current programs and/or spending any reserves the school district may have accumulated. It is conditions such as these which have forced school systems into bankruptcy, caused them to close the schools earlier than scheduled and to borrow money to meet teacher payrolls. These same actions often cause Board of Education members to cut back on any and all improvements which were planned and to consider replacing the superintendent who "got us into this mess."

To refer again to the personal opulence-public squalor indictment, Americans are spending three percent of their income on tobacco and alcoholic beverages[5] and frequently (as in Temple City) spending less than that for the education of the community's children. Any system considering differentiated staffing simply needs to be aware of the public's attitude towards the cost of education and to develp a model consonant with the financial realities of the community.

The Financing of Differentiated Staffing

National conditions seem to indicate that if differentiated staffing is to be a replicable model in other educational systems around the country, it must eventually be able to sustain itself on approximately the same number of dollars as required in former organizational models. Districts may find it possible to withstand a few years of excess transitional costs, but it is unlikely that local financial conditions and the present sentiments of taxpayers will allow any plan to require a continued new flow of cash.

The position proposed by Temple City is that "differentiated

---

[5]Bureau of Labor Statistics, Los Angeles County, 1971.

staffing should be a rearrangement of existing personnel expenditures and not depend on new monies except during transitional stages."

Associate Teacher Financial Trade-Offs

Associate teachers enter on the salary schedule of Temple City's schools at the same rate of pay as beginning, fully credentialed teachers in comparable districts. They progress normally on the schedule for a five-year period.

This progression is automatic and based solely on time served. Associate teachers who reach the top of their salary schedule (approximately a midpoint between the beginning and the top of the traditional salary schedule) do not automatically become staff teachers. All associate teachers are eligible to apply for any "advanced teacher" opening in the system for which they are credentialed and feel qualified. The candidates for an opening are screened by a selection committee composed mainly of teachers in a department, team, or school where the opening exists. The selection committee is developed by the senior teacher and it makes the final recommendation to the Board of Education.

If an associate teacher reaches the top of his salary schedule and has been unsuccessful in vying for a staff teacher position, he remains at the top of the associate teacher schedule. Associate teachers are only able to become staff teachers (or higher) if openings exist and if they are successful in competing with their peers for those openings.

As the number of associate teachers in the district increases, the number of dollars available to pay for senior and master teacher leadership increases. Temple City has done a three-year follow-up study on the replacement of departing staff teachers by associate teachers and found there has been a net savings of $660 per associate teacher employed.

The study assumed that if the average cost of employing an associate teacher was compared to the average replacement of a staff teacher under former employment practices, the difference (savings) could be attributed to the differentiated staffing structure. The traditional structure did not offer the same conditions. Inexperienced teachers were placed in roles equal to experienced teachers and expected to function independently. Under differentiated staffing, the associate teacher becomes a member of a team and is provided with in-service education, daily services of a senior teacher and scaled-down responsibilities. Thus, the $660 does not represent savings accrued due to the accumulation of a number of associate teachers at the top of their salary schedule, but represents money saving due to *new employment policies.* As associate teachers do reach the top of their schedule, savings will accrue rapidly.

Figure 9-1 indicates the phase-in timetable of associate teachers in Temple City. The chart was developed in 1969-70 and the figures for that year and 1970-71 are actual rather than projected. The figures are arrived at by (a) computing the $660 associate teacher entry level differential and (b) comparing associate teacher progress on the associate teacher schedule to that of former teachers on the traditional schedule. As associate teachers do reach the top of their salary schedule, the $660 figure remains a savings but of course becomes a minimal figure as one considers the financial outcomes which occur when a district does not automatically award staff teacher status to every teacher. Temple City has no associate teachers who have been at the top of the associate teacher schedule for more than one year.

Temple City appears unable to hire as many associate teachers on the "projected" time line as first anticipated. Teacher turnover has been substantially reduced, not only in Temple City, but nationally. Teachers are not moving from one district to another at the rate they formerly did. As a result, in Temple City, fewer associate teachers are being employed each year than projected.

Project Year	Projected Number of Associate Teachers	Annual Savings Differential
1969-70	24.5	$14,756
1970-71	35	24,127
1971-72	45	29,970
1972-73	55	36,630
1973-74	65	43,290
1974-75	70	46,620

Figure 9-1

Until Temple City reaches its quota of associate teachers, they must phase in the entry of the teaching hierarchy. Figure 9-2 illustrates the present and the projected distribution of teachers in Temple City.

PRESENT			PROJECTED
35 associate teachers	20%	40%	67 associate teachers
110 staff teachers	65%	40%	68 staff teachers
24 senior teachers	15%	17%	30 senior teachers
1 master teacher	1%	3%	5 master teachers
170 total staff			170 total staff

Figure 9-2

Projections versus Reality

As Figure 9-2 indicates, Temple City has more senior teachers than might be expected, having reached only approximately half of its projected associate teacher total (35 of 67). The decision to employ more senior teachers than the income generated by trade-off ratios would call for was reached by the district senate. They felt it was better to have 24 senior teachers functioning at reduced rates of pay and commensurately reduced responsibility levels than to have 12 fully functioning senior teachers.

Each year, based on the number of dollars available to sustain the cost of senior and master teachers, the district senate will revise the salary and responsibility levels and the number of persons holding hierarchical positions.

During 1971-72, the senate, for the first time, decided to pay all senior teachers a flat rate of $1300 each in addition to their regular salary. In previous years rates had varied from $2500 to $1000, depending on the variables in each school. Some schools such as Oak Avenue Intermediate were able to provide an environment which enabled a senior teacher to fully perform his leadership roles. Other schools which were moving towards a comprehensive program of improvements were unable to provide the senior teachers with the degree of freedom and support the program required.

Since most schools now can provide an enabling environment for a fully functioning senior teacher, it becomes a matter of distributing the financial resources which are available among the teacher leaders.

New formulas are being developed which will allow some senior teachers to work 11 or 12 months (with appropriate vacation allowances) and others to work 10 or 11 months. There is an inclination among several leaders in Temple City to allocate the funds for senior and master teachers in the same manner that SATIP funds were administered, that is, to announce the total amount available and to request bids (proposals) from senior and master teachers for specific services they wish to render. This would, according to its advocates, enable senior teachers to operate at different levels of responsibility and encourage more imaginative and accountable forms of leadership.

Temple City's plan of differentiated staffing has been widely reported. Most of what is written about Temple City is based on projections. The Temple City model, however, is much more fluid and responsive to emerging conditions and needs than the literature would indicate. As one can see, the salary levels, actual vis-à-vis projected numbers in each category, and responsibility levels are subject to annual negotiation.

One of the greatest strengths of the Temple City model is its adaptability. This trait appears to be attributable to the manner in which decisions are made. As long as power is shared, the organizational structure will tend to reshape itself easily and in a way which meets the needs of most of the participants.

Differentiated Salary Schedules

Temple City's financial goals have remained constant during the past five years. They remain committed to having senior teachers and master teachers paid at a level which prevents them from being financially attracted to administrative roles. As projections become realities, the goals will come within reach.

The current associate teacher salary schedule in Temple City places their top earnings at the midpoint of the traditional schedule. The staff teacher's schedule is the traditional salary schedule (see Figure 9-3) beginning with Step 6. Readers will recall that all staff teachers employed prior to the initiation of the project (1967-68) were "grandfathered" and allowed to retain staff teacher status and remain on the traditional salary schedule.

STANDARD TEACHERS' SALARY SCHEDULE 1970-71

STEPS	CLASS 1	CLASS 2	CLASS 3	CLASS 4	CLASS 5
*1-3	7,539	7,953	8,422	8,922	9,503
*4-5	8,378	8,853	9,332	9,876	10,561
**6-7	9,104	9,618	10,123	10,706	11,458
**8-9	9,854	10,426	10,967	11,606	12,466
**10	10,449	11,293	11,665	12,351	13,256
**11			12,513	13,446	14,590

*Present Temple City Associate Teacher Salary Schedule
**Present Temple City Staff Teacher Salary Schedule

Class 1 = B.A. and Regular Credential
Class 2 = B.A. plus 18 credits
Class 3 = M.A. or Sec. Cred. or B.A. plus 36 credits
Class 4 = B.A. plus 54 or M.S. plus 18 credits
Class 5 = M.A. plus 32 or Doctors or B.A. plus 72 plus M.A.

Figure 9-3

Figure 9-4 is a proposed differentiated salary structure which deletes credits and degrees and restricts experience to a maximum of five years at any one level. It is not in use in Temple City (or elsewhere of which this author is aware). It is quite representative of the ideal situation proposed by the original Temple City Steering Committee and remains a viable goal in the minds of many in Temple City.

PROPOSED DIFFERENTIATED SALARY SCHEDULES

1	2	3	4	5
		Associate Teacher		
7,000	7,500	8,000	8,500	9,000
		Staff Teacher		
9,500	10,250	11,000	12,000	13,000
		Senior Teacher and Principal		
14,500	15,250	16,000	16,750	17,500
		Master Teacher and Assistant Superintendent		
18,000	19,000	20,000	21,000	22,000

Figure 9-4

Our Salary Schedule, Not Theirs

One benefit of placing principals and assistant superintendents on the same pay scale as senior and master teachers is that they will not have to negotiate separately for salary increases. Currently, there are two salary schedules: one for teachers and one for administrators. This need not be so under differentiated staffing: there could be one set of salary schedules which cover all certificated personnel exclusive of the position of superintendent. Mutual salary schedules would allay many of the misunderstandings and hard feelings which have occurred in the past when administrators negotiated separately from teachers for salaries. In recent times, it has been a focal point in bargaining talks. Teachers want their salary adjustments to keep up with administrators or vice versa. Teachers in one district in Southern California are pointing out that their administrators rank fourth in the county in pay, while the teachers rank thirtieth in the county in pay. Needless to say, they have a bargaining point.

Since principals and assistant superintendents usually are employed for twelve months, it would be possible for a district to employ a senior teacher or master teacher on a ten- or eleven-month contract and pay them 10/12 or 11/12 of the annual salary. Aside from being a method of phasing in differentiated staffing at reduced rates, it provides reduced work years for individuals who prefer not to be employed twelve months.

**Teacher Supply and Demand and Its Effect
on Salary Schedules**

According to a U.S. Office of Education report it may be possible to generalize about the national scene and teacher shortages. The Report states, "Due to the declining birth rate, the recent general teacher shortage may disappear over the next few years. In fact, by 1975, it is possible that the supply of persons trained to teach will exceed the demand."[6]

This is an indication that nationally there will be less movement from district to district due to fewer openings. Schools such as Temple City have historically had a teacher turnover rate of 20 to

---

[6]A U.S.O.E. Report, "The Education Professions," 1968, OE-58032.

25 percent annually. The current teacher labor market has resulted in a sharp decrease in turnover, bringing it down to an annual rate of five to ten percent.

In addition, the large number of applicants for each opening provides for careful screening and selection procedures in contrast to the times when school systems would employ a "warm body." As a result, extremely competent new teachers are being employed. They tend to be career oriented and will be encouraged to remain with a school system longer than their "warm body" counterparts of former decades.

Reduced turnover will ultimately result in most teachers automatically advancing to the upper end of the salary schedule.

Figure 9-5 illustrates the distribution of Temple City's teachers over the past seven years. Note that in 1964-65, 75 teachers, or 50 percent of the staff, were on the lower half of the salary schedule (Classes I and II). That percentage dropped to 32 percent on the lower half in 1969-70. As associate teachers are added annually, the percentage should work its way back to 50 percent by 1974-75. Eventually, in Temple City, no staff teachers will be in Class I or II, as they either gain credits and move across the schedule or leave the district. Associate teachers will occupy Class I and II and when promoted will go to Class III.

SEVEN-YEAR ANALYSIS OF STAFF DISTRIBUTION ON SALARY SCHEDULES

	1964-65	*1965-66*	*1966-67*	*1967-68*	*1968-69*	*1969-1970*	*1970-71*
Class I	53	43	39	36	28+3AT*	14+24AT	14+35AT
Class II	22	30	31	28	30	23	25
Percentage	(50%)	(47%)	(43%)	(39%)	(34%)	(32%)	(37%)
Class III	34	35	34	37	52	50	39
Class IV	22	23	28	29	32	44	47
Class V	20	24	31	32	34	34	37
Percentage	(50%)	(53%)	(57%)	(61%)	(66%)	(68%)	(63%)

*Associate Teacher

Figure 9-5

As teacher turnover is reduced and the percentage of teachers on the upper end of the salary schedule is increased, a district's personnel costs will ascend rapidly. Average salaries will run higher each year and adjustments such as cost-of-living increases will escalate at commensurately rapid rates. For instance, a relatively small district with 200 teachers incurs a substantial financial impact when the average teacher's salary increases from $9,000 to $10,000 annually due to normal increments and cost-of-living increases (200 teachers x $9,000 = $1,800,000 compared to 200 x $10,000 = $2,000,000. This results in a $200,000 budget increase). In the same manner, if most of a district's teachers are at or near the top of the salary schedule, a five percent cost-of-living increase can cost much more than if there was a normal distribution of the salary schedule (5% of $14,000 = $700 compared to 5% of $7,000 = $350).

This points out, rather dramatically, the results of an automatic progression system. As most of a district's teachers move to the top of the salary schedule, average salaries and annual adjustments escalate at a rate which will greatly increase the cost of educating a student. When average salaries jump from $9,000 to $12,000 over a five-year period, the budget increases nearly 25 percent and the number of teachers remains constant. Taxpayers see the increase as unreasonable, given the conditions that (1) the schools are not 25 percent more effective, and (2) the average salaries of the taxpayers have not shown such dramatic increases. The taxpayer's primary defense is to restrict the ceiling of the salary schedule. The situation becomes more baffling when one considers the fact that many young, able and ready new teachers, available at beginning rates, are seeking and not finding employment. The law of supply and demand seems to have no impact on current cost factors. There is no shortage of teachers, yet the average annual salary (due to automatic step progression, degree and/or unit credits, and cost-of-living increases) of teachers is climbing rapidly.

Associate Teachers and the Problem of Promotions and Earnings

Perhaps the most radical notion of differentiated staffing is the associate teacher concept. The associate teacher is a fully qualified, credentialed teacher. It is frequently asked "Why must they be 'frozen' at the end of their fifth year of teaching unless they have earned a promotion?"

In confronting this issue it must be recalled that what exists generally in the United States is a single salary schedule which moves all teachers along automatically and which could, if teacher turnover continues to be reduced, eventually place all teachers at or near the top of the salary schedule. As has been indicated, one would expect to find about 50 percent of a teaching staff on the lower half of the salary schedule. This has not been due to imposed limitations, but to the natural distribution of inexperienced and experienced teachers.

With teacher turnover being greatly reduced largely due to factors of supply and demand, average salaries paid by a district are increasing annually. The ramifications of this annual escalation as it affects the salary potential of outstanding teachers are pointed out in the following:

> Single salary schedules inevitably result in relatively low maximum salaries. Since all teachers are eligible to receive the maximum, and since teachers are a large occupational group, any schedule with high maximums encounters strong community opposition. Communities are, or may be, willing to pay outstanding teachers outstanding salaries, but they are not going to pay *every* teacher such a salary.[7]

Perpetuating the traditional automatic promotion system simply limits the likelihood of rewarding outstanding teachers with salaries adequate to prevent them from being lured into administration or other higher-salaried occupations. The traditional system makes no distinction between exemplary and incompetent teachers. All are rewarded equally. Marmion and Weber sum it up well: "What tends to happen is that the single salary schedule (and the mass lock-step of which it is a part) is quite adequate for the incompetents and mediocrities—usually adequate, that is, to put a body in front of every class—but not good enough to attract and hold many first-rate teachers."[8]

If an associate teacher is unable to advance to the rank of staff teacher after five years of experience—due to his failure to convince his peers that he has the competence to do so—it is not a tragedy for the profession. The fact that everyone who enters teaching is promoted automatically to the top whether they are competent or not is a tragedy.

[7] Myron Lieberman, *The Future of Public Education* (Chicago: University of Chicago Press, 1960), p. 260.

[8] George Weber and William H. Marmion, "Merit Pay and Alternative," Council for Basic Education, Occasional Paper Number 16, May, 1969, p. 1.

Most competent associate teachers will in time advance to higher ranks—the most competent advancing first. One assumption of this plan is that the schools have a need for different levels of competency among their staff. All teachers need not be (a) research oriented (master teachers), (b) experts in the act of leading and training teachers and organizing resources for students (senior teachers), (c) outstanding teachers (staff teachers) or (d) professionally competent teachers (associate teachers). Some of each category are required to effectively meet the needs of students.

One problem which Temple City and others must face is, that it takes considerable time to build a cadre of associate teachers sufficient in number to support the cost of a complete contingent of senior and master teachers. Temple City expects to eventually employ 40 percent of their total staff as associate teachers. If teacher turnover is down, some of the associate teachers who are employed at the beginning of the project may justifiably "need promoting" prior to the district's reaching the 40 percent ratio. This has happened in Temple City. The result is that some associate teachers are being promoted in spite of the ratio problem and the number of dollars for teacher leadership is simply less than desirable. Decisions to make adjustments such as this are local in nature and no rigid guidelines seem advisable.

The Inequities of Single Salary Schedules

Historically, single salary schedules were an object of great attention and considered an important goal by the teacher's professional associations. This concern developed because teachers were at the mercy of administrators who individually negotiated each teacher's salary.[9] As one might suspect, the criteria for making decisions about salary rates, employment conditions and dismissal were vague and applied arbitrarily.

It seems the conditions which generated the need for single salary schedules have passed. Politically oriented financial rewards and penalties which once existed are gone. However, the present inequities of the single salary schedule remain. The next logical

---

[9]Raymond C. Callahan, *Education and the Cult of Efficiency*, pp. 120-121.

step seems to be to individualize the salary schedule on the basis of performance and responsibility as judged by one's peers.

Attendant Costs for Which to Plan

Differentiated staffing as a comprehensive concept embodies other changes beyond credentialed staffing costs. The changes have financial implications and should be part of a district's planning.

Among the early arguments in favor of differentiated staffing was the idea that teachers perform a multitude of nonprofessional tasks. It is proposed that "housekeeping chores" such as collecting lunch money, typing dittoes, and running duplicating machines should be done by paraprofessionals. The expenditure of funds for this purpose will probably improve education, but as some observers would caution, perhaps not. Simply relieving teachers of nonprofessional tasks does not guarantee greater attention to professional tasks. Teachers' job descriptions should be stated in performance terms to reflect new uses of time compared to former patterns. The cost of this type of paraprofessional, one who aids teachers, can be estimated rather minimally at a rate of one aide per ten teachers.

Aside from aides who serve teachers is the paraprofessional who serves students. Flexible schedules will, especially in a school organized along departmental lines, necessitate the utilization of paraprofessionals to serve students in areas of independent study, such as media centers and subject-matter resource centers. This expense can be determined by counting the number of resource centers planned and the estimated capacity of each. The paraprofessional in this situation assumes responsibility for the flow of all materials in the resource center and the general demeanor of students.

Flexible scheduling will normally result in remodeling costs. The extent of these costs is relative to the structural properties of the space available. Some space can easily be modified due to the presence of nonbearing internal walls. However, in many older structures it is more difficult and expensive. Some have attempted to not remodel traditionally constructed schools and yet moved toward variable-size groups. They have found they wasted too much space and were unable to provide an adequate number of student stations for independent study. This was largely due to the fact they scheduled small groups of 10 to 15 students into spaces built to hold 30 to 40 students. A dividing partition in this situation would have allowed two small groups to meet in one room and resulted in the release of another room for such uses as teachers' offices, resource centers, labs, student centers, a professional library, or a central campus word-processing center.

Most school buildings have some large group space; however, those which have an inadequate amount will find it an expensive conversion cost. Included are such factors as air conditioning, audio-sound systems, larger projection and screen equipment, and specialized seating.

New resource centers, labs and expanded library-media areas require new types and quantities of furniture, audio-visual materials and equipment and engineering improvements such as electrical outlets, added ability to facilitate increased ingress and egress needs, and improved lighting and accoustical arrangements.

It is not possible to generalize about remodeling costs; however, Oak Avenue School with an enrollment of 700 students did expend $78,484 in making their transition from a traditional to a flexible facility. $28,200 of the total was required to air-condition two large group areas and a library/media center. Inexpensive indoor-outdoor carpeting cost $10,291. Some of the carpeting was worn thin within a two-year period. In areas with less foot-traffic it remains in use. Figure 9-6 is an item summary of Oak Avenue School's remodeling costs.

Item	Cost Estimate
Air conditioning for library/media center and two large-group areas	$28,200
Ceiling tile for the above	3,300
Office air conditioning	1,172
Lumber	4,750
Paint	500
Carpet	10,291
Study carrels	15,022
Electrical supplies and labor	1,970
Plumbing and heating	1,772
Room darkening	643
District labor force	10,589
Total	$78,209

Figure 9-6

Specific changes at Oak Avenue School included: (a) converting six former classrooms to resource centers (in three instances the space was inadequate for the need by the end of the first year and these resource centers—math, social studies, and language arts— now occupy approximately 2000 square feet each), (b) purchasing 160 study carrels (each was electrically equipped), (c) dividing six former 30- by 32-foot classrooms into 12 seminar rooms. Each of the six rooms already had two exits. This enabled the district to build complete partitions. The partition consisted of a fiber-board-covered frame, paneled on each side. When planning a remodeling project, it is important to consider (a) lighting switches (usually there is one control switch for a 30- by 32- foot room; thus dividing the room requires rewiring), (b) heating and air-conditioning vents (quite often the outlet and recirculating vent are poorly located to facilitate partitioning), and (c) room darkening (most seminar rooms will require altered darkening curtains). District employees (regular maintenance staff) did the remodeling which resulted in substantial savings.

The district constructed a new library at Oak Avenue School (6000 square feet) during the third year of the project, which relieved their space problem.

The resource centers and library/media center at Oak Avenue School were equipped (media hardware and software) at a cost of $50,000. The school was quite barren of audio-visual materials prior to that time. It would be misleading, however, to suggest that a school of 700 should expect to spend $50,000 on audio-visual support materials. Many traditionally scheduled schools are well equipped and would find this item to be of minor importance.

It is significant to know that print and nonprint "circulation" is five times greater under the differentiated staffing program. This results in an increase in repairs and replacements. Temple City employed a district audio-visual repair and maintenance man after differentiated staffing was initiated due to the larger inventory and subsequent service needs.

Most of these attendant costs are "one-time" expenses which a school incurs with the inception of a program. The largest recurring cost which may not have been a previous expense to a district is the presence of an increased number of parapro-fessionals. Temple City feels this expense is attributable to flexible scheduling; however, since some form of flexible scheduling is needed to permit differentiated staffing to function well, it is a concomitant expense of the new program. It represents Temple City's largest new and ongoing financial expenditure.

Efforts to hold this cost category down include (a) establishing a six-hour work day for paraprofessionals, (b) limiting their work year to days when the students are in school, and (c) recruiting community volunteers to assist with the tasks which normally are done by paraprofessionals.

A small but important expense for which one should plan is the increased flow of printed matter. All of Temple City's schools now use more paper, and have greater needs for typing, reproduction, collation, and stapling of materials and for added general clerical assistance. Some of their schools have developed central "paper-processing centers" with automatic equipment which is operated by full-time clerks. These centers are very important to a school, yet the space, equipment, and staff are usually an added cost. These centers also are excellent training sites for students in the business education field.

SUMMARY

The public appears to be in no mood to endorse new educational programs which will create increased, long-range costs. They are demanding an educational system which clearly exhibits a relationship between the increased cost of education and its level of productivity.

Differentiated staffing as a system increases the potential for program accountability and at the same time provides a means to stabilize the spiraling cost of professional salaries. The benefits of a differentiated staffing structure can be gained without expending more dollars for teachers' salaries than are presently being spent. The plan can function on a pay-as-you-go basis by utilizing associate teacher trade-off.

The cost of paraprofessionals, remodeling, and equipping will vary but are needs for which to plan.

It seems certain that single salary schedules will be set at income levels relative to the community's value of the average, not the outstanding teacher—especially as greater numbers of teachers inhabit the top levels of the salary schedule.

TEN

In-Service Education

A Philosophy of In-Service Education

In-service education may be the only means to achieve educational change which will endure. Change which is forced on teachers tends to have poor results. Force can be construed as "any change you expect teachers to institute which they do not understand and/or with which they do not agree." Teachers have been able to effectively resist the exhortations of change agents. This resistance takes on many forms such as (1) closing their door and doing things as usual, (2) saying "I tried it and it didn't work," or (3) overtly or covertly undermining the change.

Differentiated staffing assumes teachers and administrators must systematically undergo personal learning experiences if they are expected to become committed to new and improved ways of educating students. Change in this environment is based on knowledge, not coercion. A major challenge for school systems is to incorporate mechanisms which institutionalize in-service education as a valued constant. In-service in this regard becomes an integral part of the school's educational program.

The philosophy behind this assumption is that no educator ever attains all of the knowledge and skills which are available. Establishing a system which continues to improve the expertise of educators is a formal means of saying that learning is a life-long experience for everyone. It takes one back to the idea of life being a continuing series of discoveries and that new knowledge and skills reveal new needs.

People and other organisms are growing, responding, becoming creatures. Standing still amounts to moving in reverse since the environment around a person is moving forward. Behavioral scientists refer to "entropy" as the "random distribution of energy."[1] They indicate this randomness results in inefficiency and that organisms which behave in this manner are "winding down,"—moving toward a dysfunctional existence and ultimately dying unless corrections are made (negative entropy).

People cannot stand still and remain abreast of those who are moving. Schools should carefully plan to provide teachers and administrators with renewal experiences and not leave such experiences to random selection. Systematic use of new information is the "import of negative entropy,"[2] a characteristic of an open system.

The Priority of In-Service Education in the Public Schools

There are two recurring problems relative to renewal in education. First, research and development is not systematically provided for. In fact, educators seldom have a specific person employed to perform this function. Second, even if research and development was available to the classroom teacher, schools make few formal provisions and/or requirements for its disbursement.

Teachers are employed a few days before school opens and often released from duty the day after school closes in June. They are assigned classes and supervision duties which take their entire day. Most elementary teachers haven't the time to go to the restroom, much less "plan for instruction." They are with children all day. Most secondary teachers have a "conference period" in which they are expected to plan, grade papers, confer with students or parents, and so on. There is no significant provision for on-the-job, in-service education.

In-service education for teachers often takes place after a full day of teaching in the late afternoon or evening. College and university classes, which teachers must take to gain salary credit, can hardly be called in-service education. Teachers consider most of the courses which they take for salary and degree credit "interesting, but irrelevant" to the task of teaching.

---

[1]James G. Miller, "Toward a General Theory for the Behavioral Sciences," in *Organizations*, p. 46.

[2]Ludwig von Bertalanffy, "General System Theory—A Critical Review" in *Organizations*, p. 12.

It is strongly recommended that districts allocate significant time and resources to the in-service education of teachers. Local conditions will determine the best time and the number of dollars available. Some options for scheduling in-service education include: (a) beginning the school year ten days earlier than normal. In-service for educators can be scheduled once a month and classes not held, (b) hold classes for the minimum allowable day (usually four hours) and schedule in-service weekly or monthly during the remainder of the day, (c) hold classes one day less per month to enable teachers to have in-service and extend the school year by eight to ten days, (d) rotate specialist teams who will teach a unit or topic to a group of students whose teachers are then released for in-service, (e) pay teachers a stipend or offer them salary credit for completing prescribed courses of in-service education. (f) initiate a home-study week once each quarter of the school year. Students could be working on assignments and self-initiated contracts independently of teachers while the entire staff is involved in in-service education.

Controlling the Quality of In-Service Education

It is important, especially if the idea is new in an area, to institute "quality controls" on the in-service program. If the program is going to cost the taxpayers money, it would be appropriate to "objectify" the goals of the in-service program. For instance, if a senior teacher is offering a workshop for teachers on a particular topic such as "How to write behavioral objectives" or "Introduction to video tape recording," the senior teacher should specify what each participant is expected to know or to be able to do after having participated.

The public is unlikely to support programs with poorly defined objectives. If, on the contrary, educators can "guarantee" that teachers will emerge with some new, practical skills and/or understandings (measurable) as a result of having participated in an in-service session, funding and support are more easily secured.

Historically, in-service education has been "set up" by administrators for teachers. Differentiated staffing provides a structure to avoid that. Teachers should participate in defining their in-service needs. The program can then be expected to assume relevance for them.

In addition to having a voice in the type of in-service they have, teachers should evaluate the quality of in-service education. Each training session should be evaluated and subsequent sessions should be modified in light of those evaluations.

Another means of increasing accountability in in-service education is to provide systematic follow-up for all in-service sessions. This can be accomplished by asking participants to invite their senior teacher to view an "application" of a new skill or understanding in the classroom. The test of an in-service education program then becomes its applicability in the classroom.

Training the Trainers

Schools often regard in-service education as something outside experts do to inside amateurs. To the contrary, in-service sessions become most meaningful when participated in collegially in a teacher-to-teacher manner. Each of the participants is a potential trainer.

A district should invest a number of months in assessing the strengths and weaknesses of its own personnel before planning for in-service education. They may find individual skills present of which they were unaware and in other cases may discover some weaknesses exist in terms of internal resources. In the latter situation, it will be necessary to import some assistance. The district should be certain that a teacher from within the district is assigned to attend any training sessions offered by an outside resource. It would be the teacher's responsibility to gain the necessary personal competence to eventually assume that particular training offering themselves.

Readers will recall that the APSTRAT model gives strong indications that learners who know they are to become teachers of the skill or understanding involved make better students. That model also accentuated the value of peer-to-peer as compared to superior-to-subordinate instruction. Again accountability is important and participants should expect the training/education to accomplish the stated objectives.

The Link Between In-Service Education and Evaluation

Evaluation is intended to be a helpful function. It is not meant to harm people. To be helpful, it should be connected directly to in-service education. Every teacher should have "professional growth plans." These plans, in order to be implemented, frequently require training/education. When a staff or associate teacher discusses his professional growth plans with a senior teacher, they are sharing them with a person charged with the responsibility of helping them attain these growth experiences.

In-service education should reflect the personal professional growth needs of the district's teachers. The follow-up on in-service becomes "evaluation" in the sense that it is the application of professional growth plans.

Is It In-Service "Education" or "Training"

Since the issue of training has been referred to as the acquisition of technical skills and education as the development of the full potential of each individual, the question arises as to whether in-service is to address itself to one or the other of these functions.

Obviously, the answer is both. Nevertheless many will be tempted to focus on the training aspect to the near exclusion of the educational aspect. It is much simpler to teach a person a technical skill. It is more measurable; the variables can be relatively controlled; and it limits possible philosophical disagreements by not having to be concerned with them. There is a vast difference between learning to develop an audio-tutorial program and being concerned about the manner in which one views his fellow man.

Most would agree it is important to deal with how a teacher feels about a student, his potential and background. It is more difficult to plan in-service education relating to philosophical issues, but it is nontheless important.

Broadening the view of in-service to include administrators too, it is possible to specifically consider the philosophy of the school and in so doing, to address the question of the role of the administration in shaping that philosophy. Silberman aptly describes the problem: "What is wrong with the administration of the public schools has far less to do with the fact that principals and superintendents are poor administrators or poor politicians, however, than with the fact that they are poor educators."[3]

---

[3]Charles E. Silberman, *Crisis in the Classroom,* pp. 506-507.

Temple City's Collegial Approach to In-Service Education

Temple City developed leadership training programs in which all senior and master teacher candidates (self-nominated) and administrators received a variety of inputs ranging from "cultural pluralism" to "training in the use of inquiry methods with small groups." Most of the training resources came from outside the district. Over the course of a year, leadership people gained considerable exposure and some expertise.

The district senate then endorsed a plan whereby regularly scheduled in-service sessions would be offered to all teachers, paraprofessionals, credential candidates and citizen observers. All participation except by the teachers was voluntary.

The plan called for in-service sessions to be scheduled once a month. Schools were to individually lighten the load of their staffs in any way possible on in-service days. Some were able to schedule "minimum days," and others only shortened their days. Leadership people were asked to assess the needs of their teams and to then offer workshops in their areas of competence. Each workshop leader had other leaders available to assist him as workshop coordinators. The leaders/coordinators developed descriptive information about their offering which was assembled in a booklet and distributed to all teachers, credential candidates, and paraprofessionals, and made available to the community.

Participants were to list in rank order the six workshops they preferred to attend. They were assigned to the workshops on the basis of first come, first served. When a workshop reached capacity enrollment people were then assigned to their second choice, and so on. The number of offerings varied from 12 to 20 during the year. Figure 10-1 is a sample sign-up sheet indicating titles of one set of workshops. Figures 10-2 and 10-3 are samples of workshop descriptions.

TEMPLE CITY UNIFIED SCHOOL DISTRICT
Sign-up sheet for
"A Collegial Approach to In-Service Education"
January 13, 19____Grade level or
Name_____ School_____ subject area _____

Select six topics from the list below in which you would like to participate on January

13. Write a (1) beside your 1st choice, a (2) beside your 2nd choice and so on. Every effort will be made to place you in the training activity of your highest choice.

A complete description of each workshop is provided in the following pages.

RANK CHOICE	*WORKSHOP TOPIC*	*LOCATION*
_____	#1 Workshop in Adv. Video Tape Recording	Oak Library
_____	#2 Workshop on An Analysis of Power in the Temple City School System	Student Council Rm., High School
_____	#3 Workshop on Auditory Perceptual Skills	Longden, Rm. 105
_____	#4 Workshop in Behavior Modification: An Analysis of Theory and Practice	Longden, Rm. 125
_____	#5 Workshop on Writing Behavioral Objectives	Longden Library
_____	#6 Workshop in Elementary Art	La Rosa Art Lab
_____	#7 Workshop on Individualization Instruction	Oak, Math Resource
_____	#8 Workshop on Inquiry Method	Longden, Rm. 215
_____	#9 Workshop on Intro. to Video Tape Rec.	Oak Library
_____	#10 Workshop in Micro-Teaching	Oak, Rm. 407
_____	#11 Workshop on Music in the Classroom	Memoli Hall, Longden
_____	#12 Workshop in Slide-Tape Presentation	Longden Media Center
_____	#13 Workshop in Small Group Instruction	I.R.C. Conf. Room
_____	#14 Workshop on Movement Exploration (K-6)	Cloverly Cafetorium
_____	#15 Workshop on Reading Methods and Activities	Cloverly Library

Please list the name of the workshop in which you participated the last time. _____

Return this sheet to your building principal on *Wednesday, January 13*. Be sure you put your name in the space provided. This same sheet will be returned to you indicating the workshop number to which you have been assigned.

WORKSHOP #_____   For your convenience, a location map is on the reverse side of this sheet.

Figure 10-1

WORKSHOP IN SLIDE-TAPE PRESENTATION

DESCRIPTION

The purpose of this workshop is to prepare its participants with the "know-how" of consolidating sight and sound for a well-planned slide-tape program—a powerful tool for educating, entertaining and influencing an audience. Each participant will be given the opportunity to organize a group of slides, write brief narrations, cue slide changes, synchronize slides with narrations, and present a short program. In order to be more meaningful it would be advisable that each participant provide a group of slides (15 to 20) on a central theme, such as: travel log, explanation of a concept, illustration of a story or poem, etc.

PERFORMANCE OBJECTIVES

A. Participants will be able to:
  1. Organize a group of slides that will accomplish a given objective in a proper sequence.
  2. Write a short narration for each slide.
  3. Provide cue marks for each slide change.
  4. Operate a slide projector.
  5. Operate a tape recorder (Cassette).
  6. Synchronize the slides with the narrations.
  7. Give a short slide-tape program.
  8. Critique the effectiveness of their colleagues program.
B. Maximum number of participants—15
Coordinator—George Lebrecht
Assistant—Ed Aguirre

Figure 10-2

WORKSHOP IN SMALL GROUP INSTRUCTION

DESCRIPTION

The purpose of this workshop is to initiate dialogue between teachers in different disciplines and with different levels of experience in small group instruction. Although our aim is to provide each participant with specific skills that can be used in the classroom, we do not expect you to become an expert in small group instruction in 2½ hours. Our hope is to explore small group techniques and behaviors and allow each of you to "practice" with a group of five or six students. In order to save time, it would be helpful if you could prepare in advance a five-minute lesson that could be used to practice some of the small group techniques that you learn during the workshop. This workshop is most appropriate for teachers of grades 4 through 12.

PERFORMANCE OBJECTIVES

Participants will be able to:
  1. Identify the small group type (inquiry, socratic, brainstorming, etc.) when given a description of a teaching situation.
  2. Select *one* of the above Glatthorn small group types and use a group of five or six students to demonstrate the role of the teacher.
  3. When given a list of teacher behaviors in small groups, match them to the inquiry, socratic or brainstorming technique.
  4. List a minimum of three techniques (strategies) that could be used to stimulate student discussion and interaction in small groups.
  5. List a minimum of three methods for evaluating student progress in small groups.

Coordinator—   Dean Berry
Assistants—   Tony Melton
                      Shirley Rosenkranz
                      Dick Johnson

Figure 10-3

TEMPLE CITY UNIFIED SCHOOL DISTRICT

TO: District Staff and Associate Teachers,   December 11, 19___
                  Interns and Student Teachers

FROM: Bruce Caldwell

SUBJECT: Evaluation of December 9 Workshops

Please complete the following form and return it to the school secretary by Wednesday, December 16. The forms are to be anonymous; however, the secretary will need to check you off as you turn it in.

The summary of this information will be presented to the district senate and the Board of Education, and to the U.S.O.E.

WORKSHOP ATTENDED_____

1. Please rate the training on a scale of 1-10 as it compares to college or university education classes you have taken. (#1 if the training was worse, #10 if the training was much better).

       1   2   3   4   5   6   7   8   9   10

2. The training was intended to offer you new skills or ideas. Can you specify any of either you acquired?
     1._____
     2._____
     3._____
     4._____

3. What advice (constructive criticism) would you offer the workshop coodinator and assistants in order to improve their offerings, organization, etc.?
     1._____
     2._____
     3._____

4. What new workshop topics would you like to see offered in future sessions?
     1._____
     2._____

5. Do you feel you want to take the same workshop again, but would like to cover higher-order skills or more depth?
     Yes _____No _____Comment _____
     _____
     _____

6. Do you feel your workshop leaders should have been augmented or replaced by an outside expert?
     Yes _____No _____Comment _____
     _____
     _____

7. Was it a good idea for your workshop to use pre- and post- test (if your workshop did)?
     Yes _____No _____Comment _____
     _____
     _____

8. Do you need further assistance in planning and implementing the skills and ideas you gained from the workshop in your classes?
     Yes _____No _____If yes, please specify_____
     _____
     _____

General comments about the length of time for training, frequency of training, size
of training groups, etc. _____

_____

_____

_____

_____

Figure 10-4

The workshops were informal, partially social (coffee and
dessert), and generally integrated in terms of grade level and
subject area distribution. Very few community members or paraprofessionals joined or observed the sessions; however, the invita-
tion was always extended. On several occasions the workshop
coordinators were not district employees and frequently non-
leadership personnel offered workshops.

Every participant was given a workshop evaluation form which
when completed would be returned to the workshop coordinator
(see Figure 10-4). In addition, each coordinator completed a
self-assessment of their workshop. On the basis of evaluative
feedback, workshops were modified, deleted or repeated. The
evaluation instrument also requested participants to indicate in-
service needs they each felt were not yet being offered, and gave
them an opportunity to volunteer to lead a workshop themselves.

Pre-Service Education

Temple City has initiated a new program for credential candidates which has been an important addition to their training
program. Differentiated staffing complements this program very
well.

Teacher-training institutions in California have traditionally sent
"student teachers" to public school sites during their last year of
preparation. The student teacher usually remained at the school
for three to four hours a day for one semester. This system
contributed many inadequacies including: (1) student teachers do
not move from "theory to practice" until they have completed
more than 80 percent of their teacher preparation program
(2) They come to the public school at random times (the college's
class schedule and the public school schedule do not coincide since
most colleges have adopted the quarter system). (3) They do not
stay long enough to really get acquainted. They are finished with
the program just as they are starting to become effective. (4) Their

professors may or may not have ever taught in the public schools. (5) The college training courses are at best "simulated activities," lacking the realities of a school.

The Temple City schools and the Department of Secondary Education at California State College, Los Angeles (and specifically Dr. Mariann Wagstaff) agreed that an alternative model should be developed to address itself to the problems outlined. The model has the following characteristics (it has been operational since 1968 and is now participated in by the University of Massachusetts and Pasadena College as well as the Department of Elementary Education at CSLA).

- Student teachers will be assigned to the public school site during their last year of preparation for the public school calendar year. While at the public school site they will receive a number of credits commensurate with a full academic load as an education major at the college. They receive specific credit for specific "education courses" they would have normally taken.

- The cooperating college will announce the "clinical training" opportunity and initially screen applicants. The school district then screens all candidates. Final approval is granted by senior teachers who assist with the supervision and instruction of the student teachers and determine their placement within the school.

- The college will assign one or more professors (based on the number of student teachers) to work at the public school site with the students. It is this "clinical professor's" responsibility to meet regularly with the students in seminars and monitor their progress as well as offer them learning experiences. The clinical professor is expected to summon "college resources" for specific training experiences as needs arise. The clinical professor is the student teacher's link with the college and its formal requirements.

- The student teachers must complete minimal training objectives during the year. Most of these are met in the daily course of their work in the classroom. They do participate in district in-service education (one of the students offered a workshop in 1971).

- Normally student teachers are assigned to one team and often to a particular teacher. They can and do move to other teachers and curriculum areas as personal needs become known.

- They are to function in the total role of teacher from the perspective of classroom students. They are part of the district's pre-school workshops, as well as team and staff meetings, and are to be as familiar with their new assignment as any beginning teacher. Summer contacts between the supervising teacher and the student prior to the opening of school are common.

- They normally work and study a full day at the public school site and are on the same general schedule as the teachers, although exceptions are made.

Several distinct advantages accrue to both the school and the student. Under this system there is reciprocity. The student teacher and supervising teacher invest a great deal in each other and receive considerable in return.

The student-teacher is well prepared to accept his first teaching position, having been in the classroom functioning as a teacher for a year. Temple City anticipates hiring all of its new associate teachers from each year's group participants. This eliminates the dilemma and inefficiency of attempting to employ a new teacher on the basis of an interview.

The presence of a second full-time teacher in a classroom greatly benefits students. For those who fear calling a "trainee" a "teacher," they should recall that the old model confers the title of teacher on the student-teacher after routine training but largely because they have completed the "state requirements" for a credential. The state will grant program participants an "intern credential" in the event that a district feels they need the legal protection. If the student-teachers are always "subject to the supervision of a credentialed teacher," it isn't necessary.

The participating professors become very involved with the public schools and the efficiency and effectiveness of their role is increased.

Most trainees are assigned to a team situation: they gain considerable benefit from working with a number of teachers and in receiving senior teacher services. These benefits include: (a) being able to observe several different teachers and to learn different skills from each of them, (b) having an opportunity to work with a larger number of students and yet being able to specialize in subject areas with small groups of students, (c) being able to work directly with and to request specific services from a senior teacher, (d) having access to a wider variety of teacher-developed materials, (e) being able to participate in team planning and team decision-making situations.

The colleges and school district mutually establish objectives for the trainees and work together in developing special seminars for trainees where district personnel offer specialized in-service education. Currently the college and school district are opening portions of the clinical laboratory program to undergraduates. It is anticipated that college students who have an interest in teaching will be able to spend a significant amount of time on the public school site before they have to make a career decision.

SUMMARY

In-service education is a means of renewing the skills and knowledge of a systems professional staff. It is an absolute necessity if continued improvements are an objective of the system. In-service education becomes a vehicle for introducing change on a knowledge base.

Substantial resources should be initially directed to this need in the form of time and money. The maintenance of a peer-directed, collegial model of in-service education is not costly but does continue to require released time for teachers.

In-service education is a natural outgrowth of evaluation. Individual professional growth plans become the content of in-service programs.

Pre-service education programs based on extended "clinical experiences" are a valuable means of gaining greater services from student-teachers and professors of education, as well as providing credential candidates with an in-depth teaching experience.

ELEVEN

A Summary and
Some Personal Advice

D.S. Is a Delivery System, Not a Product

Innovative terms such as differentiated staffing, flexible scheduling and multi-unit schools are representative of processes. They are administrative structures which function as delivery systems. They are means by which planners can reach toward goals.

A unique characteristic of differentiated staffing is that it utilizes a multiple, interrelated set of delivery systems. Differentiated staffing, fully implemented, is a comprehensive plan. It will have an impact on virtually every facet of the school system. It should not be considered a technique to merely establish a differentiated set of salary schedules or a device to share decision-making. Narrow perspectives of differentiated staffing will result in only partial changes. Most "innovative injections" end up in philosophical conflict with existing structures and therefore in unproductive competition.

D.S. Assumes There is Inherent Value and Potential in People

Differentiated staffing lends structure to a philosophy. The basic rationale for differentiated staffing rests on some personal and organizational assumptions about the nature of man. If one views the "potential" of most men in limited ways, considering them to be incapable of higher-order contributions and in effect needing to be forever guided, directed and manipulated for their own good, then differentiated staffing is not a desirable alternative. Conversely, if one views man as an entity worthy of "equalness," with great potential, desiring responsibility and wanting to achieve success, then differentiated staffing is a structure which provides a means for one to integrate his practice with his theory.

Schools in a Democratic Society Should be Democratic

The schools, in recent decades, have become training institutions almost to the exclusion of education. Training is necessary to produce good technologists, but as Maslow points out:

> ... this (training) is an amoral enterprise, carried on in just about the same way ... in a fascist, or nazi or a communist authoritarian society as in a democratic society ... In the authoritarian society freedom, autonomy, self-sufficiency, curiosity, free probing, free questioning, are all very dangerous; in the democratic society, of course, they are exactly the opposite; i.e., they are extremely desirable and even necessary.[1]

Education in a democratic society is to produce more than qualified technologists. We must be concerned with providing an environment which "develops the maximum potential of each learner." The environment in schools should be democratic in nature. Traditional, rigid, authoritarian structures are antithetical to the belief that man has intrinsic worth and potential. They foster distrust and are a haven for authoritarian characters who feel their view of another man's needs and his potential are more accurate than the view the man himself possesses.

The Essential Characteristics of a Comprehensive D.S. Plan

Differentiated staffing is a framework which provides an enabling structure for the implementation of an educational system congruent with democratic principles. The "essential" characteristics of differentiated staffing that have been outlined in this book are: (1) participative management, (2) student involvement in decision-making, (3) increased personal responsibility and accountability, (4) increased tolerance for diversity and individuality, (5) program accountability (minimal performance objectives for participants at all levels, (6) rewards for teacher initiative, (7) continuous curriculum and instructional renewal, (8) Collegiality among participants, (9) differentiated responsibilities and rewards,

---

[1] Abraham H. Maslow, *Eupsychian Management,* p. 65.

(10) minimal impact on district budgets, (11) a career in the classroom for outstanding teachers, (12) variable course structures and uses of time and space, (13) perpetual in-service education, (14) clinical pre-service education, (15) inverse evaluation (those being served indicate the quality of service, from students upward), (16) the elimination of "automatic" promotions for teachers.

Differentiated Staffing Requires "Behavioral" Changes of Leaders

Many leaders are intuitively effective leaders. Without conscious effort, they tend to improve the feelings and productivity of the participants in the organization. Differentiated staffing *formalizes* and provides an ongoing structure for effective leadership behavior. There is considerable agreement among behavioral scientists, sociologists and organizational theorists that effective leader behavior has common properties. Some of these include:

Adaptability—Leaders must consider local variables such as the maturity of the followers (social, emotional, and intellectual), logistical constraints, the technical skills of the participants, past failures of the organization, and the expectations of formal sources of power as they make decisions. In essence, there is no one correct leader behavior. One must assess the situation and make leadership decisions accordingly.

Sharing Power—Power is the link to freedom. Freedom is a precondition of self-actualization. If individuals are to develop their potentials, they must exercise them. Capacities are needs and must be used or else they will diminish. Leaders who relinquish power are more effective, in the final analysis, than those who retain it.

Concern for Human Needs—Task-oriented authoritarians who have few concerns with the personal needs of individuals tend to have short-lived success. Leaders who wish to endure and who are interested in fulfilling long-range goals generally show concern for the personal needs of their followers.

Goal Integration—Leaders and followers alike are individual members of a coalition. The coalition (organization) has goals. Goals of individuals and goals of organizations are most effectively met when they are not mutually exclusive. It is the leader's task to attempt to integrate personal goals (needs) with organizational goals.

Open Communication—Leaders must be receptive to all types of feedback. Where dissent is considered disloyalty, trust cannot be generated. It is proposed that conflict be considered functional and that harmony is the result of a blend of "diverse" strengths. Effective communication depends upon feedback from interacting groups and individuals. Feedback has been found to be a means of improving leader behavior.

Teachers are not Equal or Interchangeable

Teachers have a variety of skills with different levels of competence. They are valued on a continuum from outstanding to poor. Yet teachers in most schools are given equal levels of responsibility and are placed on a single salary schedule which has automatic increases based on experience and credits.

One basic assumption of differentiated staffing is that teachers are different. Due to their differences, they should be given responsibilities and remuneration which are consistent with their contributions. These additional responsibilities go beyond class-room teaching skills. They include research, curriculum develop-ment, in-service education and leadership. In order to reward outstanding teachers who accept expanded responsibilities, it is necessary to have them employed under different financial condi-tions than their colleagues who have less demanding roles. Out-standing teachers should not be lured from the classrooms to administration by salary increases. In addition, administrative services should not be rewarded at a rate greater than outstanding teaching services.

Students Need a Variety of Services from a Staff with Specialized Skills

The tasks within schools are diverse in nature and require different types of service agents. The needs of students are not effectively or efficiently met by a staff with equal responsibilities and skills. Students need services from a staff with a variety of individual talents including (a) administration and organization, (b) research and development skills, (c) curriculum renewal and development, (d) instructional competency, (e) counseling ability. It would be either a waste of resources or an impossible task if each teacher were expected to perform all of these services.

Leadership Is a "Service" Function

Differentiated staffing restructures the classical leadership role from that of a dominant authoritarian to that of a facilitator or service agent. This change is based on the assumption that the goals of the organization are, for the most part, implemented and therefore controlled by teachers, not administrators. Since teachers are in key positions regarding goal accomplishment, they become the focal point, if not the raison d'etre, of an organizational hierarchy. The hierarchy and all support services of the system exist to increase the effectiveness of the interaction and improve the results which occur between the school's teaching resources and its students. Therefore, positions of members of the hierarchy, as well as those who provide support services, are ancillary in nature. Given this condition, leaders must be responsive and accountable to the needs of those being led or served.

D.S. from a Student's Perspective

Differentiated staffing formally involves students in decision-making. Feedback from students regarding their views and feelings is considered essential. Differentiated staffing heightens the expectancy level of the school for its students. It is assumed that the behavior of students often fulfills the expectations of the staff. Differentiated staffing incrementally raises responsibility levels for students by involving them in decision-making, by giving them increased degrees of self-directed learning opportunities, and by accentuating the use of intrinsic motivators. These improvements are intended to help students mature and become "fully functioning" individuals.

One goal of differentiated staffing is to move from a normative, group-oriented organizational structure to one which caters to the personal needs of individuals. This will involve improvements which include the flexible use of time and space, multiple modes of instruction, and a counseling system based on collegial relations.

Differentiated staffing rewards outstanding teachers and thus encourages them to remain teachers, much to the benefit of students. It also places all teachers under the leadership of outstanding teachers, thereby increasing the scope of influence of these new leaders.

Differentiated staffing provides for the establishment of "baseline" educational objectives for students and minimal performance levels for teachers, resulting in an increased level of system accountability.

Schools and the Process of Change

Schools should not act as though they are mechanistic, closed systems; they are organic, open systems. The nature of the former is that of a static, unchanging system. The latter system is considered to be one which is continually adapting to the needs of its external and internal patrons (forces). Change in this sense becomes a life-maintenance function (homeostasis). Resistance to change or "random" behavioral changes are in discord with manifest needs and lead to either a dysfunctional system or one which is moving toward extinction (entropy). Organisms which appear to remain motionless in an evolving, dialectical society are, in effect, moving in reverse.

Differentiated staffing is a self-renewal model which builds in feedback mechanisms (cybernetics). For example, roles are defined which charge leaders with the retrieval, translation, and implementation of research, and policies exist which require leaders to be responsive to feedback from followers. These inputs are the basis for decision-making at the personal and organizational level.

Differentiated Staffing and Self-Actualization

Schools in a democratic society must display an increased awareness of what it means to develop the maximum potential of each learner. It is critical that schools in democratic societies provide for the full range of human endeavor, from training (skills and knowledge) to education (individual attitudes, needs, hopes, ideals, and feelings). Education is a much broader concept than training and is a peculiarity of institutions that feel increased personal effectiveness is relative to increased personal freedom. In the absence of personal freedom, self-actualization is simply rhetoric.

Self-actualization implies responsible behavior. Irresponsibility is to be considered as unhealthy for the individual as it is the organization. Immature people must be given incremental opportunities to grow to maturity by accepting increased personal responsibilities. Freedom for immature people remains a goal, not a starting place.

D.S. Introduces New Variables and Difficulties

Democratic processes are slower than those which are authoritarian. There are some who will want to return to speedy decisions. Others, especially those exercising power as a teacher for the first time, will want to be involved in every decision, even those which are irrelevant to their role and expertise.

As teachers make policy decisions and administrators become colleagues with teachers, the labor-management gap diminishes. Some representatives of professional association feel this merger will weaken bargaining positions.

Comprehensive change requires greater planning, is more expensive, and forces many participants into anxiety-producing situations. New roles must be learned; former peers become leaders and generalist coordinators may be displaced. These difficulties represent challenges with which a district must plan to cope.

Financial Realities

Differentiated staffing is not intended to save money on teachers' salaries. It is a plan to distribute the same funds presently paid to teachers on a differentiated set of salary schedules instead of a single salary schedule. Constant ratios between associate teachers and senior and master teachers must be developed and maintained if a district is to function on a pay-as-you-go basis. If associate teachers must be "phased in" due to reduced teacher turnover, money available for senior and master teachers will be limited.

Support services such as flexible scheduling, resource centers, and independent study materials are costs which accompany differentiated staffing. Expenses such as these generally return to normal after the programs are established. Paraprofessional support is a continuing long-range expense which a district should anticipate.

Training the Staff

Differentiated staffing builds in perpetual in-service education. The job descriptions of leaders incorporate the training and service needs of their teachers. As leaders evaluate staff, they are simultaneously developing professional growth plans for each teacher. It becomes their task as leaders to provide or make available appropriate in-service opportunities.

In-service education should hold a place of priority in the district's schedule. The quality and productivity of in-service programs must be of visible worth to the community if substantial amounts of time are to be invested in such programs.

Pre-service education should be a program of greater duration and substance than it has traditionally been. A clinical, on-site program for student teachers and professors can result in increased benefits to teacher training institutions and to the public schools.

SOME PERSONAL ADVICE TO POTENTIAL IMPLEMENTORS

Temple City is not "The" Model of Differentiated Staffing

It would be very appropriate for a district investigating differentiated staffing to systematically consider existing local conditions before committing themselves to a program of change. A number of means to make an assessment exist. Two of the most common are the Program Evaluation Review Technique (PERT) and Force Field Analysis. Excellent information on both techniques is available.

Assessments have a bearing on model building. It would be an error to accept the Temple City model without modification. Local variables will undoubtedly necessitate a "personalized" model which best meets local needs.

It seems important to point out that even though the Temple City model is an effective model it is, nevertheless, *a* model. The model that "works" to the satisfaction of those affected by it should be considered "best." Beware of "D.S. model peddlers," heralding their ideas as superior. They have forgotten differentiated staffing is a structure, a device, not an end or a goal. Their much ado reminds one of the poignant statement, "Pomposity is the triumph of style over substance,"[2] offered by Postman and Weingartner.

---

[2]Neil Postman and Charles Weingartner, *The Soft Revolution,* p. 35.

Driving and Restraining Forces

Force field analysis provides a conceptual tool for determining the power of driving forces and restraining forces. Driving forces, according to David Jenkins, " . . . are pushing . . . they tend to initiate change and keep it going," while restraining forces " . . . may be likened to walls or barriers."[3] Proposals for change can be analyzed to determine their success potential by considering local driving and restraining forces.

For instance, the driving forces in Temple City when they initiated their program were stronger than the restraining forces. They had a visionary, positive, humane superintendent, who was highly committed to improving education. He worked closely with a board of education which also believed in the goals of Temple City and was a public advocate of improved education. (Improved is a much less inflammatory term than changed.)

The Temple City plan earned a degree of legitimacy when it was endorsed by national educational figures such as Dwight W. Allen. The plan received an important assist when the Kettering Foundation funded the costs of project planning.

In addition, the project was dramatic enough in scope to capture the imaginations and interest of participants. They sensed they were involved in a revolutionary concept. Temple City also had a cadre of intelligent, creative, hard-working leaders (and teachers) who had the "personal power" to lend impetus to the project. Many supported the project simply because they had faith in the people who were working on it.

Financially the situation was very encouraging in Temple City, although it is a relatively poor district whose citizens pay one of the highest tax rates in Los Angeles County. Temple City had passed a bond issue prior to their committment to differentiated staffing. The remaining funds were sufficient to remodel old structures and to construct new library-media centers in each school. Temple City was also the recipient of three small, but important, ESEA Title II, Phase 2 grants to develop the print and nonprint resources of the new library-media centers. Another key

---

[3]David H. Jenkins, "Social Engineering in Educational Change: An Outline of Method," *Progressive Education,* Vol. 26, May 1949, p. 193.

source of funds was the National Defense Education Act which provided matching funds for the purchase of media hardware and software for resource centers. Finally, the passage of the Education Professions Development Act coincided with Temple City's need for funds to train teachers and administrators to perform their new roles.

There was and still is resistance to change in Temple City. Ultraconservatives exist who consider the movement in Temple City as extreme liberalism. They were and remain a potent force. They generally are prepared to blame every social ill, local and otherwise, on the new program. They tend to distrust any sources of power within the schools and consider advocates of change to be disloyal and unpatriotic.

There are teachers within the system who are finding new behaviors to be difficult. They desire to see the students as evolving, becoming, potentially great humans but in practice continue to display a lack of trust and a lower than desirable level of expectations. For example, some teachers declare that extrinsic motivators are inadequate, yet they continue to rely on "letter grades" as a source of control over students. The pressure remains on the student, not the teacher, to produce. As Postman and Weingartner say, "In most jobs, if a man does not do what he is paid to do, he is considered a failure. In teaching, when that happens, the *student* is considered a failure."[4]

Temple City recently completed a survey of its 217 teachers. The survey was conducted by an outside consultant with the charge that strict confidentiality be observed. The board of education wanted honest opinions of its teaching staff regarding their feelings about the Temple City program. There were 203 questionnaires returned. Teachers were asked to agree, be neutral or disagree with each of 37 items.[5]

An analysis of the data indicates that 89 percent of those surveyed felt that "Teachers who receive services should evaluate those who provide services," yet only 46 percent felt that same standard should apply at the next level. Most teachers *do not want* "Students at the secondary level to evaluate the effectiveness of

---

[4]Neil Postman and Charles Weingartner, *The Soft Revolution,* p. 117.

[5]A complete list of items and a summary of the returns appear as Appendix 5.

classroom instruction." As the data indicates, inconsistencies remain in Temple City between what is "right for me" and what is "right for others."

Additional restraining forces in Temple City included: (1) a lack of technical competence to perform new roles (2) old and traditionally constructed facilities, (3) a staff with considerable experience in traditional educational programs (inertia), (4) pressure on local members of the teacher's union from national and state AFT offices to "move slowly," (5) inadequate experience with shared power and teachers functioning as "equals," (6) too much national visibility which caused "professional learners" to be anxious, (7) reduced teacher turnover, (8) increased teacher workload.

This last restraining force was made apparent by the high school staff in Temple City on a survey completed in March 1972. The high school staff has been involved in a "total implementation" of the Temple City model only since September 1971. A citizen's committee which works with the high school staff wanted to know how the staff felt about the new program and, particularly, flexible scheduling. Two of the three highest percentage items on the returns indicated teacher workload and teacher fatigue were "greatly increased." Only the "utilization of the school's physical facilities" ranked as high.

The Transition from Dreams to Reality

When "planning a project" or as some say, "dreaming a dream," people often get very excited and enthusiastic. As one moves from dreams to realities, many of the participants have difficulty translating ideas to action. The idea was fine as long as it didn't require *personal* behavioral change. Planners will find it is relatively simple to gain agreement with ideas or goals. Achieving a commitment to act is a separate and more formidable task. Cultural minority leaders, ministers and psychologists all are involved daily with patrons who are intellectually committed to improving the situation but who find actions more difficult than words. Earl Pullias states this dilemma well: "The tragic gap between what we would like to be and what we are, in a deep sense, expresses the very nature of human life."[6]

---

[6]Earl V. Pullias, *A Teacher is Many Things*, p. 75

For those who are concerned with behavior modification, sufficient evidence exists to indicate that men can and do change. Goble tells the story of a former criminal who became a leader in rehabilitating other criminals. His warden, Clinton Duffy, was told by a reporter, "You should know leopards don't change their spots." Duffy snapped back, "You should know I don't work with leopards, I work with men and men change every day."[7]

Sharing Power is not Easy

Districts which intend to initiate differentiated staffing must seriously consider the ramifications of shared power. *No single factor is of greater significance in a differentiated staffing structure than the sharing of power.* Decision-making is decentralized and position power, as a base for decision-making, is replaced by knowledge and expertise. Power in this situation revolves among leaders. When those who have power feel they want to share it, they ought to listen carefully to an observation submitted by Paul Lawrence. Lawrence was asked to comment on his present view of a paper he wrote in 1954 about resistance to change. He states, " . . . the view of participation as a technique for securing compliance with a predetermined change was a widespread and seductive one in 1954—and it is not dead yet."[8] Lawrence is reminding us that the calculated sharing of power in order to manipulate or co-opt followers is a temptation too often pursued by leaders.

The Pacing of Change and the Tenure of Leaders

Rates of change are often a subject of debate. It is the author's opinion that rapid and comprehensive changes are more likely to endure than timid changes—however, the leaders are less likely to survive. Leaders who want to be liked by most and who would intend to remain in a system for longer than three to five years should pace their introduction of changes.

The question becomes one of personal style and philosophy as well as the urgency of the situation. One doesn't want to "lead" if

---

[7]Frank Goble, *The Third Force in Psychology*, p. 139.

[8]Paul R. Lawrence, "How to Deal with Resistance to Change," *Harvard Business Review*, January-February 1969.

it means perpetuating a system with which one is in disagreement philosophically—especially if one feels he is running a race that he will never finish, much less win. It is a little like fighting a fire with a garden hose. You only win after the damage has been done.

Contrary to what has been said until now, visionary leaders with technical competence and charisma are not usually concerned with assessments, pacing, and the needs of individuals. They are too impatient and eager to dwell on such matters. They move directly to the heart of the issue, make sweeping changes, and do what they can to "unfreeze" the system sufficiently enough that it can never be quite the same. This type of leader is usually predisposed to the reality that his tenure will be brief but dramatic. If one feels that the system or situation is in such deplorable condition that "participative change" will not result in changes, coercion becomes the only productive alternative. It is the author's opinion this is an unhealthy change strategy if one purports to be as interested in the personal growth of others as he is in the growth and development of an institution and its leaders. Coercive change models are likely to result in a backlash which will entrench divisions among people and create an air of distrust that will be difficult if not impossible to counterbalance.

Finally, aside from the consideration that implementing differentiated staffing has been hard work and has taken many extra hours, is the fact that it has been exhilarating, challenging, and a source of great personal growth for this author. I feel that the rationale for some form of differentiated staffing is so pervasive and compelling that it will in time exist as a normal organizational format for schools.

Appendix 1

SOCIAL SCIENCE SENIOR TEACHER
JOB DESCRIPTION/EVALUATION INSTRUMENT

Oak Avenue Intermediate School

	ACCOM-PLISHED	NOT ACCOM-PLISHED*	NOT APPLICABLE*

I. Scheduling Responsibilities

    A. Establishes teacher work loads, schedules which are proportionate and equitable (70 percent must agree workload is equitable) to include:

        1. amount of curriculum preparation;

        2. number of large group presentations;

        3. number of low-ability, high-ability classes;

        4. preparation for two grade levels or more;

        5. number of electives taught   _____   _____   _____

---

*   Please specify.

Comments

B. Establishes with teach-
    ing staff appropriate
    student placement cri-
    teria to include:

    1. past performance
       (grades)

    2. past achievement
       tests

    3. other affective cri-
       teria or anecdotal
       data   _____ _____ _____

Comments

C. Coordinates the place-
    ment of 90 percent of
    the students in appro-
    priate learning levels   _____ _____ _____

Comments

D. Responsible for the
    placement and coordi-
    nation of student tea-
    chers and observers in
    the program.   _____ _____ _____

Comments

II. Curriculum Responsibilities

    A. Responsible for the de-
        velopment and distri-

bution of all teacher-
produced materials:

1. write or assists tea-
chers in writing per-
formance objectives;

2. writes or assists tea-
chers in writing cur-
riculum packets or
materials;

3. responsible for dis-
tribution of curricu-
lum materials to tea-
chers   _____   _____   _____

Comments_____

_____

B.   Establishes appropriate
     evaluation instru-
     ments/strategies to
     measure curriculum
     objectives   _____   _____   _____

Comments_____

_____

C.   Responsible for curri-
     culum articulation
     with the Master Tea-
     cher:

1. reports back on
Master Teacher's
evaluation of Oak
Social Science Pro-
gram (at least once a
semester);

2. reports to staff on

goals and objectives
established by the
Vertical Committee;

3. Responsible for con-
gruence of program
with total District
objective   _____   _____   _____

Comments_____

_____

III. Instructional Responsibilities

A. Performs demonstra-
tion teaching or in-ser-
vice training at least
two times per semester
for the purpose of il-
lustrating new content,
methods or materials
for either grade level
(including both grade
levels during the year)
(at least 70 percent of
staff must agree that
such demonstrations
are worthwhile)   _____   _____   _____

Comments_____

_____

IV. Evaluation Responsibilities

A. Completes all formal
evaluation of staff and
Associate Teachers (in-
cluding those without
tenure and those not

meeting   department
requirements)   _____   _____   _____

Comments_____
_____

    B.   Conducts periodic con-
sultations (not less
than once per semes-
ter) with each teacher
of the team regarding
individual teacher sat-
isfaction with the pro-
gram   _____   _____   _____

Comments_____
_____

    C.   Visits each teacher in
the classroom (at least
one visit each quarter)
followed by a confer-
ence or written evalua-
tion for the purpose of
assessing the instruc-
tional appropriateness
of the content of what
is being taught and to
determine if the in-
structional mode is be-
ing properly utilized   _____   _____   _____

Comments_____
_____

    D.   Responsible for the
training and direction
of all area-based para-
professionals to in-
clude:

       1. conducting regular
discussions with the
staff (at least once

each quarter) regarding paraprofessional utilization, deployment and effectiveness;

2. maintaining communication between staff and paraprofessionals;

3. establishing clerkwork priorities (at least 70 percent of staff must agree such priorities are essential);

4. responsibility for the interviewing of paraprofessionals for employment   _____   _____   _____

Comments_____
       _____

E.   Responsible for the student utilization of area resource center:

1. reviews student usage of resource center for staff (at least once a quarter) to include:

   a. dominant types of student activities;
   b. number of student conflicts regarding equipment utilization

       c. adequacy of
          book- and mate-
          rial-based support
          systems;
       d. problems with
          student disci-
          pline;
       e. student evalua-
          tion of resource
          center   ____   ____   ____

Comments_____

_____

V.   Fiscal Responsibilities

    A.   Responsible for expen-
        diture of all depart-
        ment money for the
        following:

        1. personnel

        2. materials

        3. equipment

        4. supplies

        5. in-service (conferences,
          etc.)   ____   ____   ____

Comments_____

_____

    B.   Responsible for pre-
        senting expenditure re-
        quests to the staff for
        its consideration prior
        to presentation to the
        school Senate (at least

70 percent of the staff
must agree that the
proposed budget is re-
presentative of the in-
structional program/
objectives)   _____   _____   _____

Comments_____
_____

VI.   Communication Responsibilities

A.   If requested by the
staff, reports at each
regular department
meeting the transac-
tions of the school
Senate)   _____   _____   _____

Comments_____
_____

B.   Reports to the school
Senate concerns and pro-
posals of his area (at
least 70 percent of such
items must appear in the
written minutes of the
Senate)

_____   _____   _____

Comments_____
_____

VII.   Evaluation of Senate Role

A.   After interviewing a
Senate member, rates
the Senior Teacher in
the following areas
(first and third quarter
only):

1. ability to initiate ideas in the Senate;   _____   _____   _____

2. ability to implement Senate decisions with department;   _____   _____   _____

3. ability to evaluate and criticize Senate proposals;   _____   _____   _____

4. ability to consider and conceptualize school-wide needs, concerns, implications, etc. over area needs and requests   _____   _____   _____

Comments_____

_____

VIII. Human Relations and Leadership Variables

A. Creates an open climate for his colleagues which is characterized by:

1. high tolerance of diversity of opinion;

2. clarity of purpose of curricular and department goals;

3. good relations between members and the leader;

4. high task completion rate and a high quality of teacher/-

student work out-
put in the depart-
ment;

5. members who are
   enthusiastic about
   their work   _____   _____   _____

Comments_____

_____

B. The Senior Teacher is
    characterized by:

   1. being an accepting
      person;   _____   _____   _____

   2. ability to separate
      personalities from is-
      sues;   _____   _____   _____

   3. not belittling others;

      _____   _____   _____

   4. ability to overcome
      own biases;   _____   _____   _____

   5. being a good listener;

      _____   _____   _____

   6. ability to use direct/
      indirect methods;   _____   _____   _____

   7. knowing when to
      make closure in
      colleague relation-
      ships;   _____   _____   _____

   8. ability to act on
      others' ideas;   _____   _____   _____

   9. commanding pro-

fessional   respect;   _____   _____   _____
10. being loyal to school,
     colleagues, profes-
     sion;
                              _____   _____   _____
11. actively seeking pro-
     fessional consensus;
                              _____   _____   _____
12. being positive to-
     ward new ideas;   _____   _____   _____
13. being well organized;
                              _____   _____   _____
14. ability to commun-
     icate clearly pro-
     gram goals;   _____   _____   _____
15. being willing to de-
     vote extra effort to
     program   _____   _____   _____

Comments_____

_____

SUMMARY OF MAJOR AREAS OF RESPONSIBILITIES

Directions: A brief rating of the Senior Teacher's overall per-
              formance in the major areas of responsibility

	Performed Very Well	*Performed Adequately*	*Needs Improvement*
1. Scheduling responsibilities			
2. Curriculum responsibilities			
3. Instructional responsibilities			
4. Evaluation responsibilities			
5. Fiscal responsibilities			
6. Communication responsibilities			
7. Senate responsibilities			

8. Human relations responsibilities
9. Overall rating of performance

Recommendations for job improvement

General Comments

_____
                    Evaluator

            Quarter–1   2   3   4

Appendix 2

Directions: Please read each item carefully and decide which description is most accurate from those listed on the responding sheet. It is very important that you indicated "needed" or "not needed" for *every* item regardless of how you mark it. Use the back of the responding sheet for recording comments.

1.0 Research Responsibilities

    1.1 Disseminates orally and in writing to the Senior Teachers and staff reports and information on research and innovation in social studies curriculum development, new materials, and processes

    1.2 Reports to the total staff on the ongoing developmental activities, trends, materials, readings, etc., as they relate to social studies

    1.3 Identifies useful instructional materials, books, programs, curricula, research studies and summaries, etc., useful for demonstrating the theory and practice of new social studies and in-service programs

    1.4 Develops research and experimental design for the empirical validation of new materials, teaching strategies, and exemplary social studies programs

    1.5 Identifies and/or develops empirically reliable models for inquiry training, instructional materials development, and curriculum design

2.0 Staff In-Service Responsibilities

    2.1 Develops models for introducing innovation and conducting in-service training

2.2 Assists Senior Teachers in the design of specific in-service training programs

2.3 Assists Senior Teachers in the implementation of in-service training programs

2.4 Conducts in-service training program specifically designed for the social studies Senior Teachers

2.5 Conducts regular planning meetings for the Social Studies Vertical Committee

2.6 Contributes to the design and implementation of the EPDA Leadership Training Program

2.7 Identifies staff needs with the Senior Teachers

2.8 Respects role of the Senior Teachers

3.0 Self-Renewal Responsibilities

3.1 Develops and implements for validation exemplary teaching strategies, materials, and lessons

3.2 Attends conferences, committees, planning groups, etc. to keep abreast of current developments which may have import or implications on district curriculum development activities, teaching, materials development, or other components of the instructional program.

3.3 Participates in organizations whose purpose is the fostering of research, innovation, and evaluation of social studies education

3.4 Maintains close contact with university and other social studies leadership personnel

4.0 Coordination/Administration Responsibilities

4.1 Develops a task analysis system

4.2 Schedules a series of meetings with individual school staffs and Senior Teacher to coordinate activities and objectives

4.3 Works with representatives of the community on goal setting and implementation design

4.4 Develops a budget to finance the activities of the Social Studies Vertical Committee and the special in-service program for social studies

4.5 Maintains liaison with other district committees and the administration

4.6 Participates in the decision-making processes regarding overall curriculum development, in-service training, and facilities development by serving on various district-wide committees

5.0 Evaluation Responsibilities

5.1 Identifies and/or develops tests designed to evaluate learner behavioral change in both the substantive and higher cognitive areas

5.2 Evaluates and reports the objectives, activities, and accomplishments of the Senior Teachers and Master Teacher to the Instructional Council, the District Senate, and the various administrators

5.3 Recommends, with the advice and consent of the Social Studies Vertical Committee, specific courses of action to accomplish the curriculum and training goals of social studies in the district

5.4 Evaluates out-of-district proposals, materials and practices and reports to the Senior Teachers

6.0 Teaching Responsibilities

6.1 Teaches at least 20 percent of the working day

6.2 Demonstrates to staff and Senior Teachers new teaching strategies, new instructional materials utilization, and other exemplary teaching behaviors

RESPONSE SHEET

Key: *Needed:* You agree that it is a useful activity, goal, or
whatever.

Not Needed: You think the goal, activity, etc., unnecessary.

Performing Well: You think that the activity, goal, service,
etc. is accomplished on a regular basis and that you are
generally satisfied. Each item should be thought of as a
continuing activity, not one necessarily completed nor
capable of completion. You should judge on the basis of
your impression up to this moment.

Performing Adequately: You think that searching is happen-
ing in each category but that it is not as satisfactorily done
as you wish. Again, think of each category or item as a
developing process.

Performing Inadequately: You think that substantial improvement is needed.

Don't Know: You do not have enough information to make a
decision.

(USE BACK OF SHEET FOR COMMENTS)

NEEDED	NOT NEEDED	ITEM	PERFORMING WELL	PERFORMING ADEQUATELY	PERFORMING INADEQUATELY	DON'T KNOW
		1.1				
		1.2				
		1.3				
		1.4				
		1.5				
		2.1				
		2.2				
		2.3				
		2.4				
		2.5				
		2.6				
		2.7				
		2.8				

NEEDED	NOT NEEDED	ITEM	PERFORMING WELL	PERFORMING ADEQUATELY	PERFORMING INADEQUATELY	DON'T KNOW
		3.1				
		3.2				
		3.3				
		3.4				
		4.1				
		4.2				
		4.3				
		4.4				
		4.5				
		4.6				
		5.1				
		5.2				
		5.3				
		5.4				
		6.1				
		6.2				

Appendix 3

TEMPLE CITY UNIFIED SCHOOL DISTRICT

Citizenship Goals

Presented by
Richard Allen, Chairman, Citizens Committee
and
Clinton Boutwell, Master Teacher
June, 19__

What follows are the citizenship goals for the Temple City Unified School District developed by a study group made up of citizens of the community and social studies teachers from the District. They are categorized into three groups: (1) decision-making skills and processes, (2) baseline knowledges, and (3) self-concept attitudes and behaviors. Each category is described separately but in real life they would be integrated into the entire behaviors of young people by the time they are ready to leave school. The comments that preface each of the categories reflect the thoughts and considerations of the study group who developed the preliminary statements. These goals are intended to be the major guide to the professional staff in developing specific programs.

I. DECISION-MAKING SKILLS AND PROCESSES

To be effective, thoughtful citizens, children must learn how to make judgments about problems on the basis of careful thought. Children can learn these skills in a well-designed educational program in which they are given the opportunity to not only learn the skills of effective thinking but also have opportunities to practice them. Specifically, children need to learn and practice the following skills and processes of deciding and acting to be effective, thoughtful citizens:

A.   They must be able to recognize a problem and be able to identify why it is a problem, to society and/or to themselves.

B.   They must be able to identify the values involved, both their own and those of others to be better able to judge potential solutions more objectively, less emotionally and know what is at stake for others as well as for themselves.

C.   They must be able to gather relevant information and expert opinions and know how to analyze information sources and opinions to determine their usefulness and biases in relationship to a problem.

D.   They must be willing to withhold their judgment until sufficient information has been gathered and to avoid snap judgments.

E.   They must be able to pose tentative solutions and alternative solutions based upon the information they have and on their values toward the problem.

F.   They must be able to state the potential consequences to themselves and society if their solution was accepted; they must judge who gets helped and who gets hurt and whether or not the solutions are worth the social and personal costs.

G.   They must finally select a solution and act in such ways as to have the solution accepted by others.

H.   They must then evaluate the effectiveness of their solution and accept responsibility for their actions and decisions.

II.   BASELINE KNOWLEDGES

Even though we know that information about mankind has been growing so fast that it is inconceivable that any one person should be asked to memorize hundreds of specific facts, it is still necessary that an effective citizen be aware of certain facts that will help him be more effective. The facts that a citizen should have as part of his intellectual makeup are those that directly deal with citizenship behaviors. The children in school, then, need to know principles, values, and events that in an important way influence their decision-making and behavior. Such facts must be drawn from more than just history or civics, although those areas are important. Facts must be learned from sociology, anthropology, political science, economics, and geography to give children the necessary backgrounds for thoughtful decision-making. And all of the facts selected, must be judged on the basis of how well they will provide children with such a background and not on the basis that they seem to be good or sound or interesting. Any information learned must have lasting value to the individual over his lifetime. The facts identified below were selected on that basis. To be good citizens, then, children should know:

Our American Heritage

A.   They must know the contributions of outstanding men and women to the growth of American democracy.

B.   They must know that America is a constantly changing society and that our political, economic, and social practices and institutions have changed over time.

C.   They must know that America is a society made up of many groups; racial, linguistic, and different national heritages, all of whom have contributed to the strength and greatness of our country.

D.   They must know how Americans have settled conflicts in the past with an emphasis on democratic conflict resolution processes.

E.   They must know of the underlying principles and values of American democracy as seen through such documents as the Constitution, the Declaration of Independence, the Bill of Rights, and others.

F.   They must know of the impact of our country's geography on political, economic, and social development, and the differences and problems found in different times and places.

G.   They must know the influence of religion and religious values on the culture of the United States.

H.   They must know of the impact that technology has made on our country in terms of our wealth, values, interpersonal relations and future.

I.   They must know of the foreign relations America has had with other nations and peoples of the world.

Interpersonal Relationships

A.   They must know that a person's values, beliefs, and behaviors are to a large extent learned from the groups he grew up in and with whom he associates.

B.   They must know that a person's values, beliefs, and outlook effect the way he interprets the values, beliefs, and behaviors of others.

C.   They must know the influence of mass media on the values, beliefs, and behaviors of people including themselves.

D.   They must know that the interdependence and co-operation of people are essential for keeping a society together.

E.   They must know that values, beliefs, norms, and customs change over time.

F.   They must know that changes in our society are occurring so rapidly, in contrast with the past, that conflicts are arising in our values, beliefs, and behaviors.

G.   They must know the techniques of facing up to and accommodating themselves to a rapidly changing society.

H.   They must know that they may have, just as others do, attitudes, values, and perceptions which may distort their ability to make meaningful judgments about social and personal issues or problems.

I.   They must know the influence large organizations and institutions have on the lives, attitudes, feelings, beliefs, and behaviors of individuals, including themselves.

J.   They must know the techniques of influencing decisions within organizations.

K.   They must know that social change in a democracy is a slow process involving respect for the dignity and worth of individuals within society.

Political Systems and Processes

A.   They must know the responsibilities and rights of a United States citizen in a democracy.

B.   They must know how to utilize the due process procedures of our democratic society in effecting constructive change.

C.   They must know formal and informal workings of the local, state and federal government.

D.   They must know of the techniques of persuasion used by governmental agencies, mass media, and other organizations to gain consensus about an issue or problem.

E.   They must know the techniques useful to individuals and groups in a democracy in influencing political decision-making or in reaching some political goal.

F.   They must know that political attitudes held by people, including themselves, are to a large extent learned from the groups they grew up in and with whom they associate.

G.   They must know about systems of government other than that of the United States, including at least a communist system, a socialist system, a fascist system, and an authoritarian system.

H.   They must know the conflict resolution techniques used in a democratic, pluralistic society.

I.   They must know that political attitudes and beliefs may distort people's ability to make rational judgments about issues or problems, including themselves.

Economic Systems and Processes

A.   They must know that the basic economic problem is that there are limited resources and unlimited wants.

B.   They must know the formal and informal workings of the American economic system.

C.   They must know the advantages and disadvantages of technological innovations and growth.

D.   They must know of other economic systems than that of the United States, including at least a communist system, a socialist system, a mixed economy, a corporated state system, and a democratic socialist system.

E.   They must know that technological advances affect the traditional economic values and attitudes held by the people.

F.   They must know that most of the economic problems of the United States result from the demands of contending forces within the country for a share of the wealth.

G.   They must know the role and the influence of the local, state, and federal governments on economic decisions and practices.

H.   They must know that haphazard economic changes may produce undesirable social and political problems.

Man and Society

A.   They must know that mankind has created different cultures which contain different beliefs, values, attitudes and behaviors.

B.   They must know that differences in cultures throughout the world have historical causes and are not the result of biological differences.

C.   They must know that the attitudes, values, beliefs, and behaviors of individuals are expressive of the culture they live in.

D.   They must know the influence of religion, art, music, custom, and tradition on the attitudes, values, and beliefs of individuals.

E.   They must know the influence of the family and other face-to-face groups on the development of attitudes, values, and beliefs of individuals.

F.   They must know the effects of technology on changing values and behaviors in a culture.

G.   They must know that the natural reaction of man is to resist change.

H.   They must know that the practice of judging other cultures on the basis of one's own cultural standards may distort one's perception of that culture.

I.   They must know how cultures change and recognize those factors within their own and other's cultures.

Man-Land Relationships

A.   They must know the influences of environment on man's economic and political activities and decision-making.

B.   They must know the influences of environment of man on his environment in both the positive and negative ways.

C.   They must know the geographic factors in urban development and problems.

D.   They must know the skills and interpretative processes of geography.

III.   SELF-CONCEPT: SOCIETY AND SELF

As important as mastering the processes of rational decision-making and the accumulation of baseline information with which rational judgment may be made, is the attitude one has toward oneself: Does an individual feel confident in his abilities? Is he willing to take a stand? Is he able to take defeat as well as success and still remain self-secure? These are the kinds of questions related to self-concept. If a school is open and receptive to allowing a child to develop his full, individual potential, *if teacher behavior is geared to the unique personalities and potential of the children,* and if children find success in their school life, a positive self-concept may develop. The goals below, then, are useful to educators in guiding them in divisions about *how* the learning environment should be designed, what kinds of teacher-student interactions should take place, and a host of other factors related to the sound psychological development of children. The goal of citizenship training should be to develop in children a feeling of self-worth and confidence in their ability to effect their own lives. Specifically, children should demonstate behaviors which show that they:

A.   Have faith in themselves and believe that others trust them.

B.   Have confidence in their abilities.

C.   Are able to recognize their own mistakes and accept failure as well as success without psychological reactions.

D.   Are not threatened by new experiences.

E.   Believe they can, by personal effort, affect their own lives.

F.   Are willing to accept responsibility for their actions.

G.   Can set realistic goals in relationships to their abilities.

H.   Are aware of how others perceive them.

I.   Are willing to share their personal feelings with others.

J.   Are aware of how others feel about them.

K.   Are empathetic towards others.

L.   Recognize the needs of others and contribute to their success.

M. Are able to make decisions independently of others but are willing to seek direction from others on their own volition.

N. Can give and take in group activities.

O. Can account for distortions and biases caused by their own perceptual screen (attitudes, values, morals, etc.)

P. Can tolerate diversity, complexity, and ambiguity in a world of constant change.

Q. Are willing to propose new ideas for problem solving even when those ideas may be contradictory to "accepted" ideas.

R. Are willing to change when presented with new evidence.

S. Can recognize the biases of others.

T. Are willing to recognize and carry out their responsibilities.

Appendix 4

TEMPLE CITY UNIFIED SCHOOL DISTRICT

English Base-Line Objectives

Presented by

Jan Pitzer, Chairman,
Citizen's Committee and
Edith Ackerman, Senior Teacher
June, 19＿

THE STUDENT WILL BE ABLE:

1. Given a standardized reading test, to read at twelfth-grade level or above, displaying vocabulary and comprehension skills (for 75 percent of the students).

2. To write at least three paragraphs on one subject, with unity and coherence, using topic sentences for main ideas, supporting details or examples, and summarizing sentences. Correctness to be judged by a certificated member of the English Department.

   a. To write a rough outline, suggesting main ideas and supporting details, to accompany paragraphs written for Objective #2.
   b. To use conventions of capitalization with 80 percent accuracy.
   c. To use conventions of punctuation with 80 percent accuracy.
   d. To identify and correct fragments, run-on sentences, and dangling modifiers with 80 percent accuracy.

3. To write a business letter with complete lack of error in

format. Successful performance to be judged by a certificated member of the English Department.

4. Given a standardized spelling test, to spell at twelfth-grade level (70 percent of the students).

5. Given a standardized usage test, to distinguish between standard and non-standard use of verbs, pronouns, adjectives, and adverbs with 80 percent accuracy.

6. Given a list of ten words, to use the dictionary to locate and identify pronunciation, and find meaning and spelling of words, with 90 percent accuracy.

7. To successfully complete application forms. Performance to be judged by a certificated member of the English Department.

8. To make a short oral report of three to five minutes. Successful performance to be judged by a certificated member of the English Department.

9 Given selected material, to successfully locate, use catalogues, directories, and reference works for this purpose. Successful performance to be judged by a certificated member of the English Department.

10. Given a standardized vocabulary test, to use vocabulary at twelfth-grade level or above (for 75 percent of the students).

11. Given samples of mass media, to identify and use the three major kinds of journalistic writing: news, feature, and editorial.

12. Given reading and viewing assignments in mass media, to identify, in writing, evidences of propaganda or "slanted" presentations. Successful performance to be judged by a certificated member of the English Department.

13. Given a model of cursive writing, to legibly write all the letters of the alphabet, both upper and lower case. Successful performance will be judged by referring to a rating scale in the California State handwriting text or manual.

14. Study skills objective:

   a. Efficient studying: Given a representative reading selection, the student will be able, after ten minutes of study, to recall, in writing, the main idea and three supporting details.

   b. Note taking: When hearing a five-minute, single-concept talk, the student will take notes in a simplified, indented form covering the main idea, details and summary.

   c. Preparing for written examinations: The student will list five techniques for preparing and writing successful examinations.

   d. Preparing for oral interviews: The student will orally present five techniques used in preparing for oral interviews.

TEMPLE CITY SCHOOL DISTRICT

ENGLISH BASE-LINE OBJECTIVES (AFFECTIVE)

THE STUDENT WILL BE ABLE:

1. To recognize that there may be more than one acceptable point of view. (P. 100)

2. To recognize the importance in his life of the study of English.

3. To recognize the worth and dignity of each individual through the reading of literature.

4. To increase senstitivity of human needs and pressing social problems. (P. 108)

5. To listen to others with respect. (P. 103)

6. To become alert toward human values and judgments on life as they are recorded in literature. (P. 113)

7. To read a book for pleasure when given a choice of leisure-time activities.

8. To desire to speak and write effectively, (P. 141)

9. To desire to write legibly.

10. To take responsibility for listening to and participating in public discussion. (P. 141)

11. To be willing to take risks and to encounter difficulties in putting findings into contructive action after reading and research.

12. To participate in group processes.

13. To evaluate problems in terms of situations, issues, purposes, and consequences involved. (P. 168)

It is very difficult to measure affective objectives. Teacher observation may be one method used.

Page numbers refer to David R. Krathwohl, Benjamin S. Bloom, and Bertram B. Masia, *Taxonomy of Educational Objectives, The Classification of Educational Goals, Handbook II: Affective Domain,* (New York: David McKay Company, Inc., 1956.)

Appendix 5

Dear Educator:

Thank you for your recent inquiry concerning visiting the Temple City Unified School District. Enclosed is a packet of information to maximize the value of your visit.

In the past two years, over 2000 visitors have toured our schools. From these experiences, we have structured a variety of visitation programs. Enclosed are details of each program. Please fill out and return the bottom portion of the enclosure. This will facilitate our handling of your request.

If you have needs not apparently met by the structured visitation programs, please let us know in advance and we will try to individualize your visit.

We are restricting visitation this year to Wednesday and Thursday of each week school is in session. Special arrangements, however, will be considered upon specific request.

You will begin your visit at the Temple City Differentiated Staffing Project Training and Information Center, 9528 East Longden Avenue, Temple City. Directions: from Los Angeles take the San Bernardino or Pomona freeways to the Rosemead Boulevard off-ramp. North on Rosemead three miles (five miles from Pomona freeway) to Longden Avenue. Turn right on Longden and proceed for one-half mile to the Training and Information Center. The Center is adjacent to the school district parking lot and is clearly marked for your identification.

Several visitation programs extend from morning to afternoon. If you desire to have lunch, there are a number of restaurants within a few minutes of Temple City. A select list of these fine restaurants is enclosed.

Again, thank you for your interest.

SUPPORTED BY THE U.S. OFFICE OF EDUCATION, EDUCATION PROFESSIONS DEVELOPMENT ACT, P.L. 89-329.

OVERVIEW OF SHARED DECISION MAKING (Half Day):

An examination of the school district's shared decision-making system, including observation of a shared decision-making body in operation.

Beginning Time: 9:30 a.m.
Completion Time: 1:00 p.m.

The School District Senate is the district-wide policy-making body. It meets the first Wednesday of each month. The following encompasses a visitor's program that includes a district senate meeting as one element of the program.

Beginning time: 3:30 p.m.
Completion Time: 5:30 p.m.

- -

Please detach and return to:

> Michael W. Stover
> EPDA Information Officer
> Temple City Unified School District
> 9516 East Longden Avenue
> Temple City, California   91780

I will be in Temple City on _____ and will want to take the following tour: _____ _____
Name_____   Position_____ _____
Agency/School District_____
Address_____
      Street   City   State   Zip
Telephone_____ Number in party_____

WELCOME TO TEMPLE CITY

We appreciate you coming to Temple City to see our program in operation. The staff and administration wish to make your visit informative and productive. We have prepared a variety of written materials and video tapes highlighting elements of the local educational program. You are invited to use these resources.

Also a number of special interest program have been designed for visitors.

Since 1968 when we implemented differentiated staffing at Oak Avenue Intermediate School, we have had over 2000 visitors tour our campuses. In that time, we developed a list of most frequently asked questions about visiting:

MAY I TAKE PICTURES?

If you wish to take pictures, please clear in advance with the school principal.

MAY I MAKE TAPE RECORDINGS INVOLVING STAFF MEMBERS?

If you wish to make either audio or video tape recordings, please clear in advance with the staff member(s) involved.

MAY I VISIT SMALL GROUP CLASSES?

Visits are restricted because persons entering and leaving these classes distract staff and students.

MAY I VISIT LARGE GROUP CLASSES?

Yes, but we must request you agree to enter the classroom at the beginning of the class session and remain for the duration of the class.

MAY I QUESTION STUDENTS?

Certainly. Just one request: please do not interrupt students in resource centers or the school library. Your student tour guide should be helpful in this regard.

WHERE MAY I TALK INFORMALLY WITH TEACHERS?

If you wish to chat with staff members, the school staff room is an ideal site. Your student tour guide will show you where it is.

DISSEMINATION MENU

ENTREES *Basic Reference Sources*

NEW CAREERS IN TEACHING—DIFFERENTIATED STAFFING
Basic Differentiated Staffing Project brochure. Describes
—— the major components of the Temple City Model. 1969.

PROJECT HANDBOOK
Summary of personnel policies and procedures for the Temple City Model, including sections on collegial evaluation of teachers, selection and dismissal of staff members, and job descriptions for the various positions of the
—— staffing hierarchy. 1970.

PROJECT ABSTRACT
One-page summary of the fiscal year 1970-71 Differen-
—— tiated Staffing Project. 1970.

ORGANIZATIONAL JUXTAPOSITION: DIFFEREN-
TIATED STAFFING
This publication gives the "big picture" of differentiated staffing as a comprehensive change of how schools are
—— organized. 1970.

SIDE ORDERS *DS Components*

NEEDS ASSESSMENTS
A collection of the basic publications that formed the basis of the need assessment activity of the project's systems
—— approach to educational change. $7.50.

RATIONALE
A sampling of articles written by the project staff for professional journals describing the need for a comprehen-
—— sive model in differentiated staffing. 1970.

TRAINING PROGRAM
This publication details the differentiated staffing training program, including rationale and training strands. Also included are evaluations of the Project's Pre-School Leadership Workshop offerings of current in-service pro-
——— grams.   1970.

INDIVIDUALIZED INSTRUCTION
A sample learning activity packet and a publication describing the rationale, components, and preparation of
——— learning packets.   1970.

STUDENT/TEACHER/PARENT ATTITUDES
This publication summarized a three-month study of attitudes toward selected variables of differentiated staf-
——— fing.   1970.

PRELIMINARY FINDINGS
Includes statistical summaries of media utilization figures for traditional and innovative schools, staffing ratios, student achievement scores, and recent independent
——— evaluations of the Temple City Model.   1970.

VIEW FROM THE MOUNTAIN TOP
This publication outlines the role of school board members
——— in the educational change process.   1970.

DESSERTS   *Miscellaneous Analyses and Materials*

SALARY SCHEDULES
Associate, Standard, Senior and Master Teacher salary
——— schedules including placement criteria.   1970.

JOB DESCRIPTIONS
A sampling of performance job descriptions for Senior and
——— Master Teachers.   1970.

——— ANALYSIS OF TEACHER APPLICANTS 1967-1970

——— ANALYSIS OF VISITORS' COMMENTS 1970

——— ANALYSIS OF TEACHER ABSENCES 1970

HOW TO BUILD A DIFFERENTIATED STAFF
This publication by former Temple City Project Director Fenwick English enables the reader to become familiar with the basic terminology and concepts of differentiated staffing.

DIFFERENTIATED STAFFING: WHO IS LABOR AND WHO IS MANAGEMENT?
In this article, Project Director Bruce Caldwell discusses the changes in traditional personnel practices made by differentiated staffing. Discusses shared decision-making and the role of the educational association.

HOW TO ORDER MATERIALS

Fill out the form below and indicate in the space adjacent to the above items the number of copies desired. Copies of some publications are limited.

Name_____

Name of Agency_____

Street_____

City/State_____ Zip _____

Return this form to: Information Officer
Temple City Differentiated
Staffing Project
9516 East Longden Avenue
Temple City, California   91780

Appendix 6

Temple City Unified School District

Survey Instrument

Required Information   *Optional Information*

School_____   Subject or Grade_____
Clarification_____   Total Years Teaching_____
(Teacher, Staff Teacher,   Sex_____
Senior Teacher, etc.)

NOTE: The term "Teacher" as used in this instrument is intended to include all persons whose primary responsibility is classroom teaching.

"Formally involved" implies a recognized structural organization as opposed to temporary or ad hoc committee.

POSITION	Total Surveyed	Agree	Neutral	Disagree
1. Teachers should be formally involved in decision-making at the school level.	182	163 / 90%	10 / 5%	9 / 5%
2. Teachers should be formally involved in decision-making at the District level.	189	139 / 74%	33 / 17%	17 / 9%
3. Teachers should be formally involved in the selection of new teachers for their team or school.	187	158 / 85%	14 / 7%	15 / 8%

4. Teachers should be formally involved in evaluation of leadership personnel.

	155	19	14
188	83%	10%	7%

5. Teachers should be formally involved in evaluation before any teacher is recommended for dismissal.

	151	24	19
194	78%	12%	10%

6. A formal appeal body for personnel grievances should exist, and the majority of its members should be teaching personnel.

	158	23	8
189	84%	12%	4%

7. Students at the secondary level should be members of school and District decision-making bodies.

	87	54	50
191	46%	28%	26%

8. Students at the secondary level should be members of curriculum revision teams in every discipline.

	80	56	53
189	42%	30%	28%

9. Students at the secondary level should participate in the evaluation of educational services rendered.

	110	44	33
187	59%	23%	17%

10. Students at the secondary level should formally evaluate effectiveness of classroom instruction.

	86	49	53
188	46%	26%	28%

11. K-12 vertical curriculum committees should exist in major disciplines, and to be charged with the responsibility for

keeping their curriculum up-to-date and relevant.

	160	21	9
190	84%	11%	5%

12. Formal procedures for retrieval of research and translation into practice should be instituted in every discipline.

	136	38	12
186	73%	20%	7%

13. The District should encourage on-site pre-service training programs.

	134	37	25
196	68%	19%	13%

14. Teachers who are to receive services should determine what training and service needs are to exist.

	153	23	10
186	82%	12%	6%

15. Teachers who receive services should play the major role in selection of the service agent.

	134	31	19
184	73%	17%	10%

16. Teachers who receive services should evaluate those who provide services.

	163	15	6
184	89%	8%	3%

17. Roles and services should be defined in terms of measurable performance criteria.

	136	34	9
179	76%	19%	5%

18. When there are deficiencies in quality of professional competence, a committee of colleagues should be established to validate the charge and to assist the individual in correction of deficiencies.

	161	9	17
187	86%	5%	9%

19. Teachers should be compen-

sated at a level commensurate with their responsibility rather than having to leave the classroom in order to ascend in the profession.

191   150 / 79%   23 / 12%   18 / 9%

20. Maximum educational growth of individual learners should be the primary criterion by which all policies and programs are judged.

187   143 / 76%   22 / 12%   22 / 12%

21. Performance should be a criterion for advancement on the salary schedule.

181   94 / 52%   44 / 24%   43 / 24%

22. Roles and responsibilities should determine compensation levels.

185   128 / 67%   30 / 18%   34 / 15%

23. All certificated personnel, including administrators, should have some teaching responsibility.

192   128 / 67%   30 / 15%   34 / 18%

24. Flexibility in use of time is essential if individualization of instruction is to be achieved.

185   154 / 83%   14 / 8%   17 / 9%

25. The District should return to a more traditional decision-making process where final authority rests with the administration.

196   25 / 13%   40 / 20%   131 / 67%

26. Teacher-initiated proposals for improvement of instruction should be continued whenever funds permit.

188   175 / 93%   10 / 5%   3 / 2%

27. Parents should be involved in the establishment of long-range educational goals.

188

120	33	35
64%	18%	18%

28. Students should be involved in planning educational programs and the establishment of long-range educational goals.

188

97	44	47
52%	23%	25%

29. Instruction should focus on processes such as critical thinking and problem-solving as well as mastery of factual information.

191

180	10	1
94%	5%	1%

30. Teachers should be formally involved in District and local school budget development and allocations.

186

133	32	21
72%	17%	11%

31. School should be made a more enjoyable experience through elimination of fear of failure as a motivating factor.

189

127	26	36
67%	14%	19%

32. A systematic training program for teachers and leadership personnel should be implemented, based upon needs defined by the staff.

186

131	34	21
71%	18%	11%

33. Artificial constraints, such as grade levels and traditional report cards, should be eliminated.

203

90	35	78
44%	17%	39%

34. Leadership positions (Senior Teacher, Curriculum Associate, etc.) should be opened periodically for re-selection.

182

148	25	13
79%	14%	7%

35. The District should systematically provide for independent learning and self-instruction by students.

195	148	26	21
	76%	13%	11%

36. Students should be involved in identification of their needs and development of curriculum to those needs.

176	109	35	32
	62%	20%	18%

37. There should be greater emphasis on overcoming traditional subject-matter barriers, and development of integrated approaches to knowledge.

187	130	33	24
	69%	18%	13%

Temple City Unified School District

March 20, 19___

TO: District Senate
FROM: Robert Lundgren, Director
Differentiated Staffing Personnel
SUBJECT: *Results of Staff Survey*

In accord with action of the District Senate on February 7, 19___, the survey instrument developed to gain input on commitment of the total staff to the principles upon which the District's educational directions have been based was distributed to members of each school's certificated staff. The forms were returned to Dr. Bell, who furnished the tabulations on the attached pages. For further analysis, the frequencies were then converted to percentages.

Analysis of the data indicates several trends and inferences. 203 of the 217 forms that were distributed were returned. Areas of agreement were as follows:

90% or more agreement . . 3 items (Number 1, 26, and 29)

80-90% agreement . . . . . 8 items   (Numbers 3, 4, 6,
                                         11, 14, 16, 18, 24)

70-79% agreement . . . . . 11 items
60-69% agreement . . . . . 8 items
50-59% agreement . . . . . 3 items
40-49% agreement . . . . . 4 items

Areas of disagreement were as follows:

1-9% disagreement . . . . .16 items
9-19% disagreement . . . . 15 items
20-29% disagreement . . . . 5 items   (Numbers 7, 8, 10,
                                         21 and 28)
30-39% disagreement . . . . . 1 item   (Number 33)

Neutrality patterns included the following:

1-9% neutral . . . . 7 items
10-19% neutral . . . . 21 items
20-29% neutral . . . . 8 items
30-39% neutral . . . . 1 item

Questions number 38 and 39 asked for narrative answers related to criteria for selecting the new Superintendent, and for refinement, modification or elimination of specific current practices. No attempt has been made to reproduce all of the comments, although Dr. Bell has filed the originals of this page with Lois Taylor. 158 forms with comments were received. 94 had comments related to specific practices, and some made reference to specific aspects of District programs through their indication of desirable criteria for the Superintendent.

Temple City High School
CITIZENS COMMITTEE ON
FLEXIBLE SCHEDULING

COMPOSITE PROFILE OF TEACHER QUESTIONNAIRE
MARCH 14, 19___

	greatly	slightly	no change	slightly	greatly
	INCREASED			**DECREASED**	
1. Structured and lab time spent with students	16	13	1	9	8
2. Time available to plan assignments	7	7	9	14½	11½
3. Utilization of interdepartmental curricula	7	20	20	1	2
4. Teacher time spent on record keeping	22	16	7	3	2
5. Effective teaching time spent with students	17	10	4	8	9
6. Utilization of teaching techniques	17	20	8	1	3
7. Student-teacher contact	18	14	4	8	4
8. Preparation required for presentation to students	20	13	12	3	1
9. Continuity of teaching efforts within the department	10	19	15	2	1
10. Identification of students having academic difficulties	16	15	13	2	2
11. Preparation of materials required	21	16	12	0	0
12. Control of students	12½	8	13	9	4½
13. Professional growth (other than additional units earned)	11	12	23	0	2
14. Students receiving individual help	20	20	3	4	3
15. Student educational growth	16	15	5	6	5

16. Teacher workload	29	16	8	1	0
17. Student-teacher rapport	18	16	10	4	1
18. Responsibility of students' completion of assignments	22	12	8	5	4
19. Student use of reference material	17	21	7	2	1
20. Teacher fatigue	24	12	7	2	1
21. Students seeking help	13	20	9	4	3
22. Utilization of school's physical facilities	25	14	7	1	2

Bibliography

Allen, Dwight W. Speech delivered in Temple City, California, March 8, 1968.
—————. School of Education Catalogue, University of Massachusetts, 1972.
Argyris, Chris. *Integrating the Individual and the Organization.* New York: John Wiley and Sons, Inc., 1964.
Arnstine, Donald. "Freedom and Bureaucracy in the Schools," *Freedom, Bureaucracy, and Schooling.* Washington D.C.: N.E.A., 1971 ASCD Yearbook.
ASCD Yearbook, 1962. *Perceiving, Behaving, and Becoming* Washington D.C.: N.E.A., 1962.
Ayers, Douglas G. Speech delivered in Anaheim, California, 1967.
Bales, Robert F. "The Equilibrium Problem in Small Groups," ed. Joseph Litter; in *Organizations: Systems, Control and Adaptation* (2nd ed.), Vol. II, New York: John Wiley and Sons, Inc., 1963.
Beck, Robert Holmes. *A Social History of Education.* New Jersey: Prentice-Hall, Inc., 1965.
Bell, Gerald D. "The Influence of Technological Components of Work Upon Management Control," in *Organizations: Structure and Behavior* (2nd ed.), Vol. II, ed. Joseph Litter. New York: John Wiley and Sons, Inc., 1963.
Bill of Rights Newsletter, Vol. III, no. 2, Fall 1969.
Blau, Peter M. *Bureaucracy in Modern Society.* New York: Random House, Inc., 1956.
Broudy, Harry S., "New Problems and Old Solutions," in *Philosophy of Education* (3rd ed.), ed. Joe Park. New York: The Macmillan Company, 1968.
Brown, J.A.C. *The Social Psychology of Industry.* Baltimore: Penguin Books, Inc., 1954.
Butler, Donald J. "The Outline of a Philosophy," in *Philosophy of Education* (3rd ed.), ed. Joe Park. New York: The Macmillan Company, 1968.
Cadwallader, Mervyn L. "The Cybernetic Analysis of Change in Complex Social Organizations," *American Journal of Sociology,* LXV (September 1959)
Caldwell, Bruce G. "Differentiated Staffing, Who is Labor and Who is Management," *Educational Technology,* (January 1971)
Callahan, Raymond E., *Education and the Cult of Efficiency.* Chicago: The University of Chicago Press, 1962.
Chaffee, John Jr. and Patricia Wagner. "Teachers Do Make a Difference," *American Education,* (May 1970)
Coser, Lewis A., *The Functions of Social Conflict.* New York: The Free Press, 1956.
Cuban, Larry, "Teaching the Children: Does the System Help or Hinder, "*Freedom, Bureaucracy, and Schooling.* Washington D.C.: N.E.A., 1971 ASCD Yearbook.
Daw, Robert W. and N.L. Gage. "Effect of Feedback from Teachers to Principals," Unpublished dissertation abstract. Palo Alto, Cal.: Stanford University.
"Developing Thinking Skills," Wesleyan University,Middletown, Connecticut, Curriculum Letter no. 58.
"Development of a Low-Cost Performance-Oriented Training Model," Alexandria, Va.: Human Resources Research Organization, 1970.

Dionne, Joseph L. "The Outlook for the Future in Testing and Evaluation." Speech delivered in Los Angeles, April 1970.

Education Daily, Capital Publications, Inc., Washington D.C., Nov. 24, 30, 1971, Jan. 3, 26, 1972.

Educational Marketer, Vol. 2, no. 18, New York: Knowledge Industries Publications, Inc., 1970.

Educational Summary, Croft Educational Services, Inc., August 6, 1971.

Education Turnkey News, Vol, 1, no. 2, Washington D.C.: Education Turnkey Systems, 1970.

Elam, Stanley and Will P. McClure. *Educational Requirements for the 1970's.* New York: Frederick A. Praeger, 1967.

Froebel, Friedrick. *The Education of Man.* New York: D. Appleton Co., 1887.

Gage, N.L. "A Method for 'Improving' Teacher Behavior," *Journal of Teacher Education,* (1963)

Gardner, John. *Self-Renewal.* New York: Harper and Row, 1963.

Gellerman, Saul W. *Motivation and Productivity.* New York: Vail-Ballou Press, 1963.

Glasser, William. *Cure For Crisis.* Pasadena: Thomas Jefferson Research Center, 1971.

Goble, Frank. *The Third Force in Psychology.* New York: Grossman Publishers, 1970.

_____ and Peggy Granger. *Breakthrough in Psychology.* Pasadena: Thomas Jefferson Research Center, 1969.

Goodlad, John. "The School vs. Education," *Saturday Review,* (April 19, 1969)

Goldhammer, Keith, *et.al. Issues and Problems in Contemporary Educational Administration.* Eugene, Ore.: Center for the Advanced Study of Educational Administration, University of Oregon, 1967.

Herzberg, Frederick. *Work and The Nature of Man.* Cleveland: The World Publishing Company, 1966.

Hersey, Paul and Kenneth H. Blanchard. "Life Cycle Theory of Leadership," *Training and Development Journal,* (May 1969)

_____. *Management of Organizational Behavior,* Englewood Cliffs, New Jersey: Prentice-Hall, Inc., 1969.

Holt, John. *How Children Fail.* New York: Pitman Publishing Co., Inc., 1964.

Homans, George C. *The Human Group.* New York: Harcourt, Brace & Co., 1950.

Horne, Herman Harrell. *Idealism in Education.* New York: The Macmillan Company, 1910.

Horvat, John J. and David L. Clark. "Educational Change," in *The Teacher's Handbook,* ed. Dwight W. Allen and Eli Seifman. Glenview, Ill.: Scott, Foresman and Company, 1971.

House, Ernest R., Joe M. Steele and Thomas Kerins. "Development of Educational Programs: Advocacy in a Non-Rational System," Office of Superintendent of Public Instruction, Illinois, November 1970.

Hunter, Madeline. "The Teaching Process," in *The Teacher's Handbook,* ed. Dwight W. Allen and Eli Seifman. Glenview, Ill.: Scott, Foresman and Company, 1971.

Jackson, Philip W. "The Student's World," *The Elementary School Journal,* (1966)

Jenkins, David H. "Social Engineering in Educational Change: An Outline of Method," *Progressive Education,* 26: 7, (May 1949)

Katz, Daniel and Robert L. Kahn. *The Social Psychology of Organizations.* New York: John Wiley & Sons, 1966.

Kerr, Clarke. *The Uses of the University.* Cambridge: Harvard University Press, 1964.

Kirschenbaum, Howard, Sidney B. Simon and Rodney W. Napier. *Wad-Ja-Get?* New York: Hart Publishing Company, Inc., 1971.

Klein, Stephen P. "The Uses and Limitations of Standardized Tests in Meeting the Demands for Accountability," Center for the Study of Evaluation, Vol. 2, no. 4, January, 1971, University of California.

Landis, Paul H. *Social Control.* New York: J.P. Lippincott Company, 1956.

Lawrence, Paul R. "How to Deal with Resistance to Change," *Harvard Business Review,* (January-February 1969).

Lessenger, Leon M. "Accountability: Its Implications for the Teacher," in *The Teacher's Handbook,* ed. Dwight W. Allen and Eli Seifman. Glenview, Ill.: Scott, Foresman and Company, 1971.

Likert, Rensis. *The Human Organization.* New York: McGraw-Hill, Inc., 1967.

———— "Measuring Organizational Performance," *Harvard Business Review,* (March-April 1958)

Lieberman, Myron. *The Future of Public Education* Chicago: University of Chicago Press, 1960.

Little, Arthur D. Inc., "Teacher Supply and Demand in California, 1965-76," A report to the California State Board of Education, 1967.

Living Bible. Wheaton, Ill.: Tyndale House Publishers, 1971.

Lortie, Dan C. "The Balance of Control and Autonomy in Elementary School Teaching," in *The Semi-Professions and Their Organizations,* ed. Amitai Etzioni. New York: The Free Press, 1969.

March, James G. and Herbert A. Simon. "The Theory of Organizational Equilibrium," in *Organizations: Systems, Control and Adaptation* (2nd ed.) Vol II, ed. Joseph Litter New York: John Wiley and Sons, Inc., 1963.

Marin, Peter. "The Open Truth and Fiery Vehemence of Youth," in *This Book is About Schools,* ed. Satu Repo. New York: Random House, Inc., 1971.

Maslow, Abraham H., *Eupsychian Management.* Homewood, Ill.: Richard D. Irwin, Inc., 1965.

———— *Motivation and Personality.* New York: Harper & Row, Publishers, Inc., 1954.

———— *Toward A Psychology of Being.* New York: Van Nostrand Reinhold Company, 1968.

Mayo, Elton. *The Social Problems of an Industrial Civilization.* Boston: Harvard Business School, 1945.

McGregor, Douglas. *The Human Side of Enterprise.* New York: McGraw-Hill, Inc., 1960.

————, *Leadership and Motivation.* Cambridge: M.I.T. Press, 1966.

New Testament in Four Versions. New York: The Iverson-Ford Associates, 1963.

Nystrand, Raphael O. "High School Students as Policy Advocates," *Theory into Practice,* VIII: 4, (October 1969)

Pearl, Arthur. "Teacher Aides: Paraprofessionals,, Tutors, and Volunteers," in *The Teacher's Handbook,* ed. Dwight W. Allen and Eli Seifman. Glenview, Ill.: Scott, Foresman and Company, 1971.

Postman, Neil and Charles Weingartner.. *Teaching as a Subversive Activity.* New York: Dell Publishing Co., Inc., 1970.

————————————. *The Soft Revolution.* New York: The Dell Publishing Co. Inc., 1971.

Progoff, Ira. *The Symbolic and the Real.* New York: The Julian Press, Inc., 1963.

Pullias, Earl V. and Hames D. Young.. *A Teacher is Many Things.* Bloomington: Indiana University Press, 1969.

Raven, Bertram H. "The Dynamics of Groups," *Review of Educational Research,* XXIX: 4 (Date)

"Relevant Change and Educational Direction," A Temple City Unified School District Publication, July, 1968.

"Research Related to Academic Achievement Motivation: an Illustrative Review," W. Scott Bower, *et. al.,* in *Theory into Practice,* Vol. IX, no. 1, February, 1970.

Rogers, Carl R. "Towards Becoming a Fully Functioning Person," in *Perceiving, Behaving, Becoming,* 1962 ASCD Yearbook. Washington, D.C.: N.E.A., 1962.

Rosenthal, Robert and Lenore Jacobson. *Pygmalion in the Classroom.* New York: Holt, Rinehart and Winston, Inc., 1968.

Rothney, John W.M. "Who Gets Counseled and For What?," in *Freedom, Bureaucracy and Schooling,* 1971 ASCD Yearbook. Washington D.C.: N.E.A., 1971.

Sarason, Seymour B., *The Culture of the School and the Problem of Change.* Boston: Allyn and Bacon, Inc., 1971.

Selznick, Philip. *Leadership in Administration.* Evanston, Ill.: Row, Peterson, Inc., 1957.

Sharpe, Donald "Studying Teacher Classroom Behavior to Determine How Paraprofessionals Can Help in the Classroom," TEPS Write-in Paper on Flexible Staffing Patterns, no. 3, Washington D.C.: N.E.A., (date).

Silberman, Charles E. *Crisis in the Classroom.* New York: Random House, Inc., 1970.

Simmel, Georg. *Conflict, The Web of Group Affiliations.* NewYork: The Free Press, 1955.

Sprague, Hall T. "Human Relations School Model." Unpublished mimeographed paper. La Jolla, Cal.: Western Behavioral Sciences Institute, (date).

Strategies for Educational Change, II: 5, (April 1968) p. 000.

Taylor, Frederick W. *The Principles of Scientific Management.* New York: (publisher) 1911.

Tawney, R.H. *Equality.* London: George Allen & Unwin Ltd., 1929.

U.S. Office of Education. *The Education Professions.* OE-58032 Washington, D.C.: Government Printing Office, 1968.

Wagschal, Peter H. "Students, Teachers and Subjects: On Condensing the Trilogy," in *The Teacher's Handbook,* ed. Dwight W. Allen and Eli Seifman. Glenview, Ill.: Scott, Foresman and Company, 1971.

Weber, George and William H. Marmion. "Merit Pay and Alternatives," Occasional Paper no. 16, Council for Basic Education, May, 1969.

Whitehead, Alfred North. *The Aims of Education and Other Essays.* New York: New American Library, 1949.

Whyte, William H. Jr. "Groupthink," in *Selected Educational Heresies,* ed. William F. O'Neill. Glenview, Ill.: Scott, Foresman and Company, Inc., 1969.

Ziegler, Harman. *The Political World of the High School Teacher.* Eugene, Ore.: Center for the Advance Study of Educational Administration, University of Oregon, 1965.

Index

DATE DUE

NOV 17 '75	NOV 4 '75		